THE QUEST FOR CONSTITUTIONALISM

The Quest for Constitutionalism

South Africa since 1994

Edited by

HUGH CORDER
University of Cape Town, South Africa

VERONICA FEDERICO
University of Florence, Italy

ROMANO ORRÙ
University of Teramo, Italy

Routledge
Taylor & Francis Group
LONDON AND NEW YORK

First published 2014 by Ashgate Publishing

2 Park Square, Milton Park, Abingdon, Oxfordshire OX14 4RN
52 Vanderbilt Avenue, New York, NY 10017

Routledge is an imprint of the Taylor & Francis Group, an informa business

First issued in paperback 2020

British Library Cataloguing in Publication Data
A catalogue record for this book is available from the British Library

The Library of Congress has cataloged the printed edition as follows:
Corder, Hugh, author.
The quest for constitutionalism : South Africa since 1994 / by Hugh Corder, Veronica Federico, and Romano Orrù.
pages cm
Includes bibliographical references and index.
ISBN 978-1-4724-1631-5 (hardback : alk. paper)
1. Constitutional history—South Africa. 2. Constitutional law—South Africa.
3. Civil rights—South Africa. 4. Representative government and representation—South Africa. 5. Democracy—South Africa. 6. State, The. I. Federico, Veronica, author. II. Orrù, Romano, author. III. Title.
KTL2101.C67 2015
342.6802'9–dc23

2014021468

ISBN 978-1-4724-1631-5 (hbk)
ISBN 978-0-367-60001-3 (pbk)

Contents

Table of Cases

Notes on Contributors

Tom Bennett – BA LLB (Rhodes), PhD (UCT), Professor in the Department of Public Law and Fellow of the University of Cape Town. Research interests include African customary law, traditional African religions, ubuntu and the implications of legal pluralism in a constitutional democracy.

Edwin Cameron – Educated at the universities of Stellenbosch, South Africa, and Oxford. An academic and advocate, then Judge of the High Court and the Supreme Court of Appeal, and currently a Justice of South Africa's Constitutional Court. A distinguished author and social activist.

Hugh Corder – Studied law at the universities of Cape Town, Cambridge and Oxford. After five years at Stellenbosch as a senior lecturer, appointed to the Chair in Public Law at the University of Cape Town in 1987. Served as Dean of Law from 1999 to 2008.

Iain Currie – Advocate, Johannesburg Bar.

Francesca Romana Dau – Post-doctoral fellow in Comparative Public Law at the University of Milan. PhD in Theory of the State and Comparative Political Institutions at the University of Rome and lecturer in Anglo-American Public Law in the same university. She has been a visiting researcher in universities based in France, the United Kingdom and South Africa, and has published several essays and a book entitled *Costituzionalismo e rappresentanza. Il caso del Sudafrica* (Milano: Giuffrè, 2011).

Veronica Federico – PhD (Ecole des Hautes Etudes en Sciences Sociales-Paris), research fellow in the Department of Legal Sciences of the University of Florence, where she has taught public comparative law. Honorary Research Associate in the School of Social Sciences of the University of the Witwatersrand, Johannesburg, from 2001 to 2004, her research interests include democratic transitions, fundamental rights, African constitutionalism.

Mark Heywood – Executive Director of SECTION27 (which incorporated the AIDS Law Project in 2010). He joined the AIDS Law Project (ALP) in 1994 and in 1998 he was one of the founders of the Treatment Action Campaign (TAC). He serves on the TAC Secretariat, National Council and Board of Directors. Mark was the deputy chairperson of the South African National AIDS Council from 2007 until 2012. Mark has written extensively on HIV, human rights and the law, and with the ALP and SECTION27 has been involved in major litigation around HIV and other human rights issues in South Africa.

Tim Fish Hodgson – Bachelor of Business Science (2008) and an LLB (2010) at the University of Cape Town. He joined SECTION27 in 2011 before spending an inspiring year clerking for Justice Zakeria Yacoob at the Constitutional Court of South Africa. In 2012, he graduated with an LLM at the University of Michigan, returning to SECTION27 as a legal researcher in 2013. His work is in a variety of areas including constitutional literacy, basic education, private and public healthcare and the right to food.

Cora Hoexter – Professor in the School of Law at the University of the Witwatersrand, Johannesburg, where she teaches public law and pursues her main research interest, administrative law. A second edition of her leading text, *Administrative Law in South Africa*, was published by Juta & Co, Ltd in 2012.

Andrea Lollini – PhD (Ecoles des Hautes Etudes en Sciences Sociales, Paris). He has published widely on international and constitutional law and is Assistant Professor of Comparative Constitutional Law at the University of Bologna. He works as a permanent research fellow at the Institut des Hautes Etudes sur la Justice in Paris, and was one of the coordinators of the international research project 'Changing Role of the Highest Courts in an Internationalising World' of the Hague Institute for Internationalisation of Law (HiiL).

Tumai Murombo – Associate Professor and Director of the Mandela Institute, School of Law at the University of the Witwatersrand, Johannesburg. He is a legal practitioner admitted to practice law in Zimbabwe. Murombo is also Co-founder and Chairperson of the Board of the Zimbabwe Environmental Law Association (ZELA) and a member of the IUCN Commission on Environmental Law. He currently researches and teaches in environmental law, energy law and regulation, sustainable development, climate change law, and conservation and biodiversity law. Murombo has published and consulted in these areas internationally.

Morné Olivier – Associate Professor of Law at the University of the Witwatersrand, Johannesburg, where he teaches mainly administrative law and jurisprudence. He writes about the judiciary, and has a special interest in the selection and appointment of judicial officers. Morné frequently comments on judicial matters in the media. He and Cora Hoexter are the contributing editors of *The Judiciary in South Africa*, published in 2014.

Nic Olivier – BA (Law), LLB, BA (Hons), MA and LLD (University of Pretoria), BPhil and BA (Hons) (the former PUCHE), and Drs Iur and LLD (Leiden University). Professor and Director: SADC Centre for Land-related, Regional and Development Law and Policy (CLRDP), Post-graduate School of Agriculture and Rural Development, University of Pretoria. He was previously professor in the Law Faculties of the Universities of Pretoria, PUCHE and Natal. Since 1994, he has been involved in various projects relating to rural development, land reform, legal pluralism, cooperative governance, and the rationalisation of policy frameworks and legislation, and has on a number of occasions been seconded to the South African Government.

Nico Olivier – BPolSci, BA (Hons) Political Sciences with specialisation in International Relations, and MA (Political Sciences and International Relations). Independent policy analyst and research fellow at the Department of Political Sciences, University of Pretoria. His areas of expertise include African politics, monitoring and evaluation, higher education, cooperative governance, violence, rural development, land reform, agricultural land, and traditional leadership.

Romano Orrù – PhD in Public Law, Full Professor of Public Comparative Law at the University of Teramo. He teaches Comparative Constitutional Law and Public Law in both the University of Teramo and Bocconi University in Milan. He has extensively written on South African and African constitutional law and his research interests include constitutional adjudication, European public law, political rights and constitutional history.

Albie Sachs – Anti-apartheid legal activist, took part in the writing of South Africa's Constitution and was appointed by Nelson Mandela to the country's first Constitutional Court where he served from 1994 until 2009.

Lucia Scaffardi – PhD (Università di Bologna), Associate Professor of Public Comparative Law at the Department of Law, University of Parma. Her areas of expertise include the UK, the US and Commonwealth Countries (with special focus on Australia, Canada, South Africa); Emerging Countries (BRICS) and fundamental rights (hate speech, health rights, privacy, social rights). She is the coordinator of the 'BRICS Parma' (www.brics.unipr.it), an observatory of BRICS legal systems and their development.

Sanele Sibanda – Senior Lecturer at the School of Law at the University of the Witwatersrand, Johannesburg, where he teaches constitutional law and the law of persons. His research interests are in the areas of constitutional law, customary law reform, decolonial theory and liberation theory. He has taught, researched and published on questions related to separation of powers, administrative law, customary marriage, customary law reform and South African constitutionalism from a critical perspective.

Roger Southall – Professor Emeritus, Department of Sociology, University of the Witwatersrand, Johannesburg. He is the author of the recently published *Liberation*

Movements in Power: Party and State in Southern Africa (James Currey, London; UKZN Press, Pietermaritzburg).

Linda Stewart – BComm, LLB, LLM, LLD. Professor of Law teaching legal hermeneutics and human rights. Her research inter alia focuses on poverty and the realisation of socio-economic rights in terms of the South African Constitution.

Francois Venter – Taught law from 1974 in the Faculty of Law in Potchefstroom, North West Province, South Africa. Dean of the Faculty 2001–12. Convenor of the Technical Committee on Constitutional Affairs of the Multiparty Negotiation Process, drafting the 1993 Constitution in Kempton Park, May–December 1993. Founded *P E R* (Potchefstroom Electronic Law Journal) in 1998. President of the South African Law Deans' Association 2009–10.

Clara Williams – LLB and LLM (Child Law). Extraordinary Lecturer: Department of Procedural Law, University of Pretoria, legal researcher and legislative drafter and non-practising attorney. Since 2009, she has been involved in a number of projects for local, provincial and national government departments relating to the review of legislation, the drafting of policy documents, legislation, and so on. Focus areas include rural development, land reform, agricultural land, the rationalisation of municipal legislation, pension law and traditional leadership.

Foreword

We legal academics are a curious lot. Eternally restless, vocationally anxious, we are ever sceptical about law's pretensions, yet relentlessly search for the idealism at its core. So it is no surprise that although there is much to celebrate in South Africa's evolution in the last twenty years from a racist, authoritarian state to a constitutional democracy, this is not a book of jubilation.

Yes, let the praise-singers sing … and I will be amongst the first of them. After all, in these two decades, four presidents have vacated office without being pressurised by an army coup or massive street demonstrations; people from all over the world have flocked to observe our elections, not to determine if they are free and fair, but to see what lessons they can learn for other developing countries; armies that in the apartheid period had bitterly fought against each other have amalgamated into one service providing peace-keepers throughout the Continent; the Truth Commission helped to establish new, transparent and profound ways of examining the past with a view to promoting restorative justice in the future; government and the public administration have been completely reconstructed on non-racial lines, while schools, hospitals and residential areas have been desegregated, and we have a robust press with some of the best investigative journalists in the world. And decisions of the Constitutional Court, on which I had the honour to serve, ranging from the abolition of capital punishment, to the enforcement of social and economic rights, to the evolution of an innovative concept of living customary law, to recognition of same-sex marriages, and to the right of prisoners to vote are cited as examples of progressive legal thinking throughout the world. Yes, there are undoubtedly many things to shout from the jurisprudential rooftops.

And yet, and yet …

As Bertrand Russell said, the most powerful word in the English language is 'but'. The stocktaking in this book by leading scholars of constitutional and public law, locates itself precisely in the area of 'yes, but …'. The writers point out that just as there have been noteworthy achievements in virtually every sphere, so there have been significant shortcomings, deficiencies and threats. Great concern has been expressed about corruption and cronyism, with consequent pressures on the integrity of public institutions. And despite massive programmes of re-housing, extensive provision of electricity and clean water and the furnishing of social grants to a quarter of the population, the gap between rich and poor remains huge. Unemployment continues to be extremely high, and although the levels of violent crime have been brought down to some extent, they still remain unacceptable. True, as many authors in this volume point out, it is not the Constitution that has caused any of these problems. Yet the gap between the kind of society that the Constitution is designed to achieve and the reality on the ground continues to be vast.

Two sets of readers will be disappointed by this volume. The first will lament the absence of professorial panegyrics and sunshine legal writing. The second will bemoan seeing anything positive at all written about the contemporary scene, and not only wish the baby to be thrown out with the bathwater, but the bath itself trucked away. However, most readers, I believe, will welcome these thoughtful, nuanced and wide-ranging reflections by academics, most of whom have themselves been deeply engaged in the constitutional project.

Thus, Edwin Cameron writes bravely and memorably about starting life as a youth in a poor and fractured white family, glad to be white and ashamed of being gay, and going on to become a Justice of the Constitutional Court defending the fundamental rights of all. On a completely different tack, Sanele Sibanda shows critical spirit within the realms of critical thinking – while many of his colleagues forcefully denounce Parliament as an ineffectual lapdog of the Executive, he advances considerable detail to demonstrate that, for all its limitations, Parliament has in fact been the site of vigorous contestation that has led to meaningful outcomes.

Readers will have their own favourite topics and writers. Of special interest for me was to see how people who a couple of decades ago spoke with the sharpness and eagerness of new critical voices, have now emerged as seasoned stalwarts conveying ideas of mature constitutionalism with ingrained poise. So, anyone seeking an authoritative overview of the development of administrative law in the past twenty years, could do no better than to read the observations of Cora Hoexter. Similarly, Tom Bennett provides an authoritative retrospective of the evolution of customary law.

Finally, it should be noted that a unique feature of this volume is that it is the product of collaboration between Italian and South African scholars. (Interestingly, the editors have never met each other in person. I believe I am the only one who knows them all!) Not too long ago, South Africa was the subject of world-wide condemnation and the recipient of universal advice on how to move forward. Today, South Africa has remarkably become a universal donor as far as human rights jurisprudence is concerned. This volume is accordingly not only a tribute to the sagacity and determination of committed legal scholars as well as to modern technology. It is testimony to the richness of South African legal discourse. Its publication is proof of the existence of a trans-continental cohort of lively legal scholars willing to speak out about what they see with their eyes and hear with their ears. It is a paradox that the more trenchant and powerful the quality of scholarly critique, the more likely is it that the legal system under scrutiny will have health and vitality.

One of the pillars of constitutional democracy is an engaged and critical academia. As this book shows, South African scholars can hold their own with any in the world. And the collaboration with noted Italian jurists only adds lustre to their work.

Albie Sachs
Cape Town

Acknowledgements

This publishing project has been in production for almost twenty months. As is almost inevitable given the substantial number of authors whose work appears here and the various conflicting demands on the editors, the process has taken longer than we anticipated, but the manuscript has been finalised well before the twentieth anniversary of the advent of constitutional democracy in South Africa. We are indebted to all the authors for their good humour and patience in this process, and to Alison Kirk and her colleagues at Ashgate, for agreeing to publish this book, and then for waiting while several deadlines passed.

We are greatly indebted to Mervyn Bennun, University of Cape Town law graduate (1960) and honorary research associate (2000–2009), participant in the Congress of the People which adopted the Freedom Charter in 1955, retired law teacher from Exeter University (UK), anti-apartheid activist and dedicated South African democrat, for all his assistance in the final process of editing. Without his help, the production process would have been further delayed. We also greatly appreciate Tanya Barben's work in compiling the Index and Table of Cases.

Hugh Corder would like to record his appreciation of the tolerance of Catherine, Daniel, Juliet, James, Joanna and Lauren while he disappeared frequently to snatch time at the computer to pursue this project, and his gratitude to Veronica and Romano for their role in initiating and bringing this publication to fruition.

Veronica Federico is grateful to Hugh and Romano, their sapience has been a particular inspiration, and working with them a real pleasure; thanks also to Simone, Maddalena and Rocco who have patiently shared her South African passion, and to Carlo Fusaro and Ginevra Cerrina Feroni, for the wisdom and understanding with which they have guided Veronica's studies and work in the past two decades.

Romano Orrù wishes to thank Hugh and Veronica: Hugh for having enthusiastically accepted editorial involvement in this book and for his competence and total commitment; Veronica for her helpfulness and proficiency during all the phases of this project. Special thanks to his family – Carlotta, Matteo, Chiara and Andrea – who became intensely implicated in the *Rainbow Nation* affairs; and finally his gratitude to Giuseppe Franco Ferrari, Director of the review *Diritto Pubblico Comparato ed Euorpeo*, which was the incubator of the idea of this volume.

Hugh Corder, Cape Town; Veronica Federico, Parma; Romano Orrù, Teramo
21 March 2014 – Human Rights Day (South Africa)/UNO Anti-Racism Day
– commemorating the Sharpeville killings of 1960

Introduction

Veronica Federico, Hugh Corder and Romano Orrù

The multi-party negotiating conference mandated to write a constitution which would facilitate the transition from apartheid to democracy approved such an instrument in mid-November twenty years ago. On 22 December 1993, the Constitution of the Republic of South Africa (Act 200) was enacted almost without debate by the race-based tricameral Parliament, thus formally preserving constitutional continuity. The most significant product of the first step of a long constitution-making process, the interim Constitution (as it came to be known), opened the way for democratic elections in the country. For the first time in its history, South Africa was ruled by a fundamental law deeply imbued with constitutionalism, whose aim was to pursue 'a better life for all'. The entering into force of the interim Constitution and the elections of April 1994 were described as an historic turning-point for the entire world, a 'bridge away from a culture of authority' leading to 'a culture of justification', with the new Bill of Rights as its 'chief strut' (Mureinik 1994: 32). The final 1996 Constitution of the Republic of South Africa (Act 108), symbolically signed by President Nelson Mandela on 10 December 1996 in Sharpeville, marked the accomplishment of the constitutional and democratic transition.

Few claimed that the road to democracy, equality, freedom and social justice for South Africans was to be an easy or short one. And so it has proved. The consolidation of the democratic system, that is the 'democratic institutionalisation' (Mezzetti 2003), has turned out being a much longer and more difficult process than the already complex and demanding democratic transition, as it requires democratic values to permeate society as a whole, as well as democratic institutions and mechanisms acquiring a wide and deep social and political legitimacy.

The purpose of this volume is to contribute to a debate on what constitutionalism has meant for South Africa as a consolidating democratic state, for South Africans as citizens of the 'rainbow nation', and for the global impact of the constitutional democracy adopted for South Africa. The social project that the constitution-makers were dreaming about during the transition remains unfulfilled. The realisation of the values of the final 1996 Constitution remains unattained. The multifaceted analysis of this volume seeks to explore whether the path South African society is navigating will lead the country and its people to the full accomplishment of that social project.

Including the 1994 elections that marked the transition from the apartheid regime to democracy, South Africans have been to the polls five times to vote in national and provincial elections, including those in May 2014. In addition, local authority elections have been held four times, with the next round due in 2016. According to Dahl's (1971) widely accepted criteria for identifying a country as a democracy, fair, competitive, and inclusive elections are a crucial element, and South Africa can be regarded as a democracy in this sense. However, the African National Congress has remained the dominant party throughout the first two decades, so that the system of governance has not experimented with the alternation in power at national level that some scholars consider a milestone in the democratic consolidation process (Schedler 1998). While few would argue that South Africa is not a democracy, as several of Dahl's other criteria (civil and political rights and freedoms, inclusiveness, enlightened understanding of the choices, and so on) characterise the new political and constitutional system, an in-depth scrutiny of the salience of these elements, through an analysis of the constitutional and socio-political framework, will contribute to a better understanding of South Africa's "long march" to democracy.

Two motivations inspire the volume. Firstly, the analysis is concerned with the impact of laws and the salience of their existence and enforcement (or non-enforcement) for South Africans. We intend to situate the importance of the legal phenomenon in the broader context of the socio-political, economic and cultural democratisation process. Without consciously seeking to measure the achievements of the new democratic system, the volume asks what a constitution does, using Sunstein's approach, through the prism of South African experience. In Sunstein's words, in fact, 'the central goal of a constitution is the pre-conditions for a well-functioning democratic order, in which citizens are genuinely able to govern themselves' (2001: 6). To understand the impact of the new constitutional dispensation, borrowing from Roscoe Pound's famous formulas, on the one hand, we take into account the 'law in the books' and, on the other, we consider the 'law in action'. This means that, from the formal constitutional perspective based on an analysis of the importance of the framework of the constitutional provisions and of the evolution of the legal system, we move to an inquiry about the interaction of the legal phenomenon with the complex network of interwoven social institutions that constitute South African society. Beyond the 'universal ideal, the ideal of law as a body of precepts of universal authority, universal content and universal applicability' (Pound 1958: 16), we intend to focus on the ideal of law as a body of rules concerning relations and flowing from or attaching to relations. In short, we aspire to inquire into the social dimension of the law.

The second motivation inspiring the volume speaks to the issue of acknowledging the importance of the South African constitutional provisions for *transnational* or even *globalised* constitutionalism. We aim to discuss the innovative character of South African constitutional and legal provisions in terms of both the constitution-making process and the process of implementation of the Constitution, against the background of the heavy legacy of apartheid, the reality of everyday life, and finally against the hope and enthusiasm and civil, political and academic interest stimulated by the transition two decades ago.

Remarkably, full expression of the rule of law was first introduced to South Africa only through the interim Constitution, as the apartheid legal system was based on the sovereignty of Parliament. Since 1994, for the first time in the history of South Africa as a modern state, the legal system has been strongly anchored in a culture of justification (Van Der Walt and Botha 2000), which means that there are some limitations on governmental power that cannot be altered by means of ordinary legislation (Bobbio 1991). But South African constitutionalism goes far beyond the formal recognition of the rule of law. Indeed, the most conservative tradition of constitutionalism, with its essential distinction and balance between *iurisdictio* and *gubernaculum*, dates back centuries (McIlwain 1969). Nonetheless, we do not intend constitutionalism as a simple set of formal proceedings nor as an aseptic separation and balance of opposing powers and interests. As Habermas states, it finds its justification in certain normative principles, from the public welfare or public goods to human rights, from moral beliefs to the principle of deliberation amongst the citizenry. Constitutionalism entails the ideas of an open and democratic society and of social justice. This principle presupposes, furthermore, a framework of individual rights, which grants private autonomy and allows each citizen the capacity to exercise their equal right of political participation (Habermas 1996).

Indeed, the post-apartheid South African constitutions do regulate all the different state institutions in detail, providing for the separation of powers and all formal requirements of contemporary democracies. But they also contain normative and moral principles, they express the 'soul of the nation' (Ebrahim 1998). Dignity, equality, freedom, non-racialism and non-sexism have replaced racism, arbitrariness and inequality as the guiding principles of the very structure of the legal order.

The Constitution is not imbued with mere constitutionalism, but with 'transformative constitutionalism', that is,

> … a long-term project of constitutional enactment, interpretation, and enforcement committed to transforming a country's political and social institutions and power relationships in a democratic, participatory, and egalitarian direction. Transformative constitutionalism connotes an enterprise of inducing large-scale social change through nonviolent political processes grounded in law. (Klare 1998: 152)

The former Chief Justice, Pius Langa, described transformative constitutionalism as

> … a permanent ideal, a way of looking at the world that creates a space in which dialogue and contestation is truly possible, in which new ways of being are constantly explored and created, accepted and rejected and in which change is unpredictable but the idea of change is constant … This is a perspective that sees the Constitution as not transformative because of its peculiar historical position or its particular socio-economic goals but because it envisions a society that will

> always be open to change and contestation, a society that will always be defined by transformation. (Langa 2006: 354)

Few doubt that the constitution-making process has played a pivotal role in the South African democratic transition, and that the country has become the symbol of what constitutions and constitutionalism can achieve. It is equally true that the law is 'the primary means available to a democratic state to intervene in society'. What remains to be debated is 'the effectiveness of law as mechanism for social change' (Klug 2000: 7).

In the passage from the transition to the consolidation of the democratic system, much of the emphasis of two decades ago has now gone. Disenchantment has frequently replaced enthusiasm and the accounts of the heroic struggle against apartheid have been substituted by a critical analysis of the workings of the different aspects of the democratic system. And yet, despite all the 'dark sides' of South African democracy, the debates and analysis must not forget what apartheid was, and how deeply it scarred South African society. As the famous novelist Andre Brink stated in 1995, 'we have to expect a number of excesses and abuses: those who are now in power are not *supermen*, they are ordinary human beings. The issue is not to excuse the abuses. Nonetheless, whatever obstacle and deception, it is always exciting to feel history in the making' (1995: 35).

We need, now, to ground our discussion in the concrete South African reality. The importance of South Africa in the geopolitical arena (as powerful political actor in the African continent and more generally as representative of the requests and demands of countries of the South), in the field of legal innovation and of the circulation of legal models, and finally as moral reference point in the international community, asserts itself. As Johnston, Shezi and Bradshaw wrote at the time: 'in the absence of any very compelling single system of ethical agreement … South Africa had the merit of providing an area of substantial agreement between East and West, of what constituted acceptable and unacceptable political behaviour. Standing aside was not enough' (1993: 255).

With a population of 51.8 million people in 2011, South Africa is the fifth most populated country in Africa. According to World Bank assessments, the country is ranked as an upper-middle income economy, with the national GDP in 2012 at US$384.312 billion, which makes an average GDP per capita of US$7,508. On the other hand, given the extremely unequal distribution of wealth and of access to resources (measured by a Gini coefficient[1] of 0.63 according to 2012 Word Bank data), the average GDP per capita may be a misleading datum, if we consider that almost one-quarter of the population is unemployed and lives under the poverty line (that is, on less than US$1.25 a day). The newly released UNDP *Human Development Report* of 2012 ranks South Africa at 121, among the medium human

1 The Gini coefficient is the most commonly used measure of inequality. The coefficient varies between 0, which reflects complete equality and 1, which indicates complete inequality (one person has all the income or consumption, all others have none).

development countries (which makes South Africa the sixth ranked country for human development in sub-Saharan Africa).

South Africa is a typically divided society, where segregation first and apartheid later have separated the population according to ethno-racial factors.

Until 1994, South Africans were not one people in one country: the organisation of the state combined the typical division of the territory along geographically coherent lines with an ethno-racial division of the population, creating different communities of individuals with their own forms of government and differentiated rights and duties. Since 1950, the Population Registration Act and the Group Areas Act had classified the population into four racial groups (White, Coloured, Black and Indian), and assigned these groups to different residential and business zones. Civil, political and socio-economic rights and educational, cultural, occupational and social opportunities and economic status were determined for each individual by virtue of the group to which they were deemed to belong.

But other cleavages have built on the racial element. During apartheid, class, more or less artificially, coincided with race. Urban segregation, differentiated education policies, and the principle of separation were applied to every aspect of social, cultural, economic and even private life, and strongly contributed to strengthening the existing cleavages. About three centuries of colonial domination based on the principle of segregation and 50 years of apartheid have left scars that are difficult to eradicate. In the first decades of democracy, the inequalities of the past have not been fully redressed, and South Africa needs much more time to rebalance its social fabric, should this remain a goal to be pursued in the policy-makers' agenda.

This unequal wealth distribution is mirrored in deeply differentiated living standards, so that the richest part of the population enjoys Western consumption patterns, high standard education and health systems, and very good cultural opportunities, whereas the largest and poorest part of the population still lives in informal settlements, with no running water and little sanitation, very poor services, almost no access to higher education, an infant mortality rate four times higher than that of the richest part of the population, an extremely high unemployment rate and a much larger share of unskilled employment, where it exists. If it is true that richness and well-being are no longer formally reserved for 'net blankes – whites only' (the typical notice that after the Reservation of Separate Amenities Act of 1953 was to be found everywhere: from the benches in the parks to the beach entrances), the poorest part of the population remains black. The neo-liberal political economy which the South African government has adopted and implemented, especially during the presidency of Thabo Mbeki, has stirred up strong social criticism, but undeniably has allowed for the control of inflation and consistent economic growth.

With the highest number of infections in the world, South Africa is one of the countries most severely affected by the HIV/AIDS epidemic (which remains indeed a terrible plague in several other African countries, especially in the southern part of the continent). The epidemic, that is considered to be generalised and hyper-endemic, has an obviously strong impact on both the economic and the socio-cultural structure of society. Without anticipating the analysis of Heywood and Hodgson in this volume, it is impossible not to consider this phenomenon while analysing, for example: the progressive enforcement of socio-economic rights; its impact on economic growth; the challenges the infection poses to local government, and its corrosive effect on the inter-generational pact which the Constitution assumes as crucial for the process of nation-building, just to mention a few crucial consequences of the problem.

Nevertheless, South Africa's importance in the geopolitical arena has been growing since the democratic transition. After having been suspended in 1974 from participating in the work of the UN General Assembly due to international opposition to apartheid, South Africa was re-admitted to the UN in 1994. In 2007–2008, endorsed by the African Union, South Africa was elected as a non-permanent member of the UN Security Council. Again in 2011, the country was re-elected for a second two-year mandate in the UN Security Council. Very active in regional and sub-regional organisations, South Africa is a leading member of the African Union, the Southern African Customs Union (SACU), and the Southern African Development Community (SADC).

South Africa is the European Union's largest trading partner in Africa. Although it is also a member of the African, Caribbean and Pacific (ACP) group of countries, it is by far the strongest of sub-Saharan Africa's economies, and has a Free Trade Agreement with the EU, which was signed in Pretoria in 1999 after a long negotiating process. Indeed, South Africa was not party to the same preferential trade arrangements granted to the ACP under the Cotonou Agreement (2000). For the Economic Partnership Agreements (EPAs), which are the trade pillar of the Cotonou Agreement, South Africa joined the negotiations with the SADC EPA Group in February 2007; however, while Botswana, Lesotho, Swaziland and Mozambique signed an interim EPA in 2009, South Africa has opted not to join at this stage as its trade relations with the EU remain governed by the Free Trade Agreement. South Africa's exports to the EU are growing and their composition is becoming more diverse. This is an important signal of South Africa's economic and political strength.

Vis-à-vis the rest of the world, in the aftermath of the G-8 meeting in Evian, France, in 2003, South Africa, Brazil and India, three of the most important emerging economies, decided to intensify the quantity and quality of their political and economic relationships. They launched the IBSA initiative, a trilateral developmental initiative, to promote South-South cooperation and exchange. South Africa's becoming the 'S' in the BRICS group (Brazil, Russia, India and China) in 2011 makes even clearer the importance of the country in the international arena, as Scaffardi discusses below. In Goldman Sachs's words, these countries are not any more simply emerging economies, but real growing economies.

It is thus clear that the functioning of the constitutional system as well as the quality of democracy of one of the most important African countries is a matter of interest for African, European and international scholars and policy-makers, and not simply for theoretical reasons.

During the transition and in the first years of democracy, the South African miracle captured the attention of both the political and academic international community, and much was written on many aspects of the social, political and legal system, and of the economic, cultural and historical framework of the transition. Two decades later, South Africa is no longer so much in the limelight, and comprehensive studies on the development of the legal system and of the implications for the social configuration of power are not commonly found. We do not intend to provide a comprehensive and exhaustive analysis of the South African legal system, but to offer several standpoints and perspectives for further analysis.

Each chapter, under its specific perspective (from land reform to political rights, from local government to the green economy, and so on), will contribute to unveiling a segment of the complex general picture. Digging beneath the surface of the constitutional and legal provisions and practices, the purpose is to understand the deeper historical, political, social, cultural and economic reasons for them, and to interrogate them in order to grasp, on the one hand, the underlying logics that motivated the adoption of those provisions and practices, and, on the other hand, the real impact of those provisions and practices in deconstructing and reconstructing different social ties, that is, in transforming society.

The chapter authors are mainly South African scholars; nonetheless, the presence of foreign scholars as editors and contributors brings in new analytical angles, adding a specific comparative dimension.

The volume is organised around five general topics: the structure of the State; rights, equality and the courts; political rights and the party system; transformative constitutionalism; and the international context. As pieces of a single puzzle, each chapter is focused on a very specific topic (federalism, local government, structure of government, Parliament, equality, socio-economic rights, HIV/AIDS, the judiciary, administrative justice, political rights, land reform, the green economy, constitutional changes, legal pluralism, the right to information, the party system, constitutional case-law, the BRICS, and so on). Combining the chapters allows for an overall, and yet multifaceted, understanding of the contemporary South African constitutional system, and of how the Constitution works.

Against the segmentation of both national territory and population carried out under the apartheid regime, the democratic transition has reunited South Africa as a country and as a people. The new structure of the State, as illustrated in Federico's chapter, whether it should be considered as a federal, semi- or quasi-federal, or a centralised state with some forms of decentralisation, together with the new system of government (the quasi-parliamentarianism described by Orrù) provide the frame for the analysis of more specific aspects of South African legal order and society. Unveiling the gap between the constitutional models in theory, which are the product of a delicate and sophisticated exercise of constitutional design, and the real enforcement of those models, the first two chapters open the discussion on whether such a gap should be considered physiological and inevitable, or an alarming drift from what it should have been.

Starting from Venter's discussion of the 'completely new, consolidated, theoretically autonomous and decentralised sphere of constitutionally structured local government … in a precarious balance between a subsidiarity-like autonomy on the one hand, and the dependence on the other hand on national and provincial oversight and financing', as well as Sibanda's inquiry into the role of Parliament in a single-party-dominant system, the discourse moves to the analysis of fundamental rights and the role of the judiciary in the enforcement and protection of rights. Justice Edwin Cameron's reflection on the relevance of dignity and equality in Constitutional Court jurisprudence opens the way for a broader discussion on the role of law in the process of social change that South African society is undergoing since the democratic transition, to rebalance the inequalities of the past and to recognise the intrinsic human dignity of every person.

Since the Grootboom case in 2000, much has been written on the South African approach to the enforcement of socio-economic rights. The Constitutional Court maintained that 'our Constitution entrenches both civil and political rights and social and economic rights. All the rights in our Bill of Rights are inter-related and mutually supporting' and

> … there can be no doubt that human dignity, freedom and equality, the foundational values of our society, are denied to those who have no food, clothing or shelter. Affording socio-economic rights to all people therefore enables them to enjoy the other rights enshrined in Chapter 2. The realisation of these rights is also key to the advancement of race and gender equality and the evolution of a society in which men and women are equally able to achieve their full potential. (*The Government of the Republic of South Africa & others* v *Irene Grootboom and others*, para 23)

In a critical approach, Stewart's chapter points to the progressive technicisation and proceduralisation of needs-talk in the socio-economic rights adjudication of the judiciary, which leads to depoliticising these rights, whereas 'one possible way for courts to meaningfully contribute to the socio-economic transformation as envisioned by the transformative mandate of the Constitution is to also focus on facilitating meaningful public reasoning and dialogue in the form of political discourse and participation.'

The role of the judiciary in any legal system is never neutral, and in South Africa, this is even more evident than elsewhere. In the words of one of South Africa's most famous lawyers:

> Why is it that in this courtroom I am facing a white magistrate, confronted by a white prosecutor, escorted by white orderlies? Can anybody honestly and seriously suggest that [in] this type of atmosphere the scales of justice are evenly balanced? Why is it that no African in the history of the country has ever had the honour of

> being tried by his own kith and kin? … The real purpose of this rigid colour bar is to ensure that justice dispensed by the courts should conform to the policy of the country, however much that policy might be in conflict with the norms of justice accepted in judiciaries throughout the civilised world. (Mandela 1994: 312–13)

Nelson Mandela's initial address to the court during his trial in October 1962 was highly confrontational: much has changed since then, but, as Olivier's chapter underlines, the role of the judiciary remains a 'contested and controversial matter' in contemporary South Africa.

During the apartheid era, administrative law, as well as criminal law, were sources of oppression for the majority of South Africans. The democratisation process has liberated administrative law, together with all other facets of state institutions, and the 1996 Constitution has entrenched the right to just administrative action (s 33). In her chapter, Hoexter underlines how the inclusion of this right is remarkable, and how this might play a fundamental role in the overall enforcement of the democratic system but, 'notwithstanding what has been achieved in theory, problems such as endemic corruption and non-compliance with court orders are placing the entire constitutional project at risk.'

The relevance of political rights, and of the right to vote, may appear obvious in contemporary consolidated democracy, but the universal suffrage in South Africa was finally obtained only in 1994. Thus the right to vote occupies a special place in the framework of the Bill of Rights, and 'the constitutional judges have pushed towards a wide enfranchisement rather than disenfranchisement' as illustrated in Dau's chapter, as an instrument of nation-building. Together with the 'proper' political rights, it is interesting to follow Currie in his inquiry into the freedom of information rights, which are crucial in the structuring of the public sphere. Under the spotlight in 2012 and 2013 during the harsh debate on the Protection of State Information Bill, the implementation of freedom of information rights is ambiguous. On the one hand, these 'rights are routinely, though unevenly, invoked and relied upon. In a number of high-profile court decisions, information activists and journalists have secured important victories', but on the other hand, they are 'frequently ignored or maladministered by public bodies', so that the general picture is not as bright as it may appear. The political outcome of this involved frame is what Southall in his chapter calls the 'contradictions of party dominance', with 'the ANC that has become a victim of its own dominance, and the principal party of opposition, as presently constituted, which is constrained by its own legacy, its own constituency, and its chosen ideology'.

Within such a legal, social and political framework, the discourse moves to analyse some of the most interesting reform processes which contribute to make South African constitutionalism a 'transformative' constitutionalism. The picture becomes variegated: Corder's review of constitutional reforms in South African history 'emphasising the enormity of the shift in the basic norm which underlies the current Constitution' and 'speculating on likely pressures for further reform'; as well as the critical inquiry into the land-reform projects in which Olivier, Olivier and Williams highlight a number of key challenges and possible options to ensure that the constitutional imperative of bringing about sustainable land reform will be realised, provide different angles of analysis. In turn, Murombo's discussion of green economy policies and environmental rights adds new elements to the debate. Here, 'little has changed in how the government and industry manage natural resources ... partly due to the complex nature of the task required in promoting sustainability in a social, economic, cultural and political atmosphere full of intractable ideological contradictions.' Finally, the frame appears even more intricate, taking into consideration Bennett's discussion of the position of indigenous customary law in the democratic legal system, which offers the author the opportunity of underlining that the South African legal system has had to contend with a problem that is common to most post-colonial states: a significant gap between social classes that are marked by culture and ethnicity. Law may all too easily become a marker of cultural resistance to the interference of the central state, and, without education, income and opportunity, the disadvantaged class is less likely to accept and act on reforms promulgated by the state.

The reader should not, nonetheless, be induced to underestimate the magnitude of the South African democratisation process and the relevance of the new constitutional system in action. As well as its weight in the international arena, illustrated by the case-study of the BRICS group in Scaffardi's chapter, the impact of South African constitutional jurisprudence is remarkable. Lollini's chapter, in fact, illustrates how the South African CC's decisions are 'gradually becoming a source of inspiration for other constitutional cultures, specifically for the complexity of the issues it deals with in terms of enforcing fundamental and social rights, fighting against inequality and harmonising a multicultural society'.

Nelson Mandela's death in late 2013 marks another turning-point in South Africa's long walk to democracy. He was an immense source of value for his country and for the whole world. The new challenge is now to decide from which spring to draw inspiration for the strenuous struggle for an open, democratic and equitable society. But we remain confident. In a country where the 'constitutional vision' is 'anchored in the architectonic value of human dignity' (Eberle 2008: 3) in its special, South African meaning, the idea of Ubuntu, '*Ubuntu ungamntu ngabanye abantu*' – 'people are people through other people' – we believe there is hope for more radical social change.

References

Books, book chapters, articles

Bobbio, N. 1991. *Il Futuro della Democrazia*. Torino: Einaudi.

Brink, A. 1995. 'Lendemain du miracle', *Les temps modernes*, 585: 24–40.

Dahl, R. 1971. *Polyarchy: Participation and Opposition*. New Haven: Yale University Press.

Eberle, E.J. 2008. 'The German Idea of Freedom', *Oregon Review of International Law*, 10: 1–76.
Ebrahim, H. 1998. *The Soul of a Nation*. Cape Town: Oxford University Press.
Habermas, J. 1996. *Between Facts and Norms: contributions to a discourse of law and democracy*. Cambridge, MA: MIT Press.
Johnston, A., S. Shezi and G. Bradshaw, 1993. *Constitution-making in the new South Africa*. London: Leicester University Press.
Klare, K.E. 1998. 'Legal culture and transformative constitutionalism', *South African Journal on Human Rights*, 14(Part I): 146–88.
Klug, H. 2000. *Constituting Democracy. Law, Globalism and South Africa's Political Reconstruction*. Cambridge: Cambridge University Press.
Langa, P. 2006. 'Transformative Constitutionalism', *Stellenbosch Law Review*, 17(3): 351–60.
Mandela, N. 1994. *Long Walk to Freedom*. London: Little, Brown & Company.
McIlwain, C.H. 1969. *Constitutionalism and the Changing World*. Cambridge: Cambridge University Press.
Mezzetti, L. 2003. *Teoria e prassi delle transizioni costituzionali e del consolidamento democratico*. Padova: CEDAM.
Mureinik, E. 1994. 'A Bridge to Where? Introducing the Interim Bill of Rights', *South African Journal of Human Rights*, 10: 31–48.
Pound, R. 1958. *The Ideal Element in Law*. Calcutta: University of Calcutta Press.
Schedler, A. 1998. 'What is Democratic Consolidation?' *Journal of Democracy*, 9(2): 91–107.
Sunstein, C. 2001. *Designing Democracy: What Constitutions do*. Oxford: Oxford University Press.
Van Der Walt, J. and H. Botha, 2000. 'Democracy and Rights in South Africa: Beyond a Constitutional Culture of Justification', *Constellations*, 7(3): 341–62.

Case

Government of the Republic of South Africa & others v Irene Grootboom and others, CCT/11/00.

Map of South Africa and its Provinces. © bogdanserban / iStock / Thinkstock

PART I
The Structure of the State

Chapter 1
South African Quasi-Federalism

Veronica Federico

Introduction

Decentralisation does not necessarily increase the autonomy, power and functions of sub-national governments. Rather, the relevance of sub-national governments depends upon the interrelation between the form of the state and the system of government, on the political and socio-economic background, and on the social history of the country, as well as on the party system and institutional framework.

Since the early 1990s, decentralisation has often been a strategic element in democratisation processes and development policies in Southern Africa, and became a leitmotiv in international democratisation and developmental plans. Two decades later, it would be very interesting to embark on a discussion of the success of these policies, but the scope of this chapter is much narrower: to employ one of the typical continental European comparative public law analytical categories and tools (that is, the study of the structure of the state) to describe the contemporary South African legal system.

Indeed, much has been written on the structure of the South African State (including whether it should be described as a federal, semi-federal, provincial, decentralised, or hybrid state) by both South African and international scholars, especially during the democratic transition, and our aim is neither to provide the reader with an overview of such a broad literature, nor to suggest a new, insightful theory. Instead, we intend to focus on a few aspects of the provincial system's evolution and of the centre-periphery relations which may prove to be an interesting perspective for an analysis of the state's capacity to provide an institutional accommodation capable of responding to the needs of the people. Without detailing here the core of our analysis, whether South Africa should be considered as a federal, semi- or quasi-federal, or centralised state with some forms of decentralisation is not simply a theoretical issue. The questions concerning what tier of government (national, provincial, or local) is responsible for relevant political choices and what tier of government should be accountable for them, reveal the very nature, and quality, of the new democratic system. We believe that these also have an important impact in terms of the implementation of policies, for example in the field of service delivery, education, health care, etc.

Structure of the State before 1994

South Africa has never been a homogeneous state, either from a socio-political and cultural perspective or from an economic one, and especially not if we consider its structure.

According to the most recent demographic data referring to 2011,[1] 79.6 per cent of the 51,770,560 South Africans define themselves as African, 9 per cent Coloured, 2.5 per cent Asian/Indian, and 8.9 per cent White. South Africa is a typically divided society, where segregation first and apartheid later have separated the population according to ethno-racial factors. However, other cleavages have been built upon the racial element. During the apartheid years, class, more or less artificially, coincided with race. From urban segregation to differentiated education policies, the principle of separation applied to every aspect of social, cultural, economic and even private life, and strongly contributed to strengthening the existing cleavages.

The structure of the new state has been a crucial issue in the South African transition. Twenty years later, it remains an important element in terms of governance, democratisation, and, of course, service delivery and the amelioration of the quality of life of the most disadvantaged segments of South African contemporary society.

Indeed, decentralisation and local governance are relevant issues in the present development discourse. Since the early 1990s, decentralisation has been increasingly connected to the process of democratisation (with the assumption that a decentralised country can achieve an improved level of democratic quality), to the strategies of the fight against poverty (with the assumption that poverty reduction is positively related to decentralisation), and, in general, to the positive resolution of development problems.

> Three vantage points are especially relevant to debates about federalism: the link between federalism and democracy; the link between federalism and what we might call effective government, or policy-making capacity; and the link between federalism and the ability to manage territorially concentrated ethno-national divisions, or between federalism and varying conceptions of communities. (Simeon 1998: 3–4)

The organisation of the South African State from 1910 to 1994 combined two different principles: the typical division of the country along geographical lines, creating territorially homogeneous entities – provinces and municipalities – which enjoyed some degree of power (both legislative and executive) depending on the level of decentralisation, and an ethno-racial principle, creating different communities of individuals (perceived to be homogeneous) with their own forms

1 The latest census was held in 2011 and the basic data can be easily accessed at <http://www.statssa.gov.za/Census2011/Products/Census_2011_Fact_sheet.pdf>.

of government and differentiated rights and duties. The two principles overlapped, and produced a very confused and intertwined power structure on a twin-track decentralisation logic, in which the central power of national government remained the dominant element in almost every process of policy-making. As an informed analyst has concluded:

> The decentralisation experiments of the apartheid state were, paradoxically, grounded in an attempt to maintain central control. Decentralisation was designed to achieve at least two objectives: first to fragment the opposition by creating a set of regional and ethnic interests which would impede African nationalism; and secondly to relinquish sovereignty over parts of the space in order to satisfy the political aspiration of the majority. (Wittenberg, 2003: 24)

The idea of creating 'native reserves' where the African population could be confined dates back to early colonial times and reached its peak with the so-called 'grand apartheid' that led to the creation of the homelands, or bantustans. In the words of C.P. Mulder, Minister of Bantu Administration and Development in 1978:

> If our policy is taken to its full logical conclusion as far as the black people are concerned, there will be not one black man with South African citizenship ... Every black man in South Africa will eventually be accommodated in some independent new state in this honourable way and there will no longer be a moral obligation on this Parliament to accommodate these people politically. (Rogers 1980: 17)

This form of *divide et impera* policy carried out by the apartheid government had a very negative impact on later discussions regarding decentralisation. Any form of decentralised/federal distribution of power had to prove itself to be different in both theoretical and empirical terms to the system of apartheid. The result was that despite the advice of the international community and of experts who engaged globally in reflections and debates on the advantages of some form of federalism for the new post-apartheid South African State, the democratic constitutions (transitional and final) opted for a unitary state, with some forms of decentralisation.

Decentralisation in the Democratic State

The creation of the new South African State was characterised by a double, partially conflicting movement: on the one hand, the process of reunification of what had previously been separated by the apartheid state (the territory of the state, its population, the government structure, the vast majority of public policies – education, health, employment, the security forces, and so on); on the other hand, the process of decentralisation, which implied a complete reformulation of the country's geography both in terms of physical geography and power. This was in a country where geography has always been highly politically contested.

The final 1996 Constitution (s 40) establishes three separate, but interdependent and interrelated, spheres of government: a national government, nine provincial governments and 284 local governments, all within the general frame of a cooperative government.

The provincial sphere of government consists of legislative and executive competences, but provinces are not endowed with judicial authority. As is typical of decentralised but not federal state structures, the administration of justice remains the prerogative of the national power and is vested in the courts, which may have a provincial organisation (as is the case with South Africa), but do not depend on the provincial sphere of government either for their internal organisation (judges' recruitment, establishment of courts' seats) nor for the granting of their independence, and not even for their financial resources. Following the same principle, regional governments do not have regional/provincial police and security forces.

The legislative authority of the provinces is vested in the provincial legislature, which consists of between 30 and 80 members depending on the size of the provincial population. As with the national Parliament (Southall 2014), provincial legislatures are elected through a proportional electoral system, based on closed party-lists at the national and provincial level.

Interestingly, the first draft of the Constitution of the Western Cape was rejected by the Constitutional Court (CC) because it provided for multiple-member geographical constituencies, as opposed to the party-list proportional representation prescribed by the national Constitution. The Court judged this provision to be inconsistent with the national Constitution, as an electoral system cannot be considered to be a 'legislative nor an executive structure' (which provincial constitutions are entitled to regulate). Also, the province did not have the power to alter the electoral system (*Certification of the Constitution of the Western Cape*).

Following a ruling at the national level, Members of Provincial Legislatures (MPLs) are forced to follow a rigid party discipline by the 'anti-defection' clause, which does not allow MPLs to vote differently from their party and/or to change political affiliation during their mandate (the sanction for this is the loss of their legislative seat). Thus, MPLs are accountable in the first instance to their party rather than directly to the electorate. The legislative authority of provincial legislatures consists in passing legislation for its province in any matter of exclusive or concurrent competences (in respect to the general framework of existing national legislation), and in adopting, and eventually amending, the provincial constitution.

Despite the exclusive competences of provincial legislatures, the national Parliament can still enact legislation concerning provincial functional areas (Constitution, s 44(2)). In a comparative perspective, this provision is not unusual, as it is considered a type of guarantee for national unity even in highly decentralised states. If narrowly interpreted, it is simply a guarantee. However, if broadly interpreted – as is the case with South Africa – it considerably enlarges the legislative prerogatives of the national Parliament, to the detriment of provincial exclusive competences. In fact, in *Ex parte President of the RSA: In re Constitutionality of the Liquor Bill*, the CC underlined that 'Our constitutional structure does not contemplate that provinces will compete with each other. It is one in which there is to be a single economy and in which all levels of government are to co-operate with one another' (para 75). And 'where provinces are accorded exclusive powers these should be interpreted as applying primarily to matters which may appropriately be regulated intra-provincially' (para 51). That is to say, exclusive competences need to be interpreted in the context of those matters which can be effectively regulated in one province alone (Currie and de Waal 2001: 121).

Functional areas of concurrent national and provincial legislative competence, listed in Part A of Schedule 4 of the Constitution, cover very important aspects concerning the socio-economic development of the country and its citizens. Agriculture, education, environment, health services, housing, language policy, public transport, tourism, trade, urban and rural development and welfare services, for example, are crucial areas in order to promote a new social order, based on those democratic and egalitarian principles upon which the new South Africa should be established.

Notwithstanding provincial prerogatives, what has happened until now is that national framework legislation tends to be very detailed, regulating almost every aspect of the most sensitive issues, leaving little if any space for the provinces to perform their law-making duties effectively. This phenomenon has three different, and serious, consequences: first of all, it narrows the specific role of the provincial legislatures which is to provide provincial laws that better accommodate provincial and local needs, and which better fit the socio-economic and cultural environment. Secondly, it reduces institutional accountability and transparency, as it becomes more and more difficult to understand which legislative body is responsible for what type of legislation. Thirdly, this phenomenon fosters institutional competition (to the detriment of the principle of cooperative government for which it has been established), and intensifies institutional conflicts for the attribution of powers (Venter 2014).

Finally, when considering concurrent legislative competences, we should not forget the indirect provincial participation in the national law-making process through the National Council of Provinces, the second House of the national Parliament, explicitly designed to represent provincial interests at the national level (Sibanda 2014).

Provincial executive authority is vested in the Premier, who is elected by the members of the provincial legislature of which she or he is also a member. The Premier exercises executive authority together with the members of the Executive Council, who number between five and ten and are appointed by the Premier from among the members of the provincial legislature. Indeed, the Constitution does not provide for provincial departments, which are created by s 7(2) of the Public Service Act of 1994, and these do not have legal personality. As noted by Woolman, 'Departments do not only exist to serve the Premier. The departments are, at their most basic level, merely different manifestations of the Premier' (2009: 68). Within the provincial borders, the Premier and the Executive Council have the responsibility of implementing both provincial and national laws at the provincial level.

Provincial Constitutions

The possibility of granting provinces the capacity to adopt provincial constitutions was a much-debated issue during the constitutional negotiations, with two provinces (Western Cape and KwaZulu Natal) and some minority parties strongly advocating in its favour. Section 142 of the 1996 Constitution attributes to provinces the authority for passing provincial constitutions, within the framework of the Constitution, which must be certified by the Constitutional Court. Still, provinces enjoy quite a broad level of self-determination, as their constitutions

> … may provide for –
> *(a)* provincial legislative or executive structures and proceedings that differ from those provided for in the Constitution; or
> *(b)* the institution, role, authority and status of a traditional monarch, where applicable. (Constitution, s 143(1))

As a matter of fact, the Western Cape is the only province that has succeeded in adopting its own constitution, whereas KwaZulu Natal, the other province which 'embarked on a constitution drafting exercise, was unsuccessful since the constitutional text was not certified by the Constitutional Court' (Brand 2008: 15). All other provinces still operate under the provisions of the national Constitution.

Following a relatively long and complex constitution-making process, with an initial rejection of a number of clauses by the CC, the Western Cape provincial constitution came into effect in January 1998. Many of the provisions of this constitution restate the homologous provisions of the national Constitution, with a few distinctive elements concerning official languages, the size of the provincial legislature, the establishment of specific provincial institutions such as 'cultural councils' to represent cultural and linguistic communities within the province, the Commissioner for the Environment and the Commissioner for Children, the development of provincial symbols, and a series of directive principles of provincial policy.

In KwaZulu Natal (KZN), one of the provinces which vigorously sought more autonomy for provinces during the national constitution-making process, the provincial constitution-drafting was unsuccessful: 'South Africa's successful transition to democracy reveals two advantages of sub-national constitution making for transitional federal states. Firstly, sub-national constitutions can be effective instruments in conflict management during periods of political instability.' Secondly, they 'can facilitate necessary political socialization' (Marshfield 2008: 588–9). In fact, the inclusion in the national Constitution of a provision allowing for provincial constitutions that would recognize the Zulu monarch was crucial in reaching the compromise which opened the way for the Inkatha Freedom Party (IFP) to participate in the 1994 elections (Spitz and Chaskalson 2000).

Soon after the elections, once the national Constitutional Assembly had started work, the IFP 'employed the process of negotiating a provincial constitution for the province of KZN as surrogate for its participation in the constitutional deliberations of the Constitutional Assembly' (Devenish 1999: 505). Even before the final national Constitution was approved, the KZN's provincial legislature unanimously approved its provincial constitution in March 1996. The CC, however, declined to certify the KZN constitution. In its judgment, the Court found that various provisions 'appear to have been passed by the KZN legislature under a misapprehension that it enjoyed a relationship of co-supremacy with the national legislature and even the Constitutional Assembly' (*Certification of the Constitution of the Province of KwaZulu-Natal*, para. 15). It took the provincial legislature about a decade to issue a second draft, for which the approval and enactment process is still pending. In the meanwhile, the provincial legislature approved the KwaZulu Natal Provincial Leadership and Governance Act (2005), to provide formal recognition for traditional leaders, including the Zulu king, and to establish roles, responsibilities and functions. Supplying a legal framework for the most crucial political, cultural and identity issues, with a strong mobilizing potential, seems to have greatly reduced the pressure for the adoption of a provincial constitution.

Therefore, what is the relevance of provincial constitutions? As stated by the CC, the national Constitution 'provides a complete blueprint for the regulation of government within provinces which provides adequately for the establishment and functioning of provincial legislatures and executives' (*In re Certification of the Constitution of the Western Cape, 1997*, at 15). This asserts that provinces have been designed to function effectively even without provincial constitutions. Indeed, scholars have noted that 'provincial constitutions will never amount to more than window dressing' (Woolman 2005: 21), meaning that they have very little importance as a source of substantive law. However, from a political angle, 'it is noteworthy that the only two provinces which embarked on the provincial constitutional development road are the two provinces where political parties other than the ANC played a significant role since 1994' (Brand 2008: 16). Furthermore, provincial constitutions have played an important role in the transition process. As the KwaZulu Natal case demonstrates, a 'subnational constitution-making process can induce dynamic political interaction between national and regional polities, which in turn can strengthen unstable federal systems' (Marshfield 2008: 590).

The Federal System in Action

The analysis of provincial constitutions seems to validate the thesis of a positive link between federalism (or decentralisation) and 'the ability to manage territorially concentrated ethno-national divisions' (Simeon 1998). What we will now discuss is whether in South Africa, the first two decades of this hybrid structure of the state demonstrates a positive interrelation between federalism and effective governance.

From an electoral perspective, it is noteworthy that since 1994 the ANC has won all elections for provincial legislatures except in the Western Cape (where the New National Party won the 1994 round of elections and the Democratic Alliance was victorious in 2009 and in 2014) and KwaZulu Natal (where the IFP won the 1994 elections and have since then remained the second strongest political party of the province). A discussion of these electoral results and their implications is beyond the scope of this chapter; nonetheless, it is clear that such homogeneity between national and provincial spheres of government, together with the very strict party discipline of the ANC, leaves little space for independent and differentiated provincial policy-making initiatives. Moreover, research highlights the lack of accountability of provincial governments to their provincial electorates as one of the reasons for poor provincial performance. National and provincial elections are held contemporaneously, and party lists are delivered nationally, thus 'there is no mechanism for provincial electorates to hold their provincial governments directly accountable for the choices they make on social spending' (Van Niekerk 2012: 633).

From a service-delivery angle, 'the Big 5 areas of government performance – education, health, welfare, housing and agriculture – are either within the exclusive or concurrent powers of the provinces' (De Villiers 2007: 15). Thus provinces should, to some extent, significantly contribute towards ameliorating the quality of life standards of the population. Nonetheless, three main obstacles prevent provincial governments being effective in the process of delivering a better quality of life. The first is the central dominance granted by the Constitution and the political system to the national government, which thus maintains a very close degree of control over the legislative and executive policies of the provinces (Steytler 2005). Secondly, the skills and capacity shortages, which are evident at the provincial level, result in poor governance, inability to deliver basic services, and major inequalities between provinces. Thirdly, 'an additional, and perhaps more significant, limitation on the competency of the provinces is their ability to tax' (Marshfield 2008: 594). Provinces are precluded from imposing 'income tax, value-added tax, general sales tax, rates on property or custom duties' (s 228), which are the most important revenue sources. They are, however, 'entitled to an equitable share … to provide basic services and perform the functions allocated to them'. Each year, the Division of Revenue Act establishes the division of nationally raised revenue across the three spheres of government. The Intergovernmental Fiscal Relations Act of 1997 prescribes the process for determining the equitable share and allocation of revenue raised nationally. A redistributive formula is used to divide the equitable share among provinces, that is, to balance the simple principle of proportionality with the population. The equitable share, however, takes into consideration functions allocated to provinces by national legislation only, thus 'the provinces are not entitled to additional funding for expenses created by provincial law, and they do not have the authority to raise independent revenue' (Marshfield 2008: 594–5). This process results in a severe contraction of effective provincial autonomy.

In December 2011, the national government took direct control (invoking s 100(1) of the Constitution) of Limpopo, Free State and Gauteng provincial governments to address 'underspending, overspending, and challenges with supply chain management' (Government of South Africa 2011). In Limpopo, the provincial departments that were taken over (where provincial civil servants were replaced by central government officials) included the provincial treasury, education, transport and roads, health, and public works; in Free State, the departments included the provincial treasury, police, roads and transport. In Gauteng, the 'Ministers of Health and Finance will assist the Premier and the Members of the Executive Council with: finance management issues and supply chain management issues'.

The debate surrounding the very existence of the provinces and their future is a longstanding one, which has regularly gained momentum, and then been set aside. In 2007, the Department of Provincial and Local Government (DPLG) itself initiated a policy review process with the 'task of assessing whether existing forms of governance remain appropriate to meeting the changing demands that have become routine in developed and developing countries alike' (DPLG 2007: 3). This revival of interest, which has catalysed political and academic attention for some time, has not led to significant institutional reform. The vast inequalities in education, health and basic infrastructure, such as access to safe water, sanitation and housing which was inherited from the apartheid regime, still maintain a strong provincial element (Ozler 2007: 487), as extensively demonstrated by scientific literature in very different fields.

In education, Sayed and Soudien, for example, illustrate how 'policies of educational decentralisation may exacerbate rather than reduce inequities in society; they may exclude more than include' (2005: 115). Moreover, 'weak capacity in provincial education departments hinders the translation of policy from the national level down to the school level; and without any adjustment in the provincial equitable share [of national revenues], poorer provinces will continue to struggle to fund the many schools falling into no fee poverty quintiles' (Sayed and Motala 2012: 685). If we consider access to basic services, and in particular access to water, major provincial inequalities continue to persist, and they are only partially explained by the urban/rural factor (Federico 2012: 567). Furthermore, 'recent figures reported on healthcare in the Eastern Cape indicated an infant mortality rate of 60 compared to the South African average of 45' (Van Niekerk 2012: 631). This is the consequence of the existence of significant health needs but poor administrative capacities: 'Combined with the poor governance systems characteristic of provinces with a bantustan legacy, the health system in the Eastern Cape failed to deliver adequate health services to the citizens of the province' (ibid.: 632).

The decentralised structure of the state seems therefore to be ineffective in delivering positive governance. The combination of public commitment to decentralisation (during the transition from apartheid) and constitutional provisions supporting the provinces makes overt re-centralisation difficult (Dickovick 2007: 7). Nevertheless, the debate on the future of the provinces remains open: the functions, powers, and even the number of provinces, are under scrutiny. At the 53rd ANC national policy conference, held in December 2012, it was resolved to establish an independent presidential commission to review the role of the provinces. At this stage, the re-interrogation of the state's structure seems to be having little impact on people's lives.

Conclusion

Decentralisation has played an important role in the South African democratisation process: 'Given their presumptive success in the provinces [of Western Cape and KwaZulu Natal] and expected defeat at the national level, the National Party and the Inkatha Freedom Party championed federalism and conditioned their support for democratisation to … guarantees for provinces' (Dickovick 2007: 6). Accommodating requests from minorities for political guarantees through a form of federalism was part of the negotiated democratic transition. Furthermore, constitutional engineering offered a safe riverbed for the negotiations, as it provided the adequate institutional embankments (in this case, the different decentralisation patterns) that made it possible for different people to reach agreement when agreement was necessary (Sunstein 2001: 243). Therefore, federal arrangements were in fact a type of 'peacemaking device' (Steytler and Mettler 2001: 93).

The constitution-makers, through the complex, two-stage constitution-making process, drew up a fairly sophisticated hybrid system, creating a complex mixture of opposite centrifugal and centripetal forces. Democratic constitutions, however, should not be mere documents, but pragmatic instruments, designed to solve concrete problems and to make political life run more smoothly (Sunstein 2001: 244).

Inevitably, the system-in-action has highly simplified the structure in fact, with centripetal forces, mainly derived from the strong dominant party system, prevailing. It is probably too early to judge whether or not this is harming the quality of South African democracy, but it is not too early to affirm that South African quasi-federalism has not provided a viable solution for enhancing governance and bridging socio-economic inequalities.

References

Books, book chapters and articles

Brand, D.J. 2008. 'Asymmetry in the Federal Systems, Constitutional Arrangements in South Africa', *European Diversity and Autonomy Papers, EDAP*, no. 1.

Currie, I. and J. de Waal, 2001. *The New Constitutional and Administrative Law*, Lansdowne: Juta.

Devenish, G. 1999. 'The Making and Significance of the Draft KwaZulu Constitution', *1999 Yearbook African Law*, 47.

de Villiers, B. 2008. *The Future of Provinces in South Africa*, KAS Policy Paper, no. 2.

Dickovick, J.T. 2007. 'Municipalisation as Central Government Strategy: Central-Regional-Local Politics in Peru, Brazil, and South Africa', *Publius: The Journal of Federalism*, 37(1): 1–25.

Federico, V. 2012. '"Ogni persona ha diritto all'acqua". Acqua e diritti fondamentali in Sudafrica', *Diritto Pubblico Comparato ed Europeo*, II: 351–61.

Marshfield, J. 2008. 'Authorising Subnational Constitutions in Transitional Federal States: South Africa, Democracy and KwaZulu Natal Constitution', *Vanderbilt Journal of Transnational Law*, 51: 585–638.

Ozler, B. 2007. 'Not Separate, Not Equal: Poverty and Inequality in Post-apartheid South Africa', *Economic Development and Cultural Change*, 55(3): 487–529.

Rogers, B. 1980. *Divide and Rule: South Africa's Bantustans*. London: IDAF.

Sayed, Y. and S. Motlanta, 2007. 'Equity and "No Fee" School in South Africa: Challenges and Prospects', *Social Policy and Administration*, 46(6): 672–87.

—— and C. Soudien, 2005. 'Decentralisation and the Construction of Inclusion Education Policy in South Africa', *Compare*, 35(2): 115–25.

Sibanda, S. 2014. 'A Critical Analysis in Relation to Single-party Domination', in this volume, Chapter 3.

Simeon, R. 1998. *Considerations on the Design of Federalism*, Queen's University Working Paper, 2, pp. 3–4

Southall, R. 2014. 'The Contradictions of Party Dominance in South Africa', in this volume, Chapter 11.

Spits, R. and M. Chaskalson, 2000. *The Politics of Transition*. Johannesburg: Wits University Press

Steytler, N. 2005. 'Republic of South Africa', in eds J. Kincaid and G.A. Tarr, *Constitutional Origins, Structure and Change in Federal Countries*. Montreal: McGill-Queen's University Press.

—— and J. Mettler, 2001. 'Federal Arrangements as a Peacemaking Device during South Africa's Transition to Democracy', *Publius: The Journal of Federalism*, 31: 93–106.

Sunstein, C. 2001. *Designing Democracy: What Constitutions Do*. New York: Oxford University Press.

van Niekerk, R. 2012. 'Revisiting History: The Creation of Provinces and the Politics of Social Policy in a Democratic South Africa', *Social Policy and Administration*, 46(6): 619–35.

Venter, F. 2014. 'Local Government', in this volume, Chapter 4.

Wittenberg, M. 2003. *Decentralisation in South Africa*, ERSA Policy Paper, no. 21, Johannesburg.

Woolman, S. 2008. 'Provincial Constitutions', in ed. M. Bishop, *Constitutional Law of South Africa*, Landsdowne: Juta.

—— 2009. 'L'etat, c'est moi: Why Provincial Intra-governmental Disputes in South Africa Remain Ungoverned by the Final Constitution and the Intergovernmental Relations Framework Act – and How We Best Resolve Them', *Law, Democracy and Development*, 1: 62–75.

Reports

DPLG, 'Policy Process on the System of Provincial and Local Government', Pretoria 2007.

Government of South Africa, 'National Government Intervenes in Free State, Gauteng, and Limpopo Provinces', Pretoria, 5 December 2011 <http://www.gcis.gov.za/content/newsroom/media-releases/cabinet-statements/statement-cabinet-meeting-5-december-2011> [accessed 30 June 2014].

Cases

Certification of the Constitution of the Western Cape, 1997 (12) BCLR 1653 (CC).

Ex parte President of the RSA: In re Constitutionality of the Liquor Bill, 2000 (1) BCLR 1.

In re Certification of the Constitution of the Western Cape, 1997 (9) BCLR 1167 (CC).

In re Certification of the Constitution of the KwaZulu Natal, 1996 (11) BCLR 141 (CC).

Legislation

Constitution of the Republic of South Africa, 1996.

Intergovernmental Fiscal Relations Act, 97 of 1997.

KwaZulu Natal Provincial Leadership and Governance Act, 5 of 2005.

Public Service Act, 103 of 1994.

Chapter 2
South African 'Quasi-Parliamentarianism'

Romano Orrù

Introduction

Discourses surrounding the form of the State and the system of government can often adopt the classical analytical tool of the 'separation of powers' theory, including both its vertical and horizontal dimensions. Such an approach encompasses the relationship between sovereignty and national territory (that is, the form of the state with reference to the decentralisation process) on the one hand, and the relationship between the different constitutional organs designated to dictate the political agenda of the country (that is, the system of government) on the other hand.

The South African post-1994 legal system is one of the most interesting constitutional experiences in the wave of democratisation which followed the end of the Cold War. A very significant aspect of this experience is the recourse to a sophisticated technique of constitutional engineering that facilitates the hybridisation of existing constitutional models in order to craft original solutions suitable for the context in which they must be embedded.

For this reason there is great difficulty in describing the South African case without resorting to the ambiguous formula using words like 'quasi' and 'semi'.

System of Government ('Form of Government') and Separation of Powers

As mentioned, continental European constitutional doctrine describes the system of government (or form of government) as the patterns of power distribution between the most relevant organs of the state and their interconnections. In other words, the formula is related to the constitutional distribution of competences and authority with regard to the function to determine the basic political choices of the state, which involves Parliament, Government and Head of State as power centres, i.e. the 'Big Power Triangle' (Ágh 1998: 87).

The theory of the separation of powers is therefore an inescapable element in the discussion of the South African system of government although it should not be considered the most crucial. Nevertheless, there are two relevant aspects of the doctrine which must be considered when undertaking an analysis of the South African context.

The first aspect pertains to the observation that "no legal system is a rigorous and coherent application of the principle of the separation of powers. The separation of powers, however, must be the point of attraction for any constitutional system seeking to preserve a minimum level of concrete liberties" (Silvestri 1985: 720, my translation).

The second aspect refers to the idea that "while not sufficing to clarify any difference among the different forms of government, the criterion of a stronger or weaker application of the principle of separation of powers remains essential to distinguish presidential forms of government from parliamentary ones" (Elia 2006: 2601, my translation). Indeed, a more radical separation of powers is a typical element of presidential forms of government, characterised by a dual (democratic) legitimisation, where legislative and executive powers cannot interfere with their reciprocal mandates. Whereas, at the opposite end of the spectrum, a much softer separation of powers denotes the unique, or monist (democratic) legitimisation of parliamentary systems, where (elective) legislative and (non-elective) executive powers are bound by the principle of responsible government and are dependent on the vote of confidence.

The South African system is shaped around a hybridisation between parliamentary and presidential forms of government. Therefore the theory of the separation of powers *per se* is unreliable for the classification of the form of government in the South African context. On the one side, from a static standpoint, an analysis through the principle of the separation of powers does not provide clear results, as it is often applied in a flexible way, highlighting the checks and balances mechanisms, both with reference to legislative versus executive relations, and to legislative and executive versus other typical constitutional State organs (such as the independent administrative authorities, commonly known as the Chapter 9 institutions, and the Constitutional Court (CC) with its judicial review function). On the other side, from a dynamic standpoint, even from a checks and balances perspective, the separation of powers doctrine is challenged by the political frame which is characterised by the single-party dominance of the African National Congress (ANC).

The Problematic Theoretical Definition of the South African System of Government

For some time, European public law scholars, and in particular Italian scholars, have adopted a contextual approach to describe different forms of government, combining legal and empirical data: that is, combining structural elements which are related to the formal legal system, to dynamic factors related to the functioning of the political system.

Nonetheless, the definition of the South African form of government remains problematic, from both a static and a dynamic perspective. South African and international literature often use the formulae of 'parliamentary system' or

'Westminster system' (formulae which essentially concur). However, the form of government created by the Constitution of the Republic of South Africa of 1996 does not fit exactly into these models. Through the combination of new elements borrowed from international experiences with those typical of the South African legal tradition, the constitution-makers designed a new framework of the organs responsible for determining the political agenda, as well as a new pattern of relations between these organs, giving birth to a particular type of hybridisation between parliamentary and presidential forms of government.

The Key Role of the President

One of the most striking elements of this hybridisation is the sacrifice of the double apex of the system (that is, the hendiadys Prime Minister and President of the Republic) typical of parliamentary experiences. This sacrifice leads us to classify the South African system as *quasi-parliamentary* in formal or static terms, and as *basically presidential with parliamentary aspects* in dynamic terms.

The direct election by popular vote of the Head of State, which provides a protagonist role for this organ, dominates political and constitutional realities of sub-Saharan African countries. Post-apartheid South Africa is not an exception, with its President of the Republic, who is simultaneously Head of State and Head of the National Executive. However, the provisions of the 1993 interim Constitution, and later the 1996 final Constitution, have reversed the trend set by other sub-Saharan Constitutions, where the presidential choices were made by regimes with little respect for the separation of powers and the rule of law.

In South Africa, these two principles, which typically characterise liberal democratic regimes, are neither formally nor substantially rejected. Moreover, the constitution makers have provided for an indirect election of the Head of State (a provision which is evident in very few sub-Saharan countries and elsewhere in Southern Africa is only to be found in Botswana: Constitution of 1965, ss 32 and 47).

This indirect election, together with other elements borrowed from the British tradition and other European experiences of parliamentarianism – *inter alia*, the presence of a confidence relationship between the executive (whose *dominus* is the President of the Republic) and the legislature (with mechanisms that typically reflect the German formula of the 'constructive vote of no confidence'); the fact that all members of the Cabinet except two must be members of Parliament; and the inclusion of the instrument of early dissolution of Parliament, even if under special conditions – have sometimes induced scholars to define the form of government of the new South Africa as a particular version of the parliamentary model.

A Particular Form of Hybridisation

Against the theoretical categories elaborated by public law doctrine, and especially those articulated by European scholars, the originality of some choices expressed in the post-1994 South African constitutional order is confirmed in particular by the hybrid nature of its form of government, which inclines towards a presidential system that renounces the autonomous and direct legitimisation of the Head of State through general elections and opts for the predominance of parliamentary elements, at least in legal and formal terms.

The intricate web of relations between the executive and the legislature, as well as the complex system of checks and balances (which also involves independent administrative institutions and the organs entrusted with the responsibility of judicial review) appear to be the product of the negotiations and heritage of Westminster-style constitutionalism. In fact, the structure of the form of government provided for in the 1996 Constitution largely mirrors the one designed in the interim Constitution, with the major difference being the rejection, in the final Constitution, of power-sharing mechanisms (through the instrument of the 'Government of National Unity' which was in place until the end of the first Parliament in 1999, in order to facilitate the search for a *modus vivendi* among the major political parties of the time).

Some elements of the institutional design of the new South Africa are typically drawn from the Westminster parliamentary government model, as it is particularly evident in the constitutional provisions relating to the composition, functions and activities of the national executive. The element of greatest deviation from this model is the refusal of the principle of parliamentary supremacy (this was a distinct element of the apartheid regime), which has been replaced by the supremacy of the Constitution. Adherence to the principle of the supremacy of the Constitution has important repercussions for the form of government as, on the one hand, the Head of State and the executive can exercise neither prerogative powers nor unlimited powers in a state of emergency, and, on the other hand, the ordinary dialectic of checks and balances is extended to include the CC together with the legislature and the executive.

South African System of Government 'in action'

In the South African case, we can therefore consider how the dynamic elements significantly alter the static perspective. Building on the assumption that the 1996 Constitution outlines a hybrid system combining presidential and parliamentary models, the static analysis suggests that the parliamentary aspect prevails, whereas the dynamic approach indicates that the presidential aspect is more relevant: decisive in this respect, as mentioned, is the influence of the political frame characterized by the single-party dominance. Furthermore, the socio-economic context contributes to the emphasis of the presidential aspect. In fact, the need to face the social challenges of HIV/AIDS and the legacies of the previous apartheid regime – particularly the severe socio-economic inequalities which have troubled the young South African democracy – leads to a high level of State intervention in these economic and social realities. This need also influences the structure of formal relations between the constitutional organs of the State, thus allowing a presidential system of government to prevail.

The political landscape and the party system are of significant importance in the *de facto* articulation of the system of government. South African constitution-makers drew up the 1996 Constitution with a pre-determined political scenario in mind; therefore all of the constitutional and institutional mechanisms which relate to the function of choosing the fundamental policies of the State have not been conceived blindly or under a veil of ignorance regarding the electoral force of the different political parties in the new South Africa, as the peculiarities of the constitution-making process reveal (in particular the two-step process and the idea of a Government of National Unity built upon the power-sharing system).

Returning to the analysis of the formal aspects of the system of government, the constitutional choice of having a President of the Republic who is both the leader of the dominant party in Parliament and the Head of the executive, thus substituting the figure of Prime Minister, produces a not so negligible anomaly in the operating logic of any parliamentary system. It is noticeable, however, that in the South African case the Head of State is not politically divested, and as such there is no break in the connection between power and accountability, which is typical of contemporary representative democracies. Indeed, there is not even a break of the political bond between government action and Parliament's political orientation, which is typical of parliamentary systems. Nonetheless, the South African model cannot simply be considered to be a variation of presidential systems, as the no-confidence motion, the early dissolution, as well as the parliamentary derivation of the legitimisation of the executive clearly demonstrate.

According to the Constitution, the President of the Republic cannot 'survive' the National Assembly that has elected her/him; all Ministers (except a maximum of two) must be members of Parliament; the National Assembly can oblige the executive (Cabinet and the President) to resign; and it does not face the risk of being dissolved without its consent.

The specific hybridisation between the two basic forms of government of contemporary liberal democratic constitutionalism therefore compels us to consider the new South African form of government to be an autonomous model.

South Africa as a 'Quasi-Parliamentary' System

The 'semi-parliamentary' formula, that could adequately represent – from a linguistic perspective – the South African case, is often used to describe legal systems which do not fully belong to the parliamentary system characterised by the concomitant election of Parliament and Premier (as realised in Israel between

1992 and 2001); therefore other formulae must be forged in order to grasp the specificity of the South African context. Why not use the 'para-parliamentary' or 'quasi-parliamentary' labels? These expressions better describe the cross-fertilisation between parliamentary and presidential systems as they highlight the monistic characterization of the form of government, i.e. the single electoral legitimisation of both the legislative and the executive authority.

In other words, a form of government resulting from the implantation on the parliamentary system of elements of presidentialism which can be inferred both in a dynamic perspective – due to the action of pre- or extra- legal factors: the party system, the dominant political culture, *de facto* relations between constitutional organs, *praeter-constitutionem* praxis, and so on – and in a formal and structural one, as it is the case of the constitutional provisions that frame the President in its dual role of Head of the executive and Head of State.

It is important to stress that, notwithstanding functional and political considerations, the structural differences with the parliamentary system of government remain pronounced. The absence of the Prime Minister cannot simply be glossed over following the absorption of the role by the President of the Republic. And it is not useful to consider that in the Westminster model the prominence of the British Prime Minister over the Crown makes the political scene be substantially dominated by one single institution. In the UK as in other Commonwealth countries (that is, former Dominions of the British Empire), the Head of State (the monarch in the UK or the Governor General in Australia, Canada and New Zealand) has a 'ceremonial role, of high symbolic value, but without any significant power', and yet, 'when the political system automatism (political elections which determine the majority in Parliament; the Prime Minister as leader of the winning party, leading the Cabinet) which characterises the British model stalls, the Head of State regains his/her importance through the exercise of a mediation role that can have significant weight on the political equilibrium' (Olivetti 2007*:* 532, my translation). This conceptualisation of the Head of State as a 'reserve power' (that dates back to the theory of the monarch as '*povuoir neutre*' expressed by Benjamin Constant in his *Principes de Politique* of 1815) or as a 'crisis manager' (Esposito 1960: 236, my translation) during functional difficulties encountered by the system or in case of deadlock is of crucial importance in typical parliamentary systems. This is thoroughly illustrated by the recent Italian experience and, in the Commonwealth countries experiences, it was clearly manifest in the Canadian 'King-Byng Affair' in 1926 as well as in the Australian crisis of 1975 when the Governor General dismissed the elected Prime Minister and appointed the leader of the opposition as new Prime Minister.

The Story of Polokwane, a Turning Point Missed or Taken?

As mentioned earlier, the empirical evidence suggests a different interpretation of the apparent centrality of Parliament, due primarily to the specific South

African political party arena being centred on the ANC, a *dominant* party given its numbers, although not a *hegemonic* one. It is important to point out that 'a dominant party is a party which is invested of the right to govern by a series of consecutive popular mandates obtained through regular elections' and that the hegemonic party operates in a frame in which opposition parties cannot compete on an antagonistic and equality basis and thus the alternation in power is not possible (Carbone 2006: 71, my translation). The South African case is rather different from other African countries where a single party predominates for a long period of time. In South Africa, in fact, the dominant party does not have the features of an 'authoritarian, dominant party' nor does it resemble a 'combination of personal ties and ethnic solidarities', furthermore it is not devoid of 'ideological, socio-economic or programmatic foundations' (Carbone 2006: 71, my translation).

The ANC penetration in all aspects of public administration renders the Parliament the *dominant institution* only on paper: in *praxis*, the impact of parliamentary activity (also the monitoring/control powers) on the agenda of the executive is weak. In South Africa, despite the existence at constitutional level of the institution of the 'official opposition', in practice, due to the concentration of electoral consensus on the ANC, it is evident that 'there is no credible government in waiting' (Murray 2005: 4).

To understand the reasons behind the electoral success of the ANC, we should not underestimate the party's effectiveness in capitalising upon its image as the most prominent national liberation movement on the African continent. A potential turning point could have emerged in 2007 from the turbulence within the ANC which became apparent at the 52nd Party Conference at Polokwane 'when the ANC divided into competing factions' (Klug 2010:182). The reluctance of sections of the ANC to accept the centralising attitude of – at that time – President Thabo Mbeki as well as the even stronger rejection of his neoliberal policies summarised in the 'Growth, Employment and Redistribution strategy' (GEAR), which failed to adequately address the negative economic legacy of apartheid, paved the way for a harsh confrontation with Mr Jacob Zuma, his challenger for the presidency of the party and thus for the presidency of the country. At Polokwane, both the principle of the 'dual presidency' and the capacity of the ANC to monopolise the representation of the black majority were placed into doubt. The praxis of the 'dual presidency' establishes that the guidance and maintaining of the ANC leadership (and thus its presidency) ensure both access to the office of President of the Republic and the conservation of the office itself.

President Mbeki, who could not be elected as President of the Republic for a third time, sought a third term as President of the ANC, thus attempting to break the link between the two presidencies. Defeated on that occasion by Zuma, Mbeki still remained in office as President of the Republic until September 2008, thanks to the support he could muster from a portion of the parliamentary group. This support made problematic the approval of a parliamentary motion of no confidence against him and, in short, led to the split of the ANC with the birth of COPE (Congress of the People). Given the impracticability of the early dissolution of

Parliament, Mbeki was forced to resign by the new ANC leadership in the wake of a court ruling that declared Zuma victim of unlawful judicial persecution, and the presidency was held by current deputy president Kgalema Motlante.

Hence, in the latter period of Mbeki's presidency, the dilemma of the difficult co-existence of two, highly competitive, centres of power was resolved through the removal of Mbeki and by a government crisis which was solved *praeter Constitutionem*, that is, through non-parliamentary solutions. This replicates much of the Italian constitutional experience since 1948.

Despite such circumstances, the post-Polokwane period did not lead to a significantly different political outcome: at the 2009 elections the ANC confirmed its overwhelming electoral strength (it obtained 65.9 per cent of the vote which translated into 264 parliamentary seats against the 30 seats of the Congress of the People (COPE), which received 7.4 per cent of votes). The high prevalence of one single party was reaffirmed in the 2014 elections, when the ANC, despite a slight decline of 3,75 per cent of the votes obtained, remained by far the largest party gaining 249 seats in the NA against the 89 seats won by the second political force and main opposition party, the Democratic Alliance, or DA, which collected 22,2 per cent of the votes.

The enduring context of single-party dominance after the 2009 and 2014 elections has confirmed the dynamics of the 'dual presidency' and strengthened the degree of interaction between the ANC leadership – in particular its National Executive Committee – and the executive, leading to a 'constant fluctuation of decision-making power' between the two centres of power (Klug 2010: 207).

The prominence of the executive, in particular the role of the President in the determination and implementation of the political agenda of the majority, has been particularly strengthened by Mbeki's term in office and even more so from 2009 onwards under his successor. In fact, the 'Presidency's' power has increased over time through four key political players: the President, the Deputy President, and two Ministers serving as the central planning and coordinating structure of government. The 'Presidency' represents the real political decision-maker and 'the most powerful political institution in the country' while the Cabinet remains the 'formal decision-making centre of the executive' (Klug 2010: 204).

Concluding Remarks

To conclude, the post-apartheid South African form of government outlined in the Constitution does not fit traditional models. It is true that there is a variety of different, and often very significant (Sartori 2004: 97), realisations of the parliamentary model but it is not feasible to extend such a model to include, *tout court*, the South African case as doing so would jeopardise the explanatory capacity of this model, especially if we consider – as it seems appropriate – also its dynamic profile.

The overall weakness of the parliamentary institutions due to the presence of a dominant party, the complexity and low efficiency of the parliamentary apparatus, in particular the National Council of Provinces (NCOP), as well as the high degree of executive control over the agenda of Parliament (especially when the legislative process involves financial profiles) and the difficulty of effective activation of the instruments of parliamentary oversight, given an electoral system that does not favour the contact between elected representatives and their constituencies, all point to a hybrid parliamentary-presidential system.

In the struggle between *accountability* and *party solidarity* which emerges when analysing the checks and balances system designed to contain the power of the President, it is party solidarity that prevails (Klug 2010: 221). In the praxis this prevalence of party solidarity exalts the presidential component of the form of government.

Furthermore, the system of territorial decentralisation does not work as a constraint on presidential power: on the one hand, the ANC maintains controls of the provincial governments – except for Western Cape after the 2014 elections – and, on the other hand, the NCOP has encountered serious difficulties in fulfilling its role as co-legislator. Both aspects have *de facto* neutralised the capacity of such institutions to counterbalance the centralisation of decision-making power in the leadership of the national executive (and of the ANC). In this framework, also Chapter 9 institutions have proved to be weak.

The executive power, however, has met on his way an effective institutional embankment: the judiciary and especially the CC committed to ensure the respect for the Constitution as the supreme law. On the one hand the CC has put in place a genuine counterbalance to the action of the executive considering justiciable, to some extent, the powers conferred on the President by the Constitution (for example in *Executive Council of the Western Cape Legislature v President of the RSA* 1995 and in *President of the Republic of South Africa v Hugo* 1997) and ultimately directing the action of the executive to constitutionally legitimate objectives (typically in decisions on socio-economic rights such as *Government of the Republic of South Africa v Grootboom* 2000, and *Minister of Health v Treatment Action Campaign* 2002). On the other hand, the constitutional judges did not fail to clearly identify their own limits, consisting in the fact that 'the dignity and status of the President' must be 'preserved and protected' (*SARFU 3* 2000, para 243) so that in a 'young democracy facing immense challenges of transformation' it is taken into account 'the need to ensure the ability of the executive to act efficiently and promptly' (*Premier, Mpumalanga v Executive Committee of State-aided Schools, Eastern Transvaal* 1999, para 41). In this, the CC has acknowledged the unique nature of South Africa's version of separation of powers and affirmed the indispensability of a 'delicate balancing' between these powers (*De Lange v Smuts* 1998, para 60).

Recently, however, even the control of constitutional legitimacy by the judiciary as a potential tool to limit the power of the executive is at risk. After the so called Hlophe controversy of 2008–2009 (when the CC denounced to the Judicial

Service Commission 'an improper attempt to influence [its] pending judgement in one or more cases' , the legal community has in fact expressed concerns at the appointment of the new Chief Justice of the CC in September 2011, with the background of the increased role that the CC has to play in the judicial system by virtue of the Seventeenth Amendment Act of the Constitution, of 2013. This has established the Court as 'the highest court of the Republic' whereas before it shared this prominence in the judicial system with the Supreme Court of Appeal. The concerns expressed by the legal community have thus stigmatised any possibility for the CC to be more accommodating with the executive, or at least, less reactive in the fulfilment of its prerogatives.

Finally, to really understand the current form of government in South Africa, we must move beyond the criterion of the separation of powers conceived in a traditional or abstract manner and, rather, consider the actual checks and balances that operate in the system (O'Regan 2005). As a result, labelling the new South Africa's form of government as a quasi- or semi-parliamentary system offers a way to give the appropriate emphasis to its peculiarities. On paper, the country qualifies as a parliamentary model, but in *praxis* it is more of a presidential system operating in the context of a one-party dominant system. Limitations on the powers of the President can however occur through the disequilibrium which may emerge from within the dominant party.

Nevertheless, we should note that the constitutional structure in its entirety has overall been resistant to the challenges raised by such de facto changes in the form of government. Even at the highest peak of the political crisis in 2007-2009, the hard struggle for the Presidency remained within constitutional boundaries.

The young non-racial South African democracy does however need to develop its self-protection mechanisms at political, social and cultural levels to avoid the degeneration of presidential powers which would jeopardise the separation of powers and the rule of law.

References

Books, book chapters and articles

Ågh A., 1998, *The Politics of Central Europe*, London: SAGE.

Brooks, H. 2004. *The Dominant Party System: Challenges for South Africa's Second Decade of Democracy*, EISA Occasional Paper n. 25 (accessed at http://www.eisa.org.za/PDF/OP25.pdf%20December%202013").

Carbone, G.M. 2006. *Partiti politici e sistemi di partito in Africa. Temi e prospettive di ricerca, Rivista italiana di scienza politica*, 36 (1), 57.

Corder, H. 2004, Judicial authority in a changing South Africa, *Legal Studies*, 24, 253.

De Vos, P. 2006. The Role of the National Council of Provinces in the Governance of South Africa, in J. Luther, P. Passaglia, R. Tarchi (eds), *A World of Second Chambers*, Milano: Giuffrè, 613.

Elia, L. 1970. *Governo (forme di)*, in *Enciclopedia del diritto*, vol. XIX, Milano: Giuffrè, 634.

Elia, L. 2006. *Forme di Stato e Forme di governo*, in S. Cassese (ed.), *Dizionario di diritto pubblico*, vol. III, Milano: Giuffrè, 2593.

Esposito C. 1960. *Capo dello Stato*, in *Enciclopedia del diritto*, vol. VI, Milano: Giuffrè, 224.

Gicquel, J. 1977. *Le présidentialisme négro-africain*, in AA.VV., *Mélanges offerts à Georges Burdeau*, Paris: LGDJ,701.

Klug, H. 2000. *Constituting Democracy: Law, Globalism and South Africa's Political Reconstruction*, Cambridge: Cambridge University Press.

Klug, H. 2010. *The Constitution of South Africa. A Contextual Analysis*, Oxford; Portland OR: Hart publishing.

Murray, C. 2005. *Republic of South Africa*, Forum of Federations-International Association of Centers of Federal Studies, (accessed at http://www.forumfed.org/libdocs/Global_Dialogue/Book_3/BK3-C09-za-Murray-en.pdf, December 2013).

Murray, C. and Simeon, R. 1999. From Paper to Practice: The National Council of Provinces after its First Year, *SA Public Law*, 14, 96.

Olivetti, M. 2007. *Forme di Stato e di governo*, in S. Patti (ed.), *Il diritto – Enciclopedia Giuridica*, vol. 6, Milano: Corriere della Sera-Il Sole 24 ore, 508

O'Regan, K. 2005. *Checks and Balances reflections on the development of the doctrine of separation of powers under the South African Constitution*, PER/PELJ 8 (1), 21.

Philippe, X. 2009. *La démocratie constitutionnelle sud-africaine: un modèle?*, in *Pouvoirs*, n. 129, 157.

Rautenbach, I.M. and Malherbe, E.F.J. 1996. *Constitutional Law*, 2nd ed., Cape Town: Butterworths.

Sartori, G. 2004. *Ingegneria costituzionale comparata*, 4th ed., Bologna: Il Mulino.

Silvestri, G. 1985. *Poteri dello Stato (divisione)*, in *Enciclopedia del diritto*, vol. XXXIV, Milano: Giuffrè, 670.

Southall, R. 1998. The Centralization and Fragmentation of South Africa's Dominant Party System, *African Affairs*, 97, 443.

Cases

De Lange v Smuts 1998 (3) SA 785 (CC), 1998 (7) BCLR 779 (CC)

Executive Council of the Western Cape Legislature v President of the RSA 1995 (10) BCLR 1289 (CC)

Premier, Mpumalanga v Executive Committee of State-aided Schools, Eastern Transvaal 1999 (2) BCLR 151 (CC); 1999 (2) SA 91 (CC)

President of the Republic of South Africa v Hugo 1997 (6) BCLR 708 (CC)

President of the RSA v South African Rugby Football Union (SARFU 3) 1999 (10) BCLR 1059 (CC); 2000 (1) SA 1 (CC).
The Government of the Republic of South Africa & Others v Irene Grootboom and others 2000 (11) BCLR 1169 (CC).
Minister of Health v Treatment Action Campaign 2002 (5) SA 72 (CC).

Chapter 3

Parliament and the Separation of Powers – A Critical Analysis in Relation to Single-party Domination

Sanele Sibanda[1]

> Another institution with a watchdog role is Parliament. But members of Parliament, who are supposed to be the guardians of democracy, have become the hacklers [*sic*] of opposition and cheerleaders of the executive. They have become an extension of the party caucus, forgetting that they were elected by the people of South Africa
>
> Moshoeshoe Monare, *The Sunday Independent*, 15 October 2012

Introduction

To what extent is Monare's bleak assessment borne out by the public record? This chapter seeks to evaluate such comments in the light of both its constitutional authority and the manner in which South Africa's Parliament has performed over the past twenty years.

Parliament comprises two houses, namely the National Assembly (NA) and the National Council of Provinces (NCOP). On the one hand, the Constitution establishes the NA as the house representing the people, as well as ensuring government by the people. The members of the NA, in keeping with the constitutional commitment to multi-partyism, are elected via a closed-list system of proportional representation. On the other hand, the Constitution positions the NCOP as being primarily concerned with ensuring that provincial interests are taken into account in the consideration of national issues. The NCOP is constituted by nine provincial delegations, each with ten members, that vote predominantly as blocs in representing each of South Africa's provinces. Whilst each house performs a constitutionally distinct function, Parliament is regarded compositely as the legislative branch of government, and is an independent,

1 I would like to thank Jade Aspeling and Tshepo Mothulwe for their resourcefulness in providing research assistance during my preparations for writing this chapter. I would also like to thank Bernadette Atuahene, Jonathan Klaaren and Tshepo Madlingozi for their very useful comments and insights. Finally many thanks to my editor, Silindiwe Sibanda, for her attentive editorial inputs. All mistakes or omissions remain my own.

autonomous and deliberative representative institution with national jurisdiction. As such, Parliament is central to South Africa's constitutional democracy for several reasons, including being the embodiment of its multi-party representative democracy, making law, and coordinating with, and ultimately being responsible for checking and balancing, the executive and the judicial branches in terms of the constitutionally mandated separation of powers.

While the Constitution may be clear as to what is Parliament's envisaged role, how this plays out in practice is quite another story. There are several obvious reasons why this is the case, such as the historical, political and social dynamics of post-apartheid South Africa. Therefore, any evaluation of Parliament's performance in the post-1994 period must take into account dynamics such as the African National Congress's (ANC) massive electoral support that is in part a legacy of its history as a liberation movement. The ANC's dominance in Parliament has resulted in much debate over the past twenty years, with views ranging from those contending that this need not necessarily be conceived of as a problem (Habib and Taylor 2001) to other more extreme views that consider it as veritably undermining democracy (Giliomee et al. 2001). According to Southall (2005), whose work has tracked this dominant-party debate over the entire post-1994 period, the truth probably lies somewhere in between. In terms of this view, whilst such dominance has posed challenges to South Africa's young democracy, it has not necessarily translated into egregious and wanton undermining of constitutional institutions such as Parliament.

Against this brief background, a central concern for this chapter is how, in spite of the ANC's dominance, does Parliament remain an effective branch of government, particularly in light of its crucial constitutional role when construed within the doctrine of separation of powers? Put simply, what does single-party domination mean for an effective separation of powers? Does single-party dominance necessarily weaken the functioning of the separation of powers, especially when, in keeping with parliamentary systems of government, nearly all members of the executive branch are simultaneously legislators and senior members of the governing party? Does the ANC's control of the executive and its dominance in Parliament mean that separation of powers (and the resultant checks and balances) between these two branches is rendered meaningless to such an extent that Parliament may be regarded as being little more than a 'rubber stamp'? (Barkan 2005.) Has the South African constitutional structure provided mechanisms to obviate this possibility? Adding complexity to any attempt at answering these questions is, of course, the difficulty of discerning, with forensic precision, the exact nature and limits of South Africa's doctrine of separation of powers (Seedorf and Sibanda 2008).

This chapter suggests that to characterise Parliament solely in terms of ANC dominance would miss the dynamics entailed in how opposition parties and a vast range of other social actors or extra-parliamentary forces have manoeuvred to utilise what space, influence and power they are afforded by the Constitution to exert some form of checks and balances. In other words, it will be argued that as we consider the separation of powers, we also need to consider how politically weaker minority parties and extra-parliamentary forces have attempted to counteract the political dominance of the majority party by participating in waves of issue-based oppositional moments through parliamentary processes.

This chapter consists of six parts, including this introduction. The next part outlines Parliament's role, power and functions, as well as its relationship to the other two branches. A concise critical overview of how Parliament has performed in the period post-1994 follows. The fourth part analyses the role of Parliament in the separation of powers, particularly as viewed from the perspective of a dominant-party democracy as defined by Choudhry (2009:3), and in light of the 'pathologies and symptoms of dominant party democracy' identified by him. In the fifth part, the chapter interrogates why the ANC, despite its parliamentary and executive dominance, does not always have its way in Parliament by simply using its overwhelming majority to completely marginalise minority political parties. The Traditional Courts Bill is used as a case study to illustrate the impact of opposition parties and extra-parliamentary forces in engaging in anti-domination political practices that influence the legislative processes in their favour. In the concluding part, some tentative suggestions are made as to how these anti-domination political practices may be read to inform how we understand Parliament as a national forum for the consideration of issues.

Parliament's Constitutional Mandate and its Relationship to the Other Branches

> Constitutional Principle IV in the interim Constitution of 1993 enjoined the Constitutional Assembly to incorporate separation of powers and a system of mutual checks and balances between the three branches in the Constitution. Therefore, institutional relations between Parliament and the other two branches are dictated by the Constitution's articulation of the doctrine of separation of powers which, whilst not explicitly expressed in the text, can be deduced from the structure of the Constitution. (Seedorf and Sibanda 2008: 12–20)

Section 42 of the Constitution is pivotal in defining Parliament. It sets out its bicameral structure, its central location within the constitutional democracy as the institution representing the people whilst simultaneously balancing national and provincial interests, and its constitutional role. Parliament's functions are: (1) to make law, (2) to exercise oversight over the executive branch, (3) to elect the President of the Republic, and (4) to provide a national forum for the consideration of issues whilst also taking into account how these issues impact on the provinces.

Affirming the supremacy of the Constitution, s 44(4) provides that when Parliament exercises its legislative authority it does so constrained only by the fact that it must act in accordance with, and within the limits of, the Constitution. In practice, the implications of this provision are that, outside of a court challenge to an exercise of legislative authority and any ensuing declaration of constitutional invalidity, Parliament has extensive latitude with respect to how it exercises its powers and executes its mandate. Further, as an independent branch of government, Parliament is empowered to regulate its own processes in a manner that promotes democratic accountability, transparency and public participation. In furtherance of these values, the Constitution confers parliamentary privilege on members for all speeches made in Parliament and its committees, as well as the power to summon any person to participate in its proceedings whenever necessary.

Whilst Parliament is institutionally autonomous, the Constitution permits extensive executive involvement in the legislative process, particularly within the NA. Beyond being entitled to introduce legislation, members of the executive are also responsible for developing policy, preparing and initiating legislation, and eventually implementing these laws once enacted. The relationship established between Parliament and the executive is premised on the Westminster tradition of parliamentary government with all but two members of the executive, excluding the President, simultaneously being members of the NA. The Constitution clearly envisages a close functional relationship between these two branches. In light of this relationship, Parliament (particularly the NA) is enjoined to perform an oversight function over the executive branch as a means of ensuring democratic practice and promoting good governance premised on the values of accountability, responsiveness and openness.

Parliament has little constitutional leverage over, or involvement with, the judicial branch outside of its law-making powers and its involvement in the selection and removal of judges. Instead, it is the judiciary that, by virtue of its powers of review under a supreme constitution, is able to exert significant checks and balances over Parliament where questions of constitutionality arise. In this respect, any law enacted by the Parliament that is challenged and subsequently found by a court to be without a constitutionally valid justification must be declared to be unconstitutional to the extent of such invalidity. An example that illustrates the courts' powers is to be found in the case of *Tongoane* v *National Minister for Agriculture and Land Affairs* (2010) where, despite Parliament's power to regulate its own processes, the Communal Land Rights Act was declared to be unconstitutional in its entirety by the Constitutional Court (CC) for failure to pass the Act in accordance with the correct legislative procedures. There have, over the past 20 years, also been numerous other examples of legislative provisions being declared to be unconstitutional for a variety of reasons, usually related to rights violations.

We now turn to consider the extent to which Parliament has succeeded in meeting this multifaceted mandate.

A Critical Overview of Parliament in the Post-1994 Era

One of the most pressing tasks faced by South Africa's first democratic parliament was an extensive and demanding legislative programme. Klug (2010) rightly points out that much of this was necessitated by the voluminous apartheid laws in need of review, amendment, or repeal. Added to this was the need for Parliament, in furtherance of its democratic mandate, to embark on a transformative legislative agenda that included the production of constitutionally mandated legislation, such as the Promotion of Equality and Prevention of Unfair Discrimination Act (2000), the Promotion of Administrative Justice Act (2000), and the Promotion of Access to Information Act (2000). In as far as the processing of legislation is concerned, by most accounts, Parliament has performed satisfactorily considering the sheer amount of legislation it has considered and passed in the post-1994 period (Murray and Nijzink 2002, Klug 2010).

Whereas legislating is one of Parliament's primary functions, a concern raised by many commentators relates to Parliament's failure to initiate and prepare legislation itself. In the 2009 Independent Panel Assessment Report, it was noted that, up to the time of writing, Parliament had yet to initiate or prepare legislation in spite of constitutional provisions (s 55 (1)*(b)*) empowering it to do so. Instead, it is the executive that has come to be centrally positioned in the initiation, preparation and introduction of legislation in Parliament. Pieterse (2004), describing the relationship between the two, suggests that the executive has Parliament in a 'stranglehold', whilst Murray and Nijzink (2002) note that this is in keeping with the trend in modern parliamentary systems. This implies that the executive has gained a seemingly unassailable ascendancy over Parliament in matters legislative, as it is the executive that possesses the technical expertise, institutional capacity and organisational continuity to develop a sustained legislative agenda.

Parliament has thus come to assume something of a secondary, if not 'reactive', role relative to the executive in its primary role of law-making. Parliament's secondary role is evident in its own rules, as was exposed in the 2012 CC case, *Ambrosini* v *Sisulu.* In this matter, a member of the minority Inkatha Freedom Party challenged parliamentary rules that inhibited individual members from introducing legislation in the NA without first seeking permission from a parliamentary committee. The CC found the rules in question to be unconstitutional as they were not in keeping with the values of participatory and representative democracy.

An aspect of Parliament's work that has attracted much attention is the performance of its oversight function over the executive. The Constitution is near-emphatic on the point that exercise of executive power must be subjected to constitutional checks and balances. On the one hand, it obliges the NA to put in place mechanisms to hold the executive to account and maintain oversight over it (s 55 (2)) and on the other it obliges members of the executive to be accountable both individually and collectively to Parliament, which includes providing Parliament with full and regular reports. According to Murray and Nijzink (2002: 88–9), Parliament's lack of effectiveness on this score can be attributed to several factors, including: (1) a relic of the Westminster tradition that places the oversight role primarily on opposition parties; (2) a lack of understanding by parliamentarians of what oversight entails, thus leading to a focus on making administrative heads rather than cabinet members account as the political heads of such departments;

and (3) a generally unwavering party loyalty, particularly amongst members of the governing party. This latter point is probably generally regarded as being emblematic of Parliament's shortcomings in terms of its oversight function. Klug (2010: 176–81) cites two prominent examples where ANC loyalties served to trump parliamentary initiatives to compel the executive to account, namely the Sarafina II saga (the controversial commissioning of a very expensive theatre production) and the Arms Deal Inquiry (the procurement of military equipment in 1999, dogged then and ever since by allegations of corruption at the highest level). More recently, reference to two stand-offs in 2010 involving a cabinet minister and parliamentary committees serve to further underscore this point (Ferreira 2010).

Many commentators have been critical of the control exerted by party bosses over parliamentarians as a result of the closed-list system of proportional representation practised in South Africa (Murray and Nijzink 2002). At the core of this criticism is a concern that members of Parliament in the majority party are beholden to senior party colleagues who are either in the Cabinet or in the party's executive structures, and thus control the electoral list-making processes. Choudhry (2009: 30) has described this problem as being one that manifests as a 'subordinating [of] parliamentary to non-parliamentary wings of the dominant political party'. In 2009, taking cognisance of the challenges posed by the closed-list system with regard to enabling members of Parliament to bring in an independence of mind and conscience to bear in their tasks, the Independent Panel Assessment recommended that the electoral system based on proportional representation should be replaced by a 'mixed' system. However, this recommendation has yet to achieve any serious traction.

One thread that appears to run through much of the criticism levelled against Parliament and its performance is that of the omnipresent ANC as the dominant force in both Parliament and the executive. This ANC dominance has led Choudhry to characterise South Africa as being a dominant party democracy. In doing so, he locates South Africa within:

> … a set of polities whose constitutional design is liberal democratic, which provides an entrenched framework for multiparty democracy through universal suffrage and regular elections and which contemplates political competition and the alternation of political parties in power, but in which one party enjoys electoral dominance and continues to win free and fair elections that are not tainted by force or fraud. (Ibid.: 3)

Whether one accepts the specifics of this characterisation or not, what is undeniable is the fact that contemporary South Africa certainly displays some, if not all, of these characteristic features. Of interest is the following: does the fact that a State can be characterised as a dominant party democracy pose particular challenges to the entrenchment of an effective system of separation of powers? In particular, what does single-party domination mean for the very character of Parliament if its identity (and by extension that of the executive mostly drawn from the ranks of Parliament) is virtually collapsed into that of a single political party? The next section explores these questions, in the context of Choudhry's thesis.

Parliament and Separation of Powers in the Context of a Dominant Party Democracy

Choudhry argues provocatively for an approach to constitutional interpretation that deliberately locates the notion of dominant-party democracy prominently in our understanding of the nature of South Africa's constitutional democracy. At the core of his thesis is the suggestion of the adoption of a set of constitutional adjudicative principles that may be invoked in litigation against legislative or executive schemes where single-party dominance is perceived to be used in ways that perpetuate such party's incumbency and can, further, be perceived as undermining democracy. These 'pathologies', as Choudhry terms them, manifest themselves in particular practices where a dominant party uses its majority to its own advantage irrespective of the costs to constitutional democracy. Examples cited by Choudhry include the controversial floor-crossing period in Parliament (*United Democratic Movement v President of South Africa* 2003) and the ANC's policy of cadre-deployment (*Pikoli v President of South Africa* 2010). Although he is primarily concerned with the role of the courts, particularly the CC, as 'bulwarks against a dominant political party' (Choudry 2009: 7), there is much in his thesis that is instructive as to how we consider the threats or challenges posed by single-party domination in giving life to the democratic values and ideals of the Constitution more broadly.

Ultimately, Choudhry suggests that constitutional lawyers must recognise the particular institutional challenges which dominant-party democracy poses and must develop constitutional doctrines that address them directly. For example, he recommends the development of explicit 'anti-domination', 'anti-capture', 'anti-centralisation' and 'non-usurpation' doctrines. Whilst Choudhry's thesis is undoubtedly full of important insights, it is limited in that it is court-centric and thus makes it difficult to extrapolate directly from it to our present concern with Parliament and the separation of powers. Despite this, it encourages us to look at the idea of a dominant-party democracy less as a zero-sum game, but rather as a manifestation of democracy that poses particular institutional challenges that demand deeper, more deliberate examination and creativity in order to respond to the resultant situation as *is*, rather than lamenting the lack of other idealised notions of what a modern liberal democracy *ought to be.*

Choudhry's approach would, I suggest, be in keeping with the notion espoused in 1998 by the CC in *De Lange* v *Smuts* (at paras 60–61), namely that:

> … over time our Courts will develop a distinctively South African model of separation of powers, one that fits the particular system of government provided

> for in the Constitution and that reflects a delicate balancing, informed both by South Africa's history and its new dispensation.

This could be read to mean that, when issues of separation of powers are considered in a manner that takes due cognisance of history and the current environment, it may be justified to factor in South Africa's character as a dominant-party democracy in developing an appropriate conception of separation of powers.

I suggest that such developments may already be occurring in practical terms in that Parliament, as an institution, has been used by opposition parties to great effect where they have acted in concert or in tandem with extra-parliamentary forces to check the ANC's parliamentary dominance. Extra-parliamentary forces are social actors such as organised civil society, social movements, community-based organisations, the press, and other groups, both formal and informal, that organise and mobilise either individually or collectively around specific causes in order to influence or oppose legislation pending before Parliament. Such forces have actively participated in parliamentary proceedings to voice their opposition to, or support of, a particular issue of national interest pending before Parliament. I argue that opposition parties and extra-parliamentary forces have used Parliament in ways that are analogous to the anti-domination or anti-capture practices proffered by Choudhry.

Opposition Parties, Extra-parliamentary Forces and the Separation of Powers

Most accounts of Parliament's function as a national forum for the public consideration of important issues tend to characterise it as the promotion of debate, dialogue, and more broadly the representation of a diversity of views by virtue of its multi-party composition. Seldom is this facet approached within a more critical frame that asks what it contributes to checking the powers of the executive and single-party dominance. Therefore, rather than focusing on the shortcomings in Parliament's legislative role and the performance of its oversight function, I am suggesting that a closer examination of how Parliament has been used as national forum may yield some interesting conclusions as to how we could extend our understanding of the separation of powers.

This moves the focus away from the ANC, its 'hegemony', perceptions that it is responsible for the erosion of democracy, and how it is widely viewed as blunting the constitutional checks and balances between Parliament and the executive. Instead, the question should be: what is it that prevents the ANC from simply forcing through its agenda in spite of its legislative dominance and executive control? Put slightly differently, what is it that parliamentary opposition and extra-parliamentary forces have done that has caused the ANC to act with caution and even abandon certain courses of action?

I seek to answer this question by looking at the fate of the Traditional Courts Bill (TCB). Twenty years since the end of apartheid, one of the most notorious pieces of colonial legislation partly responsible for institutionalising Black marginality, namely the Native Administration Act of 1927 (NAA), has yet to be fully repealed. In order to do so, a new traditional court structure must replace that established under the NAA. However, despite government efforts to achieve this end since 2005, Parliament has been unable to deliver such legislation. There have been two attempts at passing such legislation. In 2008, Parliament produced a TCB, but it was subsequently withdrawn (in June 2011) owing to extreme opposition emanating from both within and outside Parliament. The TCB was reintroduced in virtually the same form as the earlier version in December 2011 and met with similarly widespread consternation. Of interest here are not the many substantive and procedural concerns raised, such as the exclusion of women under the TCB or the lack of consultation during its drafting, but rather how the Bill has been and continues to be opposed in its passage through Parliament, in a manner that emphasises Parliament's role as a national forum for the consideration of public issues.

Beyond opposition parties in Parliament, the Bill has, since 2011, faced sustained and well-organised opposition from a very wide spectrum of actors. This has culminated in the formation of the Alliance for Rural Democracy, formed by rural and urban civil-society organisations across the national spectrum. Coupled with overwhelming resistance from opposition parties in Parliament, the TCB has been the subject to a highly contested and closely monitored legislative process. Further, the sustained media focus on issues relating to the TCB's passage through Parliament has also raised the stakes in alerting many sectors of society to the outcome of parliamentary proceedings, thus further widening interest in the Bill.

Although the extra-parliamentary mobilisation has been important, Parliament and its processes, including provincial hearings, have proved also to be significant sites of contestation (Makinana 2012a). Invoking the Constitution as the basis for participation, opposition and a future judicial review (if necessary), a wide array of individuals, members of Parliament and organisations have presented their views on the TCB in what can only be described as a robust, animated and drawn-out legislative process orchestrated to lay bare much that is politically problematic and potentially unconstitutional about the TCB (Makinana 2012a, 2012b). Beyond being a clear example of participatory democracy at work, the unfolding of these debates has demonstrated that Parliament and its processes present important opportunities for other groups beyond political parties to participate in influencing how legislative power is understood and used.

Whilst it is impossible to ascertain the causes with absolute certainty, three occurrences indicate that the oppositional campaign centred on Parliament has yielded results that have shifted the ground. Firstly, the ANC Minister for Women's Affairs, Ms Lulu Xingwana, openly aligned herself with those opposing the TCB by deviating from the official party line and calling into question the constitutionality of the TCB (Makinana 2012a). Secondly, after the provincial legislative hearings on the TCB held under the auspices of the NCOP to establish individual provincial voting mandates on the Bill, four provinces returned mandates not to support the Bill, whilst others offered conditional support for further deliberation on the Bill. Thirdly, despite the Department of Justice's insistence that the passage of the Bill be completed before the end of 2012, the process around the TCB remained unresolved until 19 February 2014, when it was allowed to lapse at the NCOP. This was as a result of members asking for its withdrawal upon being fully appraised by the parliamentary legal adviser as to the full extent of the concerns regarding the Bill's unconstitutionality, as well as the extent of opposition to it from a majority of the provinces (Buthelezi 2014).

What is most notable about this case study is that whilst it remains central to negotiating what is to become of traditional courts, the processes within Parliament have not been strictly limited to the political parties represented. Instead, other participants have shaped the discourse around the TCB in Parliament, and the well-orchestrated public monitoring of the parliamentary process has ensured that the issue remains prominent and that the most salient issues are communicated widely. Viewed through a separation-of-powers lens, one can start to speculate that Parliament – as a forum for the discussion of national issues – provides important opportunities for the active civic participation of extra-parliamentary forces alongside parliamentary opposition during the legislative process. Further, analysed in light of Choudhry's thesis, such access and participation have the potential to bring about the establishment of anti-capture or anti-domination political practices. Such harnessing of Parliament's institutional potential, it is suggested, points to the enhancement of South Africa's democracy in ways that promote the constitutional values of accountability, responsiveness and openness (Constitution, s1(d)). Construed thus, Parliament must be seen to be the forum for dramatically increasing the number of voices beyond those of opposition parties. Whilst not usually cast as a function associated with the performance of constitutional checks and balances, this aspect of Parliament's functions may in fact be contributing an additional dimension to the separation of powers doctrine that warrants closer examination.

Another important example that stimulates us to re-examine Parliament's potential contribution as a national forum and as a possible mechanism to force the executive to account for, and revisit, its decisions is the passage of the Protection of State Information Bill (also known as the Secrecy Bill). Whilst space does not allow for a more detailed account, it is notable that in several respects, the narrative of the legislative progress of the Secrecy Bill mirrors that of the TCB. In particular, the challenge by parliamentary opposition parties, the broad social mobilisation by extra-parliamentary forces, including the establishment of a coalition under an umbrella alliance known as Right-2-Know, and a massive information campaign supported by the press exposed likely rights violations and other possible grounds of unconstitutionality, particularly in an earlier version of the Bill that was withdrawn.

Again, were one to conduct an extensive examination of this Bill's long-running passage through Parliament, one would no doubt be struck by the level and extent of the debates that have followed the Bill since its introduction and ultimately led to many significant concessions by the executive and the ANC majority in Parliament. At the time of writing, the Bill had been passed by Parliament, but had yet to be signed into law by the President, who has referred it back to Parliament, citing the potential unconstitutionality of several clauses. Even though there remained significant disquiet from many quarters with respect to its substance, there was also overwhelming recognition of the fact that the final version was a significant improvement on earlier versions in as far as rights' encroachments were concerned. Much credit for the concessions made is attributable to sustained pressure inside and outside Parliament by opposition parties and extra-parliamentary forces.

Conclusion

Twenty years into the democratic era, the ANC's dominance of Parliament and its control of the executive has been predictably the cause of much concern. The numerous (and growing) list of examples where Parliament is perceived as having failed to fulfil its role of checking and balancing the executive, as well as developing an effective constitutional separation of powers, has instead led to what at times appears to be an over-accumulation of power in the executive. Instead of conducting a 'traditional' separation of powers analysis that focuses on the relationships between Parliament and the other two branches based on the constitutional text and the courts' interpretation, I have sought to engage in a more situated analysis of parliamentary powers with the aid of Choudhry's dominant-party democracy thesis.

Such analysis seeks to engage critically with Parliament as an independent institution that, despite the apparent 'continuities' of power between Parliament and the executive under the ANC, is, by itself, of strategic importance in preserving and advancing South Africa's constitutional democratic project. An institutional understanding of Parliament is required, that foregrounds its character as a national forum that provides space to advocate for, register and record diverse views from different parliamentary and extra-parliamentary forces as they seek to influence matters (particularly legislative ones) before Parliament. I have also sought to demonstrate that single-party dominance has not necessarily led to unbridled uses of power and flagrant unaccountability.

It is possible that, in portraying Parliament as an accessible and responsive national forum of debate, I could be accused of idealising it. Thus it could be argued that Parliament's timeworn traditions and its sometimes exclusivist and elitist practices that privilege elected political parties over any other groups have been overlooked. I would respond by pointing out that the analysis seeks to focus on Parliament and how the power it wields has been rendered more open, transparent and accessible – in short, democratised. Therefore, in focusing on these 'anti-domination' or 'anti-capture' practices, I hope to increase understanding of separation of powers as 'distinctively' located in South Africa.

A further criticism could also be levelled, namely that the analysis above fails to heed the conventional or doctrinal limits of the separation of powers by bringing extra-parliamentary forces into the reckoning. My response would be to say that, in spite of the theoretical and normative prescripts that typify contemporary understandings of separation of powers, from an historical standpoint, the doctrine's development has always been informed by an analysis of prevailing institutional functions and relationships. Ultimately, it is important to recognise that whilst significant power resides within Parliament, how that power is configured, allocated and distributed in practical terms can be as important as where the lines of separation are drawn.

References

Books, book chapters and articles

Barkan, J. 2005. 'Emerging Legislature or Rubber Stamp? The South African National Assembly After Ten Years of Democracy' <www.cssr.uct.ac.za/sites/cssr.uct.ac.za/files/pubs/wp134.pdf> [accessed 30 June 2014].

Choudhry, S. 2009. '"He had a mandate": The South African Constitutional Court and the African National Congress in a Dominant Party Democracy', *Constitutional Court Review*, 2: 1–86.

Gilliomee, H., J. Myburgh and L. Schlemmer, 2001. 'Dominant Party Rule, Opposition Politics and Minorities in "South Africa"', in ed. Roger Southall, *Opposition in South Africa's New Democracy*, p. 161 <http://www.kas.de/wf/doc/kas_5086-1522-2-30.pdf?040723124840> [accessed 30 June 2014].

Habib, A. and R. Taylor, 2001. 'Political Alliances and Parliamentary Opposition on Post-Apartheid South Africa', in ed. Roger Southall, *Opposition in South Africa's New Democracy*, p. 207 <http://www.kas.de/wf/doc/kas_5086-1522-2-30.pdf?040723124840> [accessed 30 June 2014].

Klug, H. 2010. *The Constitution of South Africa. A Contextual Analysis.* Portland, OR and Oxford: Hart Publishing.

Murray, C. and L. Nijzink, 2002. *Building Representative Democracy – South Africa's Legislatures and the Constitution.* Cape Town: Parliamentary Support Program.

Pieterse, M. 2004. 'Coming to Terms with Judicial Enforcement of Socio-Economic Rights', *South African Journal on Human Rights*, 20: 386.

Seedorf, S. and S. Sibanda, 2008. 'Separation of Powers', in eds S. Woolman and M. Bishop, *Constitutional Law of South Africa*, 2nd edn. Cape Town: Juta, pp. 1211–298.

Southall, R. 2005. 'The "Dominant Party Debate" in South Africa', *African Spectrum*, 40: 61.

Website and online material

Alliance for Rural Democracy, 2012. 'Press release: Civil society organisations in alliance to stop the Traditional Courts Bill' <http://www.lrg.uct.ac.za/usr/lrg/docs/TCB/2012/Media_Release_11042012.pdf> [accessed 30 June 2014].

Buthelezi, M. 2014. 'State at Odds with the Rights of Rural People' <http://mg.co.za/article/2014-02-27-state-at-odds-with-the-rights-of-rural-people/> [accessed 30 July 2014].

Ferriera, E. 2010. 'Defence Committee Concedes Battle with Sisulu' <http://mg.co.za/article/2010-09-15-defence-committee-concedes-battle-with-sisulu> [accessed 30 June 2014].

Defenceweb 2010. 'SCOPA Standoff Between Godi, Sisulu Continues' <http://www.defenceweb.co.za/index.php?option=com_content&view=article&id=8787:1&catid=54:Governance&Itemid=118> [accessed 30 June 2014].

Makinana, A. 2012a. 'Parliament Draws Fire on Traditional Courts Bill' <http://mg.co.za/article/2012-10-25-parliament-draws-fire-on-traditional-courts-bill> [accessed 30 June 2014].

—— 2012b. 'Traditional Courts Bill Revamped Beyond Recognition' <http://mg.co.za/article/2012-09-21-00-traditional-courts-bill-revamped-beyond-recognition> [accessed 30 June 2014].

Moshoeshoe, M. 2012. 'Public Protector Madonsela's Office is Our Only Hope', *Sunday Independent*, 15 October, p. 16.

Cases

De Lange v Smuts 1998 (3) SA 785 (CC), 1998 (7) BCLR 779 (CC).

Oriani-Ambrosini, MP v Sisulu, MP Speaker of the National Assembly 2012 (6) SA 588 (CC).

Pikoli v President of South Africa 2010 (1) SA 400 (GNP).

Tongoane and Others v National Minister for Agriculture and Land Affairs and Others, [2010] ZACC 10; 2010 (6) SA 214 (CC); 2010 (8) BCLR 741 (CC).

United Democratic Movement v President of South Africa 2003 (1) SA 495 (CC).

Legislation

Communal Land Rights Act 11 of 2004.

Native Administration Act 38 of 1927.

Promotion of Access to Information Act 2 of 2000.

Promotion of Administrative Justice Act 3 of 2000.

Promotion of Equality and Prevention of Unfair Discrimination Act 4 of 2000.

Protection of State Information Bill (2010).

Traditional Courts Bill (2012).

Chapter 4
Local Government: Between Subsidiarity and Shortfalls in Service Delivery

Francois Venter

The current system of local government deserves consideration because of its ambitious intricacy as a completely re-conceived order. It demonstrates the difficulties of marrying structural novelty with tough reality. Its pre-history is complex, its constitutional conceptualisation has not fully been realised and it is labouring under severe practical challenges.

Whereas the pre-constitutional system was notorious for the ubiquitous role of racial separation, the primary focus of the South African constitutional project since 1994 has been restitutional racial equality. This is of particular importance in the local government sphere, generally recognised as the closest interface between citizen and government.

Understanding the system requires some historical background, a consideration of the constitutional and statutory framework within which it operates, an examination of the consequences of the policy of the deployment of political cadres, and a noting of the outcome of all of these considerations on the ground.

The Constitutional Context

A short history of local government in South Africa

Local government and administration has a history going back to the late eighteenth century, beginning under Dutch colonial rule. Elements of seventeenth-century institutions of the Province Holland and nineteenth-century English structures were merged into the practical arrangements in the colonies, but adapted to local circumstances (Bekink 2006: 21, Meyer 1978: 28–42).

When the Union of South Africa was established in 1910, the South Africa Act (1909) entrusted most of the regulation and administration of municipal affairs to the provincial authorities. Due to the reality that the Union was composed of four former British colonies, two of which had a history of almost five decades of independence as republics before their annexation during the Anglo–Boer War, the constitutional arrangements gave rise to divergent local government systems in the four provinces. In the deployment of mechanisms necessary to deal with constantly increasing urbanisation, each of the provinces proceeded over the next eight decades to build on their colonial foundations. The focus was on providing local services to the almost exclusively white electorate. In terms of national policy and legislation, the black urban population was considered to be non-permanent, that is, notionally domiciled in the rural areas reserved for black occupation, temporarily providing labour in 'white' cities and towns. Provincial legislation ('ordinances') regulated local municipal administration in each province in an uncoordinated fashion. In the areas reserved for black occupation, traditional cultural structures provided a form of local administration, broadly regulated in terms of national legislation and, in what eventually became the black 'homelands', various arrangements for urban government and administration were introduced.

Before 1994, municipal authorities were not perceived so much as structures of government than as agencies responsible for the provision of services. When the Union became a Republic in 1961, and even more so when a new constitution was introduced in 1983 in terms of which those classified as 'coloured' and Indian were co-opted as minority components of the white-dominated governmental system, municipalities continued to be seen as administrations rather than belonging to a local level of government. The administration of the urbanised black population outside the reserved areas was regulated by national (parliamentary) legislation, and was partially delegated to the white municipalities.

Not surprisingly, the separate administration of urban residential areas set aside for black habitation became a political hotbed. The system of black local government generated strong political resistance within the community and although many structures were erected for the implementation of the policy, it failed completely. Attempts to reform the regulation of municipal administration and service delivery, however, still on the assumption of strict racial separation, made the black residential areas a focal point for political protest, often taking the form of violent mob action leading to brutal public murders (including 'necklacing' – setting alight a car tyre around the neck of the victim) of members of the community perceived as collaborators with the government in establishing a separate system of black local government.

By the early 1990s, it became clear that the local government system was to become an important component of constitutional and social reform. A first attempt to launch a process of reform with emphasis on negotiation within local communities was the adoption of the Interim Measures for Local Government Act of 1991. Because this Act was, as were the attempts of the 1980s, initiated unilaterally by the white government, and as little progress had at that stage been made in the field of multi-party negotiations, its legitimacy was suspect. Very little of the 1991 Act was implemented before it was repealed by the Local Government Transition Act of 1993.

The wording of the Transition Act was negotiated concurrently with that of the 1993 Constitution. Chapter 10 of this Constitution specifically dealt with local government, providing a framework for a profoundly reconceived local government dispensation to be established in terms of detailed parliamentary and provincial legislation.

By 1993, the local authorities of white urban areas (at that stage almost the only functional class of local authorities in the country) took the form of large city councils, city councils (or municipal councils), town councils (or town management councils), local councils (or local area committees), and health committees. Local authorities were classified into one of these categories with reference to factors such as the size of the urban area concerned and the extent (financial value) of the services that were provided. Generally it may be said that these municipalities were administered well and provided municipal services comparable to international standards, primarily to the white residential areas. Rural (for example, farming) areas were dealt with as not being suitable for municipal governance.

Towns and cities were managed politically by councils elected by the white inhabitants in a ward (constituency) system. As ceremonial head of a council, a mayor was elected from among the members of the council. In the Cape Province and Natal, the councils entrusted their functions to a variety of committees for dealing with details, while a system of management committees was in operation in the Transvaal and the Orange Free State. The municipal councils served for all practical purposes as the executive body of the local authority, but also to a very limited extent as a local legislature for the passing of municipal by-laws.

The local municipal administration was in the hands of a professional corps of officials in the employ of the council. The city administration was headed by a town clerk as chief executive officer. The office of town clerk was statutorily regulated as a profession. Other chief officers who headed departments in the city administration were typically the town secretary, the town treasurer, the city engineer, a head of the health department and a chief traffic officer, or chief of security services.

Although the foundations of local government have, especially since 1994, changed radically, the operational elements of the system existing in the former white urban areas formed the basis upon which the new dispensation had to be built, now naturally for the equitable provision of municipal services to the whole of the population.

After the Transition Act came into operation in 1994, it was amended repeatedly and (especially in 1996) expanded significantly. The 1996 amendments naturally related partially to the applicable provisions of the 1996 Constitution that had in the meantime come into effect.

The Transition Act contained the most important structural arrangements concerning the local government dispensation until 5 December 2000. It made provision for local multi-racial negotiating forums and for the unfolding and establishment of reconceived non-racial local government structures in various phases. This preceded the first open democratic local government elections held between November 1995 and May 1996.

The constitutional framework

Evidence that the 1993 Constitution and the Transition Act's wording was synchronised, appears especially from s 245(1) and (2) of the 1993 Constitution.

The purpose of Chapter 10 of the 1993 Constitution, containing ss 174–180, appears clearly from s 245(2) (under the heading 'Transitional arrangements'), namely to serve as a framework of principle for the further development of local government. The particulars of the new local government dispensation were to be worked out within the framework of Chapter 10 of the 1993 Constitution. What was made clear right from the outset was that local government was to attain a status in law much more elevated than the previous system.

The 1993 Constitution further set up a compulsory framework, not only for rolling out the statutory regulation of the newly conceived local government system, but also for the constitutional regulation of this governmental sphere in the final (1996) Constitution. The mechanism by means of which this was achieved, took the form of the 'Constitutional Principles' enshrined in the 1993 Constitution, with which the final Constitution had to conform.

When the Constitutional Court was called upon to certify the new constitutional text in 1996, it found that the first draft indeed failed to comply with the Constitutional Principles pertaining to local government, in that it did not provide for a framework for the structures, appropriate fiscal powers and functions of local government, for formal legislative procedures to be adhered to by local government legislatures, or for appropriate fiscal powers and functions for different categories of local government. These shortcomings were then duly remedied by the Constitutional Assembly.

Chapter 7 of the final Constitution contains provisions intended to enable the full constitutionalisation of local government. Thus its newly acquired status as one of three spheres of government, sharing (at least in theory) the same constitutional status as the national and provincial spheres, became entrenched. What remained to be done, however, was the establishment in terms of national legislation of a final structure and regulatory statutory framework for putting flesh on the constitutional bones, as it were. This process actually began even before the adoption of the 1996 Constitution when the Development Facilitation Act of 1995 was passed by Parliament for the purposes of facilitating 'the implementation of reconstruction and development programmes and projects in relation to land'. The rest of the statutory construction was completed in the following five years.

The new constitutional arrangement required the whole of the national territory to be placed under the authority of local governments. This new arrangement was introduced by s 151(1) of the 1996 Constitution, which provides that 'The local sphere of government consists of municipalities, which must be established for the whole of the territory of the Republic.' This is known colloquially as 'wall-to-wall local government'.

Local autonomy qualified by provincial and national oversight

During the drafting of the 1993 Constitution, the complexity of internal boundaries within the Republic required an objective approach to future demarcation, especially of provincial boundaries. The Negotiating Council of the Multi-Party Negotiating Process therefore appointed a demarcation commission to investigate and propose a regional demarcation to be regulated by a new constitution. The result was the delimitation of nine provinces, only two of which correlated with the former provinces of the Republic, the other seven having newly demarcated boundaries. The demarcation of municipalities within the nine provinces, however, had to wait for the finalisation of the design of the future local government system.

The prominent placement in the new constitutions of provincial government raises the question of the nature of the Republic's form of state. Apart from the opening statement in s 1 of the 1996 Constitution – that 'The Republic of South Africa is one, sovereign, democratic state' – no specific constitutional terminological indications of the form of the state are to be found. The historical evolution of the Union of South Africa from a near-federation in 1910 to complete centralisation by 1983 was suspended with the introduction in 1994 of constitutionalism. The nature of the form of state at the time of the new beginning was, however, not named. A possible, though not institutionalised, theoretical designation for the South African state, might be 'composite' state (Venter 1997: 56–8). The introduction of local government as an autonomous sphere of government enhanced, at least notionally, the theoretical viability of such a characterisation of the form of state.

From the theoretical perspective of structural decentralisation of local government, the constitutional provisions are clear: the democratically elected municipal council is endowed with legislative and executive authority over matters allocated to it in terms of the Constitution, not to be interfered with by the provincial and national authorities beyond the limits explicitly allowed for by the Constitution. These limits are various in nature, co-determined in practice by the status and capacity of a specific local government, with, however, the possibility of intervention by the relevant provincial executive when 'a municipality cannot or does not fulfil an executive obligation in terms of the Constitution or legislation.' Such intervention can, in terms of s 139, take the form of directives that corrective steps are to be taken, taking over the obligations concerned or the dissolution of the municipal council, and the appointment of an administrator to take corrective steps until a new council can be elected. Such steps may be taken by the provincial executive only with the knowledge and concurrence of the national executive and the provincial and national legislatures.

These arrangements, realistic for a newly designed and untested system of local government in a process of establishment and transition from a previous order different in nature, do however allow the provincial and national spheres of government to compromise the autonomy of individual municipalities, if not of the local government sphere as a whole. These mechanisms have the potential, especially if municipal councils lack capacity or become dysfunctional, to at least temporarily bar decentralisation and local autonomy.

It appears therefore that, despite the elevation of local government to the status of a constitutionally founded governmental sphere, its position can only properly be understood relative to the provincial and national spheres. The constitutional status of local government does not preclude the need (and practice) of it being supervised by the national and provincial spheres. All three spheres of government must, however, in terms of s 41(1)(*g*) of the Constitution and in the spirit of cooperative government, 'exercise their powers and perform their functions in a manner that does not encroach on the geographical, functional or institutional integrity of government in another sphere'.

Cooperative government

An interesting element of the 1996 Constitution is Chapter 3 under the heading 'Cooperative Government.' Both the 1993 and 1996 Constitutions were drafted making liberal use of comparative insights gleaned from especially German and Canadian constitutional law. No doubt the Canadian notion of 'cooperative federalism' (Hogg 2006: 150–53) and the German concept *Bundestreue* (described in the 'First *Rundfunkurteil*' of the *Bundesverfassungsgericht*), served as models for the introduction of cooperative government to South African constitutional law. A significant difference, however, between the South African and German concepts is that cooperative government has been written into the South African Constitution as a set of principles constituting binding obligations, whereas *Bundestreue* would appear not to take the form of a substantive legal rule, but to be more in the nature of a guiding principle, the substance of which is sometimes contested (Egli 2010: 167).

Inter-governmental litigation on relative competencies is not precluded by the notion of cooperative governance and a few disputes of this nature involving local government have had to be resolved judicially. Such disputes naturally arise from the constitutional mechanisms of the allocation of 'functional areas' of exclusive and concurrent competence to primarily the national and provincial spheres, but also incidentally to the local government sphere. This is regulated by specific provisions of the Constitution relating to the legislative competence respectively of Parliament and the provincial legislatures. The powers and functions of municipalities regarding the relevant functional areas are primarily granted in s 156 as executive and administrative competencies, but municipalities are also empowered to make and administer by-laws on such matters, although any conflict between a by-law and provincial or national legislation renders the by-law null and void. From this, it should be clear that the autonomy of local government does not allow for claims to exclusive or even concurrent legislative or executive authority.

Difficulties regarding a clear demarcation and definition of functions and duties of different levels (or spheres) of government are endemic in composite states.

Much room for speculation and dispute was created by the constitutional lists in Schedules 4 and 5 of the Constitution, for example, roads and traffic are listed for all three spheres of government, and determining which aspects should be considered to be the responsibility and within the competence of which sphere, was left open. Given the fact that local governments are not allowed any exclusive or concurrent competencies, it becomes a matter of dealing with the overlap of competencies, a situation that tends to produce either the avoidance of responsibility (especially where funding is concerned), or incursion beyond the constitutionally contemplated allocation of governance functions (Steytler and Fessha 2007).

Categories of local government

Section 155 of the 1996 Constitution provides for the establishment of three categories of local government, Category A being a single-tier municipality having 'exclusive municipal executive and legislative authority in its area', Categories B and C being two-tier municipalities. Essentially, Category A municipalities take the form of metropolitan local governments with authority over all the functional areas listed in Schedules 4B and 5B of the Constitution. In Category B, local municipalities of smaller cities and towns are to be found, and Category C comprises district municipalities covering non-urbanised areas, sharing jurisdiction with various Category B municipalities within its district. Details of this constitutional framework are provided for in the Local Government: Municipal Structures Act of 1998.

The Legislative Framework

As the process of reconfiguring local government unfolded in three phases in terms of the Local Government Transition Act of 1993, further national legislation was being prepared for the comprehensive regulation of local government. The final stage was reached in December 2000 when municipal elections were held across the country for the establishment of 283 municipalities. In terms of s 159 of the Constitution, municipal councils are elected for terms of five years.

The reconceptualisation of local government entailed a particular emphasis on developmental functions, founded upon the wording of s 153 of the Constitution. This ideal was intended to be given more substance in terms of the Local Government: Municipal Structures Act.

Section 23 of the Local Government: Municipal Systems Act of 2000 furthermore requires municipalities to undertake 'developmentally oriented planning' in the spirit of ss 152 and 153 of the Constitution and Chapter I of the Development Facilitation Act of 1995, which comprehensively lays down 'general principles for land development'.

The complexity of the constitutional and statutory allocation of functions to the various spheres of government clearly shows up in the 2010 judgment of the Constitutional Court in *Johannesburg Metropolitan Municipality* v *Gauteng Development Tribunal*. The Court found that the statutory allocation of the functional area of municipal planning to any other sphere of government than local government was inadmissible.

In addition to the parliamentary statutes mentioned above and significant remnants of pre-constitutional provincial ordinances, the raft of laws regulating local government, each individually complex and voluminous, include the following:

- Organised Local Government Act of 1997,
- Local Government: Municipal Demarcation Act of 1998,
- Local Government: Municipal Electoral Act of 2000,
- Local Government: Municipal Finance Management Act of 2003,
- Intergovernmental Relations Framework Act of 2005 and
- Municipal Fiscal Powers and Functions Act of 2007.

This amounts to over-regulation, which has aptly been referred to as 'the strangulation of local government'. Steytler (2008: 520–21) described the forms that strangulation by over-regulation takes as follows:

> A direct command that effectively eliminates discretion is certainly the clearest form. The more invidious form is when it is indirect where the sheer complexity or cost of regulation stifles initiative. This often is linked to the uniformity of the legal regime; for the more capable municipalities it is a bearable burden, but for the lesser endowed ones it becomes an obstacle in the way of governance.

Subsidiarity

The South African constitutional project undertaken over the past two decades has received many accolades. There are various reasons for the praise, usually in the first place for the successful political negotiation of a compact between diametrically opposed parties against a background of police and military containment of revolutionary ambitions, serious public violence, social instability and economic isolation. The constitutional products of this process have also received many compliments as exemplary of advanced liberal democracy and democratic constitutionalism in tune with the best of its kind in this era. Twenty years since the inception of South African constitutionalism the Constitution survives undiminished, an impressive volume of often-cited constitutional jurisprudence has been produced, the legal system as a whole has changed radically in the process of its constitutionalisation, and essentially all elements required for the operation of the institutions provided for in the Constitution, including local government, have been set in place.

An interesting question that arises is whether the notion of subsidiarity can be read into the local government arrangements provided for in s 156(4) of the

Constitution, which requires the national and provincial governments to assign some of the matters within their jurisdictions to local governments if they 'would most effectively be administered locally'.

When the 1993 and 1996 Constitutions were negotiated, some of the participating parties actually promoted subsidiarity as a constitutional principle. Some scholarly writing on subsidiarity in the South African Constitution has also appeared (De Visser 2010, Du Plessis 2006), but the courts have not as yet utilised the notion for the purposes of interpreting the constitutional distribution of legislative and executive competencies.

De Visser's comparative description of subsidiarity as it is understood and applied in various legal systems and his analysis of s 156(4) and related constitutional provisions lead him to the conclusion that the subsidiarity model of the Constitution is different from the concept of subsidiarity as it is understood in Germany and Europe. The Constitution, he argues, has a top-down approach, which implies a centralised view of the allocation of powers, meaning that what is not expressly allocated to local government in Schedules 4B and 5B, stays with the national and provincial spheres, except if an efficiency test in favour of decentralisation is passed. Put differently, he argues that s 156(4) does not create an automatic bias for the allocation of decentralised local competencies, but should rather be seen as a functional mechanism driven by the ideal of developmental governance. De Visser doubts the justiciability of the provision due to the courts' reluctance to be engaged in adjudicating disputes turning on policy.

However that may be, subsidiarity has the potential of growing in theoretical and interpretational significance if the system of local government, or at least meaningful pockets within it, become successful. Unfortunately, stark reality on the ground does not inspire confidence in achieving success.

Stark Reality

The comprehensive and in some respects admirable constitutional and legislative framework for local government in South Africa exists within a reality which places the effective operation of this framework under severe stress. Whereas the industrialised metropolitan areas where the country's economic activity is focused have the appearance of success due to large revenues, expenditures and infrastructure in contrast to most other municipalities (South African Cities Network 2011), they are facing essentially the same challenges as do the rest. At the core of this difficulty lies the high and growing degree of inequality in the distribution of family income: according to the Gini coefficient index where 0 equals full equality and 100 complete inequality, South Africa scored 59.3 in 1994 and 65 in 2005 (CIA World Factbook 2013). Given the ongoing trend of urbanisation (UN Department of Economic and Social Affairs 2009), this translates into growing city populations suffering under conditions of poverty and crying out for municipal and other services. Add to this the high levels of unemployment, and the fact that local government is for the citizen the first tangible manifestation of the state.

With the democratisation of local government came the local reflection of national politics. Since 1994, the African National Congress (ANC) has held an overwhelming majority of votes in all spheres of government. This has had a direct impact on the manner in which political and managerial positions are awarded and consequently on the effectiveness of governance. It is obviously difficult for the ANC to find sufficient numbers of capable local politicians and qualified managers from among their own number to fill the thousands of posts left vacant in the course of the systematic purging since 1994 of municipal administrations of experienced officials employed under the previous dispensation. The ANC's response to this situation has been a system of centralised 'cadre deployment', meaning the placement of trusted supporters in key positions in, amongst others, the municipal structures, often regardless of their experience, skills, or qualifications. One of the consequences of this practice has been that the dividing line between municipal administration and the political executive has been compromised.

Cadre deployment is an overt policy of the ANC deeply rooted in its revolutionary history and the organisation's conception that 'the revolution' is still continuing, despite its having been in power since 1994. This is clearly evident from a recently released 'policy discussion document' (ANC 2012: 27), in which the mechanism of cadre deployment is both expressly confirmed and its deficiencies recognised. The document laments the lack of 'a coherent cadre policy' as the cause of 'the vicious cycle of internal problems over the past decade-and-a-half', since it leaves 'the revolution ... to survive on sheer luck'. The document acknowledges the fact that the ANC has been 'deploying comrades into positions of serious responsibility and authority without adequate preparation', that cadre deployment has consequently been discredited, and that it 'destroyed some of our comrades who ultimately could not perform and had to be removed' (ibid.: 27–8). Nevertheless, the document goes on to emphasise the importance of its cadre deployment policy and confesses that 'What remains a challenge is that the process is yet to reach a point where the best cadres who combine integrity with competence are deployed' (ibid.: 64). Regarding deployment of 'cadres' in the public service, the purpose is stated to be to place them 'in all key sites of struggle and centres of power and influence' and points out that it was accepted already in 2002 that the integrity of the process was suspect due to 'internal tensions and factionalism, fuelled by perceptions of "jobs for pals" and confusion between employment and deployment' (ibid.: 65). The intention was, however, not to terminate this failed practice, but to 'improve' the policy.

That the functioning of the local government system was flawed was acknowledged officially in the strategic plan of the national department responsible for local government, published in August 2009 (Department of Cooperative Government and Traditional Affairs 2009: 8).

Against this background, it is not surprising that public protests about poor service delivery have frequently occurred in recent years, in some cases turning to violence and destruction of property. It is clear that very few municipalities are succeeding in providing satisfactory services to their inhabitants. This is unfortunately a growing tendency attributable to proven dysfunctionality of structures, rampant corruption and incompetence of municipal councillors and officials. At the end of a comprehensive, professionally compiled, survey funded by the Canadian International Development Agency (Van Hoof 2011: 53–5), Idasa concludes that:

- Ninety per cent of the citizens are dissatisfied with the quality of service delivery provided by municipal councils despite government efforts to increase access to services;
- The gap between what people expect and what government is realistically able to deliver is increasing due to factors like population growth, international and national migration, and growing expectations;
- Democratic structures of consultation and feedback are dysfunctional, whereby councils are allowed to disregard the needs of the citizens until violent protests erupt;
- 'Basic democratic governance principles and values are increasingly sacrificed by politicians for individual benefits and political power', causing the distance between the governors and the governed to increase ominously.

Conclusion

Before its reconceptualisation over the past two decades, local government in South Africa was deemed to be composed of mere local administrations constitutionally under central control. Since 1990, much planning, legislation and policy formulation have gone into the creation of a completely new, consolidated, theoretically autonomous and decentralised sphere of constitutionally structured local government. The constitutional and legislative regulation of the local government system provides for, on the one hand, subsidiarity-like autonomy, and on the other, dependence on national and provincial oversight and financing. In addition, the pervasive politicisation of local governance, growing urbanisation and poverty have caused local government to suffer from severe skills shortages and endemic corruption.

Making this system work efficiently and effectively is proving to be a challenge apparently beyond the current ability of all three spheres of government. This lack of success is manifested in degenerating service provision and localised protest and unrest, but has as yet not translated perceptibly into democratic rejection through the electoral process of those in power. This is indicative of a limited internalisation of the essence of democracy by the largest portion of the urban population.

South Africa has, however, over the centuries proven itself to be populated by resilient citizens who have succeeded in overcoming huge obstacles and in making significant course changes when circumstances require. Research, analysis and monitoring of the progress of the sphere of local government is effectively being undertaken by internal academic institutions and NGOs, frequently supported by external funders and by researchers from Europe and North America, through which not only the weaknesses and stumbling blocks of the system are being exposed, but useful recommendations are also frequently being produced. Democracy has been introduced constitutionally for all spheres of government: the realisation of its fruits is in the hands of the electorate and its leadership.

References

Books, book chapters and articles

Bekink, B. 2006. *Principles of South African Local Government Law.* Durban: LexisNexis Butterworths.

De Visser, J. 2010. 'Institutional Subsidiarity in the South African Constitution', *Stellenbosch Law Review*, 21: 90–115.

Du Plessis, L. 2006. '"Subsidiarity": What's in the Name for Constitutional Interpretation and Adjudication?', *Stellenbosch Law Review*, 17: 207–31.

Egli, P. 2010. *Die Bundestreue – Eine Rechtsvergleichende Untersuchung*. Zürich/St. Gallen: Dike Verlag.

Hogg, P. 2006. *Constitutional Law of Canada*, student edn. Scarborough: Carswell.

Meyer, J. 1978. *Local Government Law*, vol. 1. Durban: Butterworths.

Steytler, N. 2008. 'The Strangulation of Local Government', *Tydskrif vir die Suid-Afrikaanse Reg*: 518–35.

—— and Y.T. Fessha, 2007. 'Defining Local Government Powers and Functions', *South African Law Journal*, 124: 320–38.

Venter, F. 1997. 'Aspects of the South African Constitution of 1996: An African Democratic and Social Federal *Rechtsstaat*?', *Zeitschrift für ausländisches öffentliches Recht und Völkerrecht*, 57: 51–82.

Website and online material

ANC. 2012. 'Organisational Renewal – Building the ANC as a Movement for Transformation and a Strategic Centre of Power: A Discussion Document towards the National Policy Conference', Version 9, 10 April 2012 <http://www.anc.org.za/docs/discus/2012/organisationalrenewalf.pdf> [accessed 21 April 2012].

CIA World Factbook 2013 <https://www.cia.gov/library/publications/the-world-factbook/fields/2172.html?%20countryName=&countryCode=&regionCode=> [accessed 21 March 2013].

Department of Cooperative Government and Traditional Affairs, 2011. *Strategic Plan FY 2009–2014* <http://www.dplg.gov.za/index.php/documents/cat_view/162-strategic-plan.html> [accessed 23 December 2011].

South African Cities Network, 2011. *State of City Finances Report 2011* <http://www.sacities.net/images/stories/2011/Publications/State_of_City_Finances_Report_2011.pdf> [accessed 23 December 2011].

United Nations' Department of Economic and Social Affairs – Population Division, 2009. *World Population Monitoring – A Concise Report.* New York: United Nations.

Van Hoof, P., ed. 2011. *The State of Local Governance in South Africa from a Citizen Perspective* <http://www.idasa.org/media/uploads/outputs/files/the_state_of_local_governance_in_south_africa_from_a_citizen_perspective.pdf> [Accessed 22 August 2012].

Cases

'First' *Rundfunkurteil*. BVerfGE 12, 205.

Johannesburg Metropolitan Municipality v Gauteng Development Tribunal 2010 (6) SA 182 (CC).

Legislation

Development Facilitation Act 67 of 1995.

Intergovernmental Relations Framework Act 13 of 2005.

Interim Measures for Local Government Act 128 of 1991.

Local Government: Municipal Demarcation Act 27 of 1998.

Local Government: Municipal Electoral Act 27 of 2000.

Local Government: Municipal Finance Management Act 56 of 2003.

Local Government: Municipal Structures Act 117 of 1998.

Local Government: Municipal Systems Act 32 of 2000.

Local Government Transition Act 209 of 1993.

Municipal Fiscal Powers and Functions Act 12 of 2007.

Organised Local Government Act 52 of 1997.

PART II
Rights, Equality and the Courts

Chapter 5

Competing Notions of the Judiciary's Place in the Post-apartheid Constitutional Dispensation

Morné Olivier

Introduction

In democracies across the globe, the role of the judiciary is contested and controversial. South Africa is no exception. Since about 2005, the governing African National Congress (ANC) has become very critical of the courts and the judiciary, claiming particularly that their powers to review and set aside legislation and executive conduct are too expansive and have been misapplied, leading to interference with the work of government. The complaints centre mostly on cases involving the separation of powers, including the implementation of socio-economic rights and the review of presidential acts.

The dividing line between the various arms of government and their respective functions is perhaps not as fixed in South Africa as in some other jurisdictions. The Constitutional Court (CC) has stated that in developing a 'distinctively South African model of separation of powers', what is required is a 'delicate balancing ... between the need, on the one hand, to control government by separating powers and enforcing checks and balances, and, on the other, to avoid diffusing power so completely that the government is unable to take timely measures in the public interest' (*De Lange* v *Smuts* para 60). The judiciary's part in finding this 'delicate balance' is controversial. In contention, therefore, is the proper domain of the courts.

This chapter describes and comments briefly on criticism by the governing party of the judiciary and its powers; gives two examples of recent judgments that have been criticised; describes and comments on the judiciary's response to the criticism, and explains what form the dialogue between the judiciary and the other arms of government in a constitutional democracy such as South Africa ideally should take. The discussion is informed by the question of the judiciary's role in the transformation of society, but first, a very brief overview of the courts' powers under the Constitution is provided.

The Courts' Powers Under the Constitution

Both the Constitution and its 1993 predecessor allocated significant powers to judges by making the courts the ultimate authority on the interpretation of the Constitution, including the Bill of Rights. The CC is the final arbiter in constitutional matters, and has the power to decide the constitutionality of legislation and executive conduct (s 167). The Court was allocated even greater powers in 2013 when it became the court of final instance in all matters – not only constitutional matters as before (see Constitution Seventeenth Amendment Act 2012). Additionally to its constitutional jurisdiction, the Court can now decide any other matter in which it grants leave to appeal, which is likely to be the exception rather than the rule. Because of this increase in the powers and influence of the CC, the selection of its judges is likely to become even more politically contentious and contested. (See generally Lewis 2005 for an early assessment of the advantages and disadvantages of making the CC the apex court.)

Once the CC makes a finding of constitutional invalidity, it must declare such law or conduct invalid to the extent of its inconsistency with the Constitution (s 172(1)(a)). The Court has a discretion to make any just and equitable order in addition to the declaration of invalidity (s 172(1)(b)), so as to mitigate any detrimental consequences of the declaration. For example, the Court could suspend the order of invalidity to allow the legislature to correct a defect, which the Court has generally been willing to do, except in cases where the provision in issue could not be salvaged (see *Justice Alliance of South Africa v President of the Republic of South Africa* below as an example).

The foundation for the exercise of these powers is to be found in certain guarantees provided by the Constitution: judicial authority is vested in the courts – not in the executive or legislature; courts are subject only to the Constitution and the law (s 165). Judicial independence is thus specifically protected, at least in theory. Organs of state are under an obligation to 'assist and protect the courts to ensure [their] … independence, impartiality, dignity, accessibility and effectiveness' (s 165(4)). The judiciary requires institutional independence not only to forge an identity that is distinct from the other branches, but more importantly to enable the performance of its constitutionally sanctioned duties.

Government, Transformation and Judicial In(ter)dependence

Transformation is the primary theme of post-apartheid South Africa and affects virtually every sphere of life. Finding a comprehensive and universal definition is challenging but perhaps not undesirable, as contestation has resulted in increased engagement with the meaning and purpose of transformation. There is substantial agreement, however, that transformation lies at the heart of the constitutional enterprise and goes beyond the reform of state institutions to the transformation of society more broadly in order to remedy past inequality, discrimination and injustice. In this respect, the Constitution's Preamble promises to heal the divisions and remedy the injustices of the past, and looks towards a better and brighter future in which all South Africans irrespective of race, gender, or creed can share equally.

What is the role of the CC and other courts in this transformation project? This is a contentious question that is inextricably linked to the place of the judiciary in South Africa's constitutional dispensation. At the minimum, the new constitutional order necessitated a change in how judges thought about and interpreted the law – an attitudinal shift away from apartheid-era executive-mindedness towards transformative, constitution-based adjudication (on transformative adjudication generally, see Moseneke 2002, Langa 2006). The act of judging in post-apartheid South Africa, therefore, could no longer be a technical, mechanical function. Instead, adjudication had to be anchored in the Constitution and its values.

Though not without criticism, the CC, as an institution of and for transformation, has taken the lead through the development of a body of law that reflects the principles and values underlying the Constitution. This has cemented the Court's place as a symbolic and substantive keystone of the post-apartheid constitutional order. Since its deeply symbolic judgment in *S v Makwanyane*, the Court has been at the forefront of fostering a culture of respect for human rights and the supremacy of the Constitution. The Court's transformative approach to adjudication is arguably most visible in the area of socio-economic rights.

The courts' power to review and determine the constitutional validity of legislation and executive conduct is an important component of transformation. This authority to hold the other two arms of government accountable is the constitutionally sanctioned way to ensure protection against the abuse of power that defined the apartheid era. In this regard, Wesson and Du Plessis (2008: 203) state correctly that 'a key outcome of transformation is an independent judiciary that regards its primary task as the implementation of the Constitution as opposed to the policies of the government of the day.'

It seems that not everyone in government shares this view. A number of recent comments by senior ANC officials, and even the President, indicates their frustration with the courts' exercise of their powers of review. For example, one senior figure warned the CC 'to leave laws made by Parliament alone' (Hartley 2011) while the Secretary-General of the party, Gwede Mantashe, reportedly called the courts 'oppositional and counterrevolutionary' (Hartley 2011) and also accused them of 'revers[ing] the gains of transformation through precedent' (Mkhabela 2011). Mantashe further said the following, which could be interpreted as a veiled threat to the judiciary:

> The independence of judiciary and separation of powers must never be translated into hostility, where one of those arms becomes hostile to the other. My view is that there is a great deal of hostility that comes through from the judiciary towards the executive and Parliament, towards the positions taken by the latter two institutions. Unless this issue is addressed deliberately it's going to cause

> instability. It undermines the other arms of government and this could cause instability. (Mkhabela 2011)

In 2011, in an address to local and foreign judges, President Zuma articulated a particular conception of the separation of powers and the role of the courts that accords with the idea of co-partnership in the pursuit of the transformation agenda – a kind of judicial *inter*dependence rather than judicial *in*dependence (Zuma 2011). A similar idea is expressed in the Department of Justice's 2012 discussion document on the transformation of the legal system and the judiciary, which also authorises a 'review' of the jurisprudence of the CC as part of 'a critical assessment of how the Constitution has changed the lives of ordinary citizens … The role played by the Constitutional Court is of fundamental importance in this process, hence the necessity to evaluate the impact of our constitutional jurisprudence on society as a whole' (Discussion document 2012 II). The assessment was later extended to include the Supreme Court of Appeal (SCA). In explaining the proposed assessment, the Presidency said that 'the outcome of this exercise will not only assist in developing value-based solutions to address the legacy of the past but will contribute in shaping our evolving constitutional jurisprudence' (Zuma 2012). This is problematic as executive 'shaping' of the CC's jurisprudence would clearly infringe judicial independence; it is not the role of the executive to act as a check on the judiciary, but the obverse. In fairness, the discussion document does not focus in isolation on the judiciary, but also envisages a critical assessment of the executive in implementing laws and judgments, as well as the establishment of a scheme to monitor and evaluate the implementation of court decisions 'by all state departments to advance the respect for the rule of law' (Discussion document 2012 VI). The contract for the review was awarded only in August 2013, to the Human Sciences Research Council (HSRC) and the University of Fort Hare. The report is due in early 2015 and, depending on its findings, there are real fears that it may provide the pretext for limiting the role of the courts in some way.

What is worrying in the President's 2011 address referred to above is the inference that when a court strikes down legislation or conduct following a challenge by opposition political parties or civil society organisations, it is in fact helping these challengers to co-govern:

> In as much as we seek to respect the powers and role conferred by our constitution on the legislature and the judiciary, we expect the same from these very important institutions of our democratic dispensation.
>
> The Executive must be allowed to conduct its administration and policy making work as freely as it possibly can.
>
> The powers conferred on the courts cannot be superior to the powers resulting from the political and consequently administrative mandate resulting from popular democratic elections.

> Political disputes resulting from the exercise of powers that have been constitutionally conferred on the ruling party through a popular vote must not be subverted, simply because those who disagree with the ruling party politically, and who cannot win the popular vote during elections, feel other arms of the State are avenues to help them co-govern the country. (Zuma 2011)

There are other examples of similar statements by the President, including those expressed at the farewell function for outgoing Chief Justice Ngcobo later in 2011. And in commenting on the *Justice Alliance* case, which is discussed in the next section, Mantashe cast aspersions on the Court by questioning both the decision and the impartiality of the CC judges who decided the case:

> That judgment looks suspicious from where I am seated. I'm not a lawyer, but the judgment is very very suspicious. You have a section in the law that has been there over 10 years, and at a point of extending the term of a judge, then it (suddenly) becomes unconstitutional. Fine, but when you look at that judgment, you begin to ask yourself, whether the judges who sat on that Bench were not interested parties in the actual appointment of a new chief justice. Where does that line stop, when you must sit and be a judge in an area that benefits you? … For a lay person like me, it seems as if they accelerate the exit of the sitting chief justice so that they can take over quicker. (Mkhabela 2011)

Worrying too are the views expressed by a deputy minister, Ngoako Ramatlhodi, questioning the sensibility of the ANC's 'fundamental and substantive concession' to agree to a constitutional democracy (Ramatlhodi 2011). Is this a call for a return to parliamentary sovereignty in which the judiciary simply enforces the will of the legislature? Former Chief Justice Chaskalson (2012: 36) asked the same question: 'If this is what they want, they should say so, so that a sensible public debate can take place around such issues.'

Challenges to a judiciary's review powers and its institutional independence are not unknown in new democracies. In fact, Friedman (2010: 4) has described 'threats to the independence of the judiciary' in these democracies as 'inevitable' (O'Regan 2012: 119 calls them 'endemic in all democracies'). But what does the criticism mean, and what implications does it hold? Does the criticism evince a misunderstanding of the courts' constitutionally prescribed role or is it a deliberate attempt to challenge the courts' power of reviewing legislation and executive conduct? Is this a call for compliance or for more critical engagement with South Africa's constitutional arrangements and the judiciary's role in terms of it? Or is it simply populist rhetoric?

Provoking Government's Ire: Holding the Executive to Account

Corder and Brickhill submit that the way the judiciary tackles the review of executive action is the real test to determine its resolve to preserve judicial independence and to hold the rest of government accountable:

> … in an era of increasing social complexity and popular expectation of the delivery of goods and services by the state, and when as a consequence the balance of power has been shifting inexorably towards the executive, the true test of the judiciary's determination to preserve its independence and hold the rest of government to account is to be found in the courts' approach to regulation of executive authority.. . (Corder and Brickhill 2014: 384)

Two cases in which the CC has reviewed executive conduct are briefly described below. In both cases, the Court assertively reaffirmed its independence and its resolve to hold the executive and legislature accountable for their actions.

In August 2011, the term of Justice Sandile Ngcobo as Chief Justice and as a CC judge was due to expire, but shortly before its end, the President, acting in terms of legislation, asked Ngcobo to remain in office for an additional five years. Ngcobo initially acquiesced but, following a constitutional challenge to the extension of his term, he withdrew his agreement shortly before the CC delivered its judgment on the challenge in *Justice Alliance of South Africa* v *President of the Republic of South Africa*. The Court found the legislative provision in issue – s 8(a) of the Judges' Remuneration and Conditions of Employment Act of 2001 – inconsistent with the Constitution, and declared it invalid. The provision allowed for a Chief Justice who had reached his term limit on the CC to continue as Chief Justice at the sole request of the President for a period determined by the President, provided it did not extend beyond the time at which the Chief Justice turned 75 years of age. The Court found that this provision and the President's conduct in terms of it had infringed s 176(1) of the Constitution, which imposes a term limit on CC justices: 'A Constitutional Court judge holds office for a non-renewable term of 12 years, or until he or she attains the age of 70, whichever occurs first, except where an Act of Parliament extends the term of office of a Constitutional Court judge.'

It was clear, the Court said, that the plain wording of s 176(1) required an Act of Parliament to extend the term of office of a CC judge, whilst s 8(a) of the Act had conferred on the President an executive discretion to request the Chief Justice to continue in office and to determine the period of the extension (para 50). This violated judicial independence and was ruled to be an unlawful delegation of legislative power. In addition, the Court found that s 8(a) differentiated between the Chief Justice and other judges of the CC in a way not permitted by the Constitution (paras 70–91 generally).

The judgment is significant for its emphasis on constitutionalism, the supremacy of the Constitution and Parliament's subservience to it. At pains to make clear its authority as the sole interpreter of the Constitution, the Court observed that it was obliged to determine objectively the meaning of the constitutional provision, irrespective of Parliament's perception or view of its meaning (para 60). The Court's focus on judicial independence, particularly within the context of the separation of powers, runs through the judgment like a golden thread. Clearly, the Court wanted to assert its own independence, and signal that independence of the judiciary is sacrosanct and a fundamental pillar of South African constitutionalism that the courts will jealously protect.

The following year, in *Democratic Alliance v President of the Republic of South Africa* (colloquially known as the *Simelane* case), the CC affirmed the judgment of the Supreme Court of Appeal setting aside the decision of the President to appoint Menzi Simelane as National Director of Public Prosecutions, on the basis that the President had not applied his mind to the appointment. The Court assertively rejected the President's argument that the review standard of rationality as it applies to executive decision making should be lowered on the basis of separation of powers (para 44), finding that the President's failure to consider a finding by an independent commission of enquiry critical of Simelane's evidence before the enquiry, as well as a recommendation by the Public Service Commission to institute disciplinary steps against him, meant that the President's appointment of Simelane had been irrational.

Of Dialogue and Engagement: The Judiciary's Response

In 2011, Deputy Chief Justice Dikgang Moseneke engaged directly with the attacks on the courts, describing its essence as follows: 'The sub-text … is that the will of the people on the project of transforming society is frustrated by the supremacy of the Constitution and the role courts fulfil in policing its compliance' (Moseneke 2011: 2)

At its core, the argument is one of majoritarianism versus constitutional supremacy, including the courts' power of judicial review. The right to participate in the democratic process is one of the cornerstones of the democratic order. But democracy in South Africa, informed by its 'wicked' past, comes with certain safeguards to prevent abuse of the kind witnessed during apartheid. Moseneke expressed it thus:

> The will of the majority when expressed in some formal act through its duly appointed and elected representatives must be given effect and courts are bound to do so, provided that the democratic will, if translated into a law, policy or conduct, bears a rational and legitimate purpose and has been passed by a procedure authorised by the Constitution. Simply put, valid laws bind everyone but one cannot by-pass the supremacy of the Constitution by merely asserting the parliamentary or executive will of the people. It must be a will expressed within the constraints of the Constitution. (Ibid.: 6)

The system of checks and balances built into the constitutional system allows for maintaining an appropriate, workable balance between the branches and their respective but complementary functions. The work of the courts, in particular the CC, 'albeit counter-majoritarian at times, is ultimately supportive of democracy. It upholds protections that ensure democratic process and protects both minority and majority rights under the beneficence of our constitutional arrangement' (ibid.: 20). Significantly, Moseneke calls the claim that constitutionalism only limits government 'misleading and potentially dangerous':

> A robust and supreme Constitution arguably can make government stronger and more stable. Institutional arrangements such as the separation of powers, checks and balances, individual civil, political, and justiciable socio-economic rights make the government more responsible, more consistent, more predictable, more just, more caring, more responsive and more legitimate in the eyes of the citizenry. (Ibid.: 17–18)

The judiciary too is subject to these institutional arrangements, and for 'a court to unduly interfere in the functions of the legislature or executive is not only constitutionally wrong, but could put a young democracy in grave danger' (Van der Westhuizen 2008: 260). Although the courts are free from the vagaries of elections and other popular forces, and their decisions are not political in the sense that they are influenced by political considerations, cases before the courts often concern issues that inevitably have political and policy implications. In such cases, the CC has for the most part shown itself to be pragmatic in its approach to interpretation and the provision of relief that, although respectful to the other two branches, does not shy away from the Court's obligation to ensure that the State observes its constitutional obligations in its policy decisions. Provided government sticks to the 'threefold framework of legality, rationality and compliance with the Bill of Rights', 'courts should not tie government's hands more than the Constitution requires' (O' Regan 2012: 132, 133). But critics argue that the CC has since 2008 become too deferential and has not gone far enough in holding government to its constitutional obligations, particularly in socio-economic rights cases.

So how should the judiciary deal with the criticism? Extra-curial responses such as Moseneke's speech can be an effective way to confront criticism head on and concurrently to inform the public of the judiciary's constitutionally prescribed role. However, the interaction between the judiciary and the other two branches envisaged by the Constitution should preferably take a more formal and structured form. Former Chief Justice Ngcobo explains: 'When courts strike down legislation or declare invalid executive decisions, this is followed by an amendment to the legislation or removal of the constitutional defect or a new policy that complies with or responds to the order of the court' (2011: 42).

In basic terms, constitutional dialogue occurs whenever a decision by a court prompts a formal response of some kind from the legislature or executive, such as the enactment of legislation or a change of policy. When the CC declares legislation or conduct invalid, it does so as one party to a 'conversation' with the other arms of government. It is not being obstructionist or anti-transformative.

The Discussion Document envisages the development of 'appropriate mechanisms' to promote regular dialogue among the three arms of the state within the confines of the separation of powers and in pursuit of the transformative goals of the Constitution. Former judge of the CC, Justice Zak Yacoob, in a direct response to the discussion document, has rejected outright any form of dialogue outside of court:

> … the conversation between the courts on the one hand the legislature and the executive on the other is of a different kind. It is not about branches of government talking to each other privately and secretly to obtain a common understanding of the needs of our country. The executive and the legislature on the one hand and the judiciary on the other should indeed talk to each other and do indeed talk to each other. But they do so in a specialised structured way. (Yacoob 2012)

The most important principle that should guide the judiciary in any dialogue with the other arms of government is the maintenance of judicial independence and the courts' constitutionally mandated obligation to act as a check on the actions of the executive and legislature.

Conclusion

Criticism of the judiciary and its decisions is to be expected and is entirely acceptable in a constitutional democracy, provided the criticism is reasoned, informed and justified. However, public confidence in the judiciary should not in the process be undermined irresponsibly and for inappropriate purposes. In South Africa, there is a fear that the current wave of rhetoric against the judiciary led by people of authority in the governing party – and therefore by implication the government – is merely a pretext for challenging constitutional supremacy. No constitution – the system of government it provides for, the powers it allocates to different arms and organs of the state, and so on – is immune from change and amendment, but in any debate about the powers of the judiciary, South Africans need to remain cognisant of their apartheid past. The constitutional negotiators had with good reason agreed on the need for a strong, independent judiciary with extensive powers to act as a check on the exercise of executive and legislative power. A judiciary with strong review powers is not an obstacle to government; it enables government to function properly within the bounds of the Constitution.

The government's view of the judiciary as a co-partner in the pursuit of transformation is misplaced. In order for the judiciary to perform its mandate, it requires independence from government – not interdependence. Judges should remain steadfastly independent and should not be dissuaded from performing their obligation to hold the other arms of government accountable to the Constitution. Without strong courts, the future of constitutional supremacy in South Africa is not guaranteed.

References

Books, book chapters, articles

Chaskalson, A. 2012. 'Without Fear, Favour or Prejudice: The Courts, the Constitution and Transformation', *Advocate*, August: 34–8.

Corder, H. and J. Brickhill, 2014. 'The Constitutional Court', in eds C. Hoexter and M. Olivier, *The Judiciary in South Africa*. Cape Town: Juta & Co.

Friedman, S. 2010. 'Winning Public Trust: Towards a Wider Agenda for Judicial Transformation', *SA Crime Quarterly*, 32 (June): 3–8.

Langa, P. 2006. 'Transformative Constitutionalism', *Stellenbosch Law Review*, 17(3): 351–60.

Lewis, C. 2005. 'Reaching the Pinnacle: Principles, Policies and People for a Single Apex Court in "South Africa"', *South African Journal on Human Rights*, 21(4): 509–24.

Moseneke, D. 2002. 'Fourth Bram Fischer Memorial Lecture: Transformative Adjudication', *South African Journal on Human Rights*, 18(3): 309–19.

Ngcobo, S. 2011. 'South Africa's Transformative Constitution: Towards an Appropriate Doctrine of Separation of Powers', *Stellenbosch Law Review*, 22(1): 37–49.

Olivier, M. 2011. 'The Judiciary in Post-apartheid South Africa', *Diritto Pubblico Comparato ed Europeo*, IV: 1473–89.

O'Regan, K. 2012. 'Helen Suzman Memorial Lecture: A Forum for Reason: Reflections on the Role and Work of the Constitutional Court', *South African Journal on Human Rights*, 28(1): 116–34.

Van der Westhuizen, J. 2008. 'A Few Reflections on the Role of Courts, Government, the Legal Profession, Universities, the Media and Civil Society in a Constitutional Democracy', *African Human Rights Law Journal*, 8(2): 251–72.

Wesson, M. and M. Du Plessis, 2008. 'Fifteen Years On: Central Issues Relating to the Transformation of the South African Judiciary', *South African Journal on Human Rights*, 24(2): 187–213.

Website and online material

Department of Justice and Constitutional Development. 2012. 'Discussion Document on the Transformation of the Judicial System and the Role of the Judiciary in the Developmental South African State' <http://www.justice.gov.za/docs/other-docs/20120228-transf-jud.pdf [accessed 23 August 2014].

Hartley, W. 2011. 'Moseneke Speaks Up Against Attacks on Constitution', *Business Day*, 30 September <http://www.bdlive.co.za > [accessed 10 August 2013].

Mkhabela, M. 2011. 'Full Interview: ANC's Mantashe Lambasts Judges' <http://www.sowetanlive.co.za/news/2011/08/18/full-interview-ancs-mantashe-lambasts-judges> [accessed 10 August 2013].

Moseneke, D. 2011. 'Claude Leon lecture 2011: Striking a Balance Between the Will of the People and the Supremacy of the Constitution' <http://www.lrc.org.za/images/stories/Desktop/2011_10_10_Claude_Leon_Public_Lecture_29_September_2011-__Moseneke_speech.pdf> [accessed 10 August 2013].

Ramatlhodi, N. 2011. 'The Big Read: ANC's Fatal Concessions', *Times Live*, 1 September <http://www.timeslive.co.za/opinion/commentary/2011/09/01/the-big-read-anc-s-fatal-concessions> [accessed 30 June 2014].

Yacoob, Z. 2012. 'Justice Zak Yacoob on the "Dynamic Constitution"' <http://constitutionallyspeaking.co.za/justice-zac-yacoob-on-the-dynamic-constitution/> [accessed 10 August 2013].

Zuma, J. 2011. 'Keynote Address to Access to Justice Conference' <http://constitutionallyspeaking.co.za/president-zumas-keynote-address-to-access-to-justice-conference/> [accessed 10 August 2013].

—— 2012. 'President Zuma's Comments on Judicial Review', 13 February <http://www.thepresidency.gov.za/pebble.asp?relid=5687&t=79> [accessed 10 August 2013].

Cases

De Lange v Smuts NO 1998 (3) SA 785 (CC).

Democratic Alliance v President of the Republic of South Africa 2013 (1) SA 248 (CC).

Justice Alliance of South Africa v President of Republic of South Africa 2011 (5) SA 388 (CC).

S v Makwanyane 1995 (3) SA 391 (CC).

Legislation

Constitution of the Republic of South Africa, Act 200 of 1993.

Constitution of the Republic of South Africa, 1996.

Constitution Seventeenth Amendment Act, 2013.

Judges' Remuneration and Conditions of Employment Act 7 of 2001.

Chapter 6
Depoliticising Socio-economic Rights

Linda Stewart

Introduction

The Constitution of South Africa of 1996 differs from classical liberal constitutions in other parts of the world and is perceived as a progressive and transformative document (Klare 1998: 153, Albertyn and Goldblatt 1998: 249, Liebenberg 2011). It firstly envisages social change of the 'country's political and social institutions and power relationships in a democratic, participatory, and egalitarian direction' through a 'long-term project of constitutional enactment, interpretation, and enforcement' (Klare 1998: 153). Secondly, and closely related to the project of transformative constitutionalism, is the recognition of socio-economic rights as justiciable rights in the Bill of Rights. Klare argues that the inclusion of socio-economic rights 'intends not merely to proclaim democratic political rights but to commit the South African people to achieve a new kind of society in which people actually have the social resources they need meaningfully to exercise their rights' (ibid.).

The Constitution guarantees a wide variety of socio-economic rights and the State has the same obligations to respect, protect, promote and fulfil socio-economic rights as it does civil and political rights. In their textual setting, most of the socio-economic rights are qualified by an obligation placed on the State to realise these rights within the boundaries of reasonableness, available resources, and progressive realisation. The rights to have access to adequate housing; health-care services, including reproductive health care, sufficient food and water; social security and appropriate social assistance; further education and access to land on an equitable basis (see ss 25(5), 26, 27, 29(1)(b)) are examples of the latter. Children's rights to basic nutrition, shelter, basic health-care services, and social services (s 28(1)(c)); the rights of detained persons and prisoners to adequate accommodation, nutrition, reading material and medical treatment (s 35(2)(e)), as well as the right to basic education including adult basic education (s 29(1)(a)) are examples of unqualified rights. There is no internal limitation requiring that the right be 'progressively realised' within 'available resources' subject to 'reasonable legislative measures'. These rights can only be limited in term of s 36 – the general limitation clause – and are perceived to be immediately realisable (*Governing Body of the Juma Musjid Primary School v Essay*, 2011).

In this chapter, I argue that socio-economic rights interpretation and adjudication is by its very nature political and the judiciary plays a significant role in shaping the political discourse on needs and poverty not only in the language they use, but also the conceptual structures and rhetorical remedies they employ and rely on when adjudicating socio-economic rights (see Brand 2009, for a similar argument). The courts' use of the 'reasonableness test' (as language and strategy) as a mechanism to defer dealing with the content of these rights may be detrimental, for it affects the ability of people outside formal political structures and government actively to participate, engage and oppose decisions on poverty, needs and social provisioning of the State. It therefore limits the transformative potential of the constitutional text, because it depoliticises socio-economic rights as part of the political discourse (Brand 2003: 33, 2005: 17–36, 2009: 3). Put differently, the reasonableness test transforms poverty and needs issues into technical and administrative issues which can only be addressed by formal political and governmental structures (based on a liberal-capitalist economic system) (Brand 2009: 72, Liebenberg 2005: 15–16).

I commence with a discussion of the challenges presented to the judiciary by the political nature of socio-economic rights and the transformative mandate of the Constitution within the broader commitment to improve the life of all and to achieve social justice through democratic values and constitutional rights. I focus on socio-economic rights cases where the courts have relied on judicial deference and turned to the reasonableness test to escape dealing with difficult technical and/or contested social questions. This is followed by a discussion of *Mazibuko v City of Johannesburg* where 'reasonableness review' has clearly been utilised to depoliticise poverty issues. I conclude by suggesting that socio-economic rights adjudication requires careful consideration and the judiciary should be conscious of the way they choose to address issues of poverty, needs and provisioning by the State.

Transformative Constitutionalism and Justiciable Socio-economic Rights

The separation of powers and judicial deference

Section 172 of the Constitution provides the judiciary with a powerful and special role that compels a court deciding a constitutional issue within its jurisdiction to declare invalid any law or conduct inconsistent with the Constitution. Section 7(2) furthermore places an obligation on all the branches of government to respect, protect, promote and fulfil the rights in the Bill of Rights. In *Glenister v President of the Republic of South Africa*, the Constitutional Court (CC) stated that this duty 'goes beyond a mere negative obligation not to act in a manner that would infringe or restrict a right'. The Court explained that it also places positive duties on the State 'to take deliberate, reasonable measures' to give effect to constitutional rights (para 105). Implied in s 7(2) 'is the requirement that the steps the State takes must be reasonable and effective'. The CC held that

> ... there are many ways in which the state can fulfil its duty to take positive measures to respect, protect, promote and fulfil the rights in the Bill of Rights. This Court will not be prescriptive as to what measures the state takes as long as

> they fall within the range of possible conduct that a reasonable decision maker in the circumstances may adopt. (para 105)

Possibly the most difficult area under the Constitution requiring a balance in the separation of powers is the interpretation and adjudication of socio-economic rights (O'Regan 2005: 126). In *Certification of the Constitution of the Republic of South Africa, 1996*, it was argued that socio-economic rights are inconsistent with the separation of powers because they required a court to enter the domain of the legislature and executive when it gives content to socio-economic rights and this will result in judicial interference with budgetary matters. The Constitutional Court (CC) reasoned that some civil and political rights such as the right to vote might have similar implications. It held, 'it cannot be said that by including socio-economic rights within a bill of rights, a task is conferred upon the courts so different from that ordinarily conferred upon them by a bill of rights that it results in a breach of the separation of powers' (para 77). The Court also held that socio-economic rights are to some extent justiciable although these rights may have budgetary implications (para 78).

Linked to the doctrine of separation of powers is the idea of judicial deference. According to this idea, courts are expected to show respect for, or submit to, the policies of the administration, the executive and the legislature (Brand 2011: 614, Davis 2006: 312, Pillay 2005: 419, Stewart 2008: 481). Judges often rely on the idea of deference to defend their refusal to engage in cases where they are expected to deal with budgetary or policy-making disputes (McLean 2009: 2). Judicial deference in socio-economic rights cases is 'the strategy of courts, when faced with difficult technical or contested social questions in such cases to leave decision of those issues, in different ways and to varying degrees, to the other branches of government' (Brand 2011: 614). When confronted with the interpretation and adjudication of qualified socio-economic rights, the CC uses judicial deference in relying on the 'reasonableness' test to measure whether the State took the necessary socio-economic measures (legislation and policy) to realise the rights.

With reasonableness review, the courts evaluate the obligation placed on the State by asking whether the measures taken are reasonable instead of defining the content of the right (Liebenberg 2010: 131–223). The Court enquires whether government policies and programmes are rational, coherent, inclusive, comprehensive, coordinated, flexible, inclusive, sensitive to various degrees of deprivation and reasonably implemented and conceived, as well as whether these measures are transparent (*Soobramoney v Minister of Health (KwaZulu-Natal)* 1997, *Government of the Republic of South Africa v Grootboom* 2000, *Minister of Health v Treatment Action Campaign* 2002). The CC in these cases refused to recognise an immediate, direct and individual entitlement to any of these socio-economic rights and evaded an explanation of the content of these rights. In turning to the reasonableness test, the Court therefore escapes difficult questions relating to its institutional capacity to address the matter as well as the specific problem presented before the Court. This approach of the Court in socio-economic rights cases has been criticised as formal/procedural constituting mere good governance principles (Brand 2003: 37). The Court has also been criticised for immediately focusing on the duties placed on government instead of defining the specific socio-economic right (Stewart 2008: 480–82). Put differently, in cases where the judiciary was expected to make a decision on the positive obligation on the state to take measures to realise a socio-economic right, the Court was reluctant to provide normative content to socio-economic rights and resorted to a procedural and formalistic approach to measure the reasonableness of the measures taken by the State (Brand 2011: 614, Liebenberg 2010: 470, 466–80, O'Connell 2011: 551–2).

Transformative constitutionalism

The Constitution is an engagement with a future that it will partly shape, and has been widely accepted as a text with a transformative vision aimed at achieving social justice and substantive equality. Klare, who coined the concept 'transformative constitutionalism', describes it as:

> ... a long-term project of constitutional enactment, interpretation, and enforcement committed (not in isolation, of course, but in a historical context of conducive political developments) to transforming a country's political and social institutions and power relationships in a democratic, participatory, and egalitarian direction. Transformative constitutionalism connotes an enterprise of inducing large-scale social change through nonviolent political processes grounded in law. (Klare 1998: 150)

Pieterse (2005: 165) argues that the Constitution 'unashamedly dictates the political vision required from its interpretative community by articulating unequivocally the political goals to which those tasked with its interpretation and concrete application must aspire'. Transformative constitutionalism furthermore demands critical approaches to law which call for a post-liberal reading of the Constitution and an acknowledgment of the open-ended meaning of legal texts (Van Marle 2003: 551, Du Plessis 1996: 218). Van Marle (2009: 289) argues that, because of the impossibility of language to convey clear meaning in the sense of producing single neutral and objective truths, any text – also the constitutional text – will be open for interpretation and the generation of different plausible interpretations.

Post-liberal thinkers contend that meaning is not discovered in text, but in dealing with the text (Du Plessis 2002: viii, Botha 2004: 249–83), and that engagement with extra-legal factors is inevitable, when interpreting socio-economic rights which pose polycentric questions (Van Marle 2009: 289). This means that the Constitution as a transformative text embodies a political character demanding positive actions from all branches of government, including the judiciary, to achieve this transformative vision (Brand 2011: 622). However, while coining the idea of transformative constitutionalism, Klare (1998: 149) also expressed his reservations on the transformative vision of the Constitution, arguing that the choice made 'to accomplish some significant portion of their law-making through adjudication is a decision fraught with institutional consequences', and questions whether it is in any way possible to expect the judiciary (as the least democratic branch of government) to bring about social, economic and political change.

Brand argues that the adjudication of socio-economic rights should be perceived as part of the political discourse in a democracy. Brand describes transformative politics as the 'capacity and space for political action intended to advance the interests of impoverished people' which is 'critical in its orientation; it is non-institutional; and it is substantive and agonistic rather than procedural and consensual in nature' (Brand 2009: 13, 15–16). Thus a democratised approach to socio-economic transformation requires 'the creation of a society in which all – perhaps in particular impoverished people – are able to participate in a meaningful fashion in the decisions that affect them and that affect the society of which they are a part'. He perceives it as a desired outcome of transformation 'alongside the physical eradication of poverty and socio-economic inequality' (ibid.: 30). He suggests that the courts should rather decline to address a matter or find ways to redirect the matter within the broader political spectrum (ibid.: 18). The following section addresses reasonableness review and how this conceptual strategy employed by the courts depoliticises poverty and needs.

Depoliticising Strategies: The Example of the Mazibuko Case

Depoliticising socio-economic rights

The proceduralisation of needs-talk in socio-economic rights adjudication indicates a definite trend in the language and strategy of the Court. This is particularly illustrated in *Grootboom*, *TAC* and *Mazibuko*. The depoliticisation process can be clearly seen in the Mazibuko case in 2008, the facts of which were as follows. Ms Mazibuko (the first applicant in the case), along with approximately twenty other people, shared a stand in the township Phiri. No one in Mazibuko's house was employed and their income consisted mainly of social assistance grants and the rent from each of two backyard shacks. In January 2004, the residents of Phiri received notice that a pre-paid water system would be put in place. The notice also indicated that if the residents decided on such an installation of the pre-paid water system, their debt in arrears would be cancelled. Mazibuko did not receive such a notice and was not consulted on the prepayment system. In October 2004, she finally surrendered to the prepayment water system, in terms of which, once the six kilolitres free water per household per month had been consumed, the water supply was automatically shut off and the consumer had to buy water credits in order to be supplied with water again. Mazibuko indicated that – with extreme care – the free water would last for ten to fifteen days. This situation fundamentally compromised their health and human dignity. The case was brought before the High Court which ordered in favour of the applicants, ruling that every resident was entitled to 50 litres of water per person per day. Respondents appealed the entire decision and the Supreme Court of Appeal then reduced the quantity of water entitlement to 42 litres per person per day provided that residents registered with the City's Register of Indigents. Unhappy with this order, the residents of Phiri turned to the CC. The case turned on two major issues: first, whether the Free Basic Water policy (including the City's decisions to supply six kilolitres of free water per month to every accountholder in the city) was in conflict with the right of access to water in terms of s 27 of the Constitution and s 11 of the Water Services Act. The second issue was whether the installation of prepaid water meters by the State was lawful (*Mazibuko* para 6). O'Regan J wrote the judgment for the unanimous court.

Naturalisation: sustainability and economic ordering

The Court explicitly recognised its own institutional limits and constraints in the adjudication of socio-economic rights and provided reasons justifying the limits and constraints. The Court reasoned that:

> National government should set the targets it wishes to achieve in respect of social and economic rights clearly. That is consistent with the founding values of our Constitution: government should be accountable, responsive and open. The minimum standard set by the Minister informs citizens of what government is seeking to achieve. (para 70).

There is, furthermore, a clear underlying message: that the Court will not question the substantive content of the obligation placed on the State, and that the Court is merely there to enquire whether the measure to realise the right in question is procedurally reasonable.

The reasoning of the CC is framed by the 'naturalisation' strategy, which is often used to depict poverty and needs, as a result of 'natural causes, wholly outside of the control of society' (Brand 2009: 65–6). For example, the Court describes South Africa as a largely arid country and depicts water scarcity as a reality, something wholly outside the control of society. It emphasises that the rights of people to have access to a basic water supply should be understood in the context of the State's duty to manage water services sustainably. The issue of water as a basic need has consequently been translated into a complex problem of sustainable water management which can only be addressed in formal political and governmental institutions.

A particular kind of naturalising strategy is to view 'liberal (or free market) capitalism' as the proper or natural economic ordering. Dugard (2010: 81) explains that water services in South Africa are 'managed largely along commercial lines' and 'water has become more of an economic product and less of a public health-related service'. The reason for this can mainly be attributed to the government's 'growing neo-liberal preoccupation', visible in several ways (ibid.: 77). These measures pressured municipalities to commercialise basic services such as the provision of water and electricity. As such, the provision of services has become the main source of revenue for most municipalities and this results in 'poor households being disconnected for inability to pay for water services' (ibid.).

Technicisation

Technicisation occurs when poverty and needs are depicted as technical, administrative and complex problems for managers and planners in formal political and governmental institutions (Brand 2009: 147). The 'technicisation of needs-talk' within political discourse is a process of translation by different discursive arenas who occupy positions of relative power to engage with and influence the meaning and content of poverty and needs-talk. The different discursive arenas consist of informal social movements and formal organs of civil society (NGOs and academia) and official arenas such as Parliament or specialist administrative agencies. When Parliament and specialist administrative agencies identify a need and speak about that need and engage in the content of that need with a specific purpose, they legitimise state intervention by translating a politicised need into an 'administrable' need. The Court recognises the inequalities in the provision of water and water services and the transformative vision of the Constitution to rectify these inequalities (paras 1–2). It contextualises the inequalities in the provision of water by stating that:

> Water is life. Without it, we will die. Despite the significant improvement in the first fifteen years of democratic government, deep inequality remains and for many the task of obtaining sufficient water for their families remains a tiring daily burden. The achievement of equality, one of the founding values of our Constitution, will not be accomplished while water is abundantly available to the wealthy, but not to the poor. (para 2)

Technicisation of the issue of access to adequate water already occurs in the final part of this introductory statement (and continues through the judgment), turning previously politicised issues into 'technical problems for managers and planners' (Brand 2009: 66–7). In the cases of *Grootboom* and *TAC*, the CC recognised its institutional incapacity to address issues of poverty and needs either because of the complexity presented by the case or to defer to other branches of government. The CC legitimises its decision by allowing other branches of government a greater margin of discretion. The CC therefore chooses to constrain its powers by making it a complicated technical issue and then by placing the (technical) issue wholly in the 'formally constituted political branches of government "whose responsibility [and right] it is to deal with such matters"' (ibid.: 154, 186). The Court's rhetoric, therefore, disenfranchises social movements, NGOs and ordinary people from the poverty-and-needs discourse.

In a democracy in which the judiciary has the power to interpret and declare legislation or government actions invalid, tension will always exist between the judiciary and other branches of government. This relationship is often adversarial, resulting in an unevenness between democracy and constitutional law (Davis 2012: 4). Central to the complex relationship between different branches of government is the question of whether there is a justification that the right of a sovereign citizenry to decide the terms of public life (democracy) may be limited in the name of the constitutional rights as contained in the Bill of Rights (constitutionalism) (Christodoulidis 2002: 108).

When attempting to resolve the paradox created by the tension between democratic will and constitutional reason, constitutional theorists either deny or avoid the tension (dualist view), or present an answer where constitutional reason prevails over democratic will or vice versa (monist view) (ibid.: 108–9). This paradox is often described as the *counter-majoritarian* difficulty which questions the law-making powers of the judiciary. Christodoulidis (ibid.: 108–12) points out that instead of viewing the problem posed between democratic will and constitutional reason as binary, we should rather approach it as a triangular relationship between the role of the courts in terms of constitutionalism (or constitutional reason), the representative branches of government (democratic will) and the people (the sovereign people). Brand (2011: 631) argues that this shift will force the judiciary to focus on the problem presented before them instead of shifting the responsibility to address the matter to other branches of government. He contends that such an approach 'would in fact seek both to engage with these problems [of institutional illegitimacy] in every case in which they arise, and to do so by looking for inventive solutions to them elsewhere than simply in a deferral to the other branches of government'. Davis (2012: 10) proposes that assessing the task of courts faced with the separation of powers principle seems to be less about the principle and more about how a court works within the confines of the principle to promote a better dialogue between the legislature, executive and the courts. He argues that such a task should be directed to 'improve the principle of democratic accountability of public institutions and their commitment to constitutional rights'.

The Court seeks refuge in structure

Under the heading 'The role of courts in determining the content of social and economic rights: the proper interpretation of s 27(1)(b) and 27(2) of the Constitution', the Court echoes the rhetoric used in *Grootboom* and *TAC* by stating: firstly, that there is no directly enforceable obligation on the State to realise the right to water (paras 48–9), and, secondly, that the Court is only capable of reviewing the reasonableness of the State's measures (para 50). It includes the Court's view that the City's Indigent registration policy is a reasonable measure to target state provision to poor households. The Indigent registration policy provides for an additional 10 kilolitres of water per month per household on condition that residents apply and it is subject to means testing (paras 98–102). Thirdly, the Court argues that it is institutionally incapable of determining the content of the right (including its minimum core) because of the complexity involved in making such decisions. The Court therefore shows deference to other branches of government to avoid infringing the separation of powers (paras 51–52, 65).

The Court proceeds to review existing State measures to enforce the right to water. The Court limits its power to adjudicate socio-economic rights by explicitly stating that:

> … it is institutionally inappropriate for a court to determine precisely what the achievement of any particular social and economic right entails and what steps government should take to ensure the progressive realisation of the right. This is a matter, in the first place, for the legislature and executive, the institutions of government best placed to investigate social conditions in the light of available budgets and to determine what targets are achievable in relation to social and economic rights. Indeed, it is desirable as a matter of democratic accountability that they should do so for it is their programmes and promises that are subjected to democratic popular choice. (para 61)

This formalistic reasoning is even more evident in the Court's investigation of the consultation process of the Free Basic Water policy. As part of the reasonableness review, the Court investigated whether the City had adequately consulted the residents before they implemented the pre-paid water system. It was argued on behalf of the City that a proper consultation process preceded the disconnection of water services to the residents. The communication of the policy changes took place through formal structures representing the community, particularly ward committees and meetings held by ward councillors. There was evidence that public meetings were held twice monthly to explain the project to community members and that community workers conducted house visits to explain the policy changes to the residents (para 133). The question is whether these measures constitute 'meaningful participation'. In contrast, it may be argued that the community had no input in the development of the policy; these measures were merely there to inform residents that policy changes were imminent and out of their control (paras 7, 10–18).

A limited account of 'democratic participation'

The Court further limits democratic participation as either a process where government can be held to account through election on certain matters or where courts may be approached to investigate the reasonableness of government measures (paras 71, 96 and 160).

In other words, the Court's limited account of 'democratic participation' excludes people outside formal political structures the space to participate, engage and oppose decisions on poverty, needs and social provisioning of the State. The Court further suggests that the only remedy available to people outside formal political structures is to turn to highly complicated, slow and expensive litigation (para 165). Realising the conundrum presented in a suggestion that the poor can only turn to courts when they disagree with the decisions of government, the Court argues that South Africa has a range of civil society and non-governmental organisations to assist the poor in the legal arena to litigate (para 165). Thus, the limited procedural perception of 'democracy' seems not to take into account the importance of meaningful public participation. The limited conception of democratic participation proposed in *Mazibuko* especially excludes impoverished people from participating in and contributing to decisions that affect them and the society of which they are a part.

To summarise, the Court depoliticises the right to water, a typical socio-economic right, firstly by turning the provision of water to indigent members of the society into a complex, administrative and technical issue, that can only be addressed by formally constituted political branches of government (technicisation); secondly, by limiting its engagement in the issue to reasonableness review (structuralisation), and finally, by showing deference to a (procedural account) of democracy and limiting questions of need within the 'liberal capitalist understandings of economic ordering' (proceduralisation). This line of argumentation leaves little scope for the future adjudication of socio-economic rights, if the judgment is to be followed.

Conclusion

As illustrated above, impoverished communities need to participate in decisions affecting their interest and needs. However, these communities struggle to participate or voice their concerns and are often left with the option of approaching those mechanisms that have been provided by the State or by formalised civil society organisations or they may turn to the courts. It is, however, problematic when courts engage in language and strategies that depoliticise the needs of impoverished communities. When dealing with the complexities and institutional difficulties presented in the adjudication of socio-economic rights cases, courts should be conscious of the language and rhetoric they use to avoid depoliticising needs talk and the participation of that community.

One possible way for courts to contribute meaningfully to socio-economic transformation as envisioned by the Constitution is also to focus on facilitating meaningful public reasoning and dialogue in the form of political discourse and participation. In *Occupiers of 51 Olivia Road, Berea Township, and Others v City of Johannesburg and Others*, the CC made an interim order compelling the parties to enter into meaningful engagement and to report back to the Court on the content of their engagement. The Court stressed that the parties should resolve the difficulties expressed in the application 'in the light of the values of the Constitution, the constitutional and statutory duties of the municipality and the rights and duties of the citizens concerned' (para 1). This resulted in a comprehensive settlement agreed between the parties. In the subsequent order, the Court explained that the legal basis of meaningful engagement as an adjudication strategy is founded on a range of constitutional provisions including s 26, which places a positive obligation on the state to act reasonably in realising the right of access to adequate housing. Liebenberg (2012: 19), however, warns that the danger remains that 'meaningful engagement as an adjudicatory strategy may descend into an unprincipled, normatively empty process of local dispute settlement.' Liebenberg further reiterates that in the context of socio-economic realities these 'judicial procedures, interpretive methods and doctrinal categories' are 'blunt instruments for dealing with particularity and difference' (ibid.: 6).

There will always be a tension between democratic will and constitutional reason in a constitutional democracy. A possible way for courts to address the tension is to view it as a problem between the sovereign people, constitutional reason and democratic will. As Brand (2011: 631) proposes:

> … this shift of perspective, should they be able to operationalise it in their doctrine, techniques and reasoning, would enable them to embrace instead of deference with its attendant problems, an approach of what can perhaps be called judicial prudence. Such an approach would, on the understanding that courts in the exercise of their review powers stand in a complex triangular relationship with the other branches of government and the rest of the world (civil society, ordinary people), indeed recognise the difficulty of the institutional problems of capacity, legitimacy, integrity and security. But such an approach would in fact seek both to engage with these problems in every case in which they arise, and to do so by looking for inventive solutions to them elsewhere than simply in a deferral to the other branches of government.

References

Books, book chapters, and articles

Albertyn, C., and B. Goldblatt, 1998. 'Facing the Challenge of Transformation: Difficulties in the Development of an Indigenous Jurisprudence of Equality', *South African Journal on Human Rights*, 14: 248–76.

Brand, D. 2003. 'The Proceduralisation of South African Socio-economic Rights Jurisprudence or "What are Socio-economic Rights for?"', in eds H. Botha, A. Van der Walt, and J. Van der Walt, *Rights and Democracy in a Transformative Constitution*. Stellenbosh: African Sun Media.

—— 2005. 'Introduction to the Socio-economic Rights in the South African Constitution', in eds D. Brand and C. Heyns, *Socio-economic rights in South Africa*. Pretoria: PULP.

—— 2009. 'Courts, Socio-economic Rights and Transformative Politics', LLD Thesis, Stellenbosch: Stellenbosch University.

—— 2011. 'Judicial Deference and Democracy in Socio-economic Rights Cases in South Africa', *Stellenbosch Law Review*, 22(3): 614–38.

Davis, D.M. 2012. 'The Relationship Between Courts and the Other Arms of Government in Promoting and Protecting Socio-economic Rights in South Africa: What About Separation of Powers?', *Potchefstroom Electronic Law Journal*, 15(6): 3–14.

Dugard, J. 2007. 'A Pro-poor Critique of Prepayment Water Meters in South Africa: The Phiri Story', *Critical Health Perspectives*, 2(2): 1.

—— 2010. 'Civic Action and the Legal Mobilisation: The Phiri Water Meters Case', in eds J. Handmaker and R. Berkhout, *Mobilising Social Justice in South Africa: Perspectives from Researchers and Practitioners*. The Hague: ISS and Hivos.

Evans, T. 2005. 'International Human Rights Law as Power/Knowledge', *Human Rights Quarterly*, 27(3): 1046–68.

Jansen van Rensburg (Stewart), L. 2008. 'The Right of Access to Adequate Water', *Stellenbosch Law Review*, 19(3): 415–35.

Klare, K. 1998. 'Legal Culture and Transformative Constitutionalism', *South African Journal on Human Rights*, 14: 146–88.

Liebenberg, S. 2005. 'The Value of Human Dignity in Interpreting Socio-economic Rights', *South African Journal on Human Rights*, 21: 1–31.

—— 2006. 'The Interpretation of Socio-economic Rights', in eds S. Woolman et al., *Constitutional Law of South Africa*, 2nd edn. Cape Town: Juta.

—— 2010. *Socio-Economic Rights Adjudication under a transformative Constitution*. Cape Town: Juta.

—— 2012. 'Engaging the Paradoxes of the Universal and Particular in Human Rights Adjudication: The Possibilities and Pitfalls of "Meaningful Engagement"', *African Human Rights Law Journal*, 12(1): 1–29.

McLean, K. 2009. *Constitutional Deference, Courts and Socio-Economic Rights in South Africa*. Pretoria: PULP.

O'Connell, P. 2011. 'The Death of Socio-Economic Rights', *Modern Law Review*, 74(4): 532–55.

O'Regan, K. 2005. 'Checks and Balances Reflections on the Development of the Doctrine of Separation of Powers under the South African Constitution', *Potchefstroom Electronic Law Journal*, 8(1): 120–50.

Pieterse, M. 2007. 'Eating Socioeconomic Rights', *Human Rights Quarterly*, 29: 796–822.

Pillay, A. 2005. 'Reviewing Reasonableness: An Appropriate Standard for Evaluating State Action and Inaction', *South African Journal on Human Rights*, 122(2): 419–40.

Stewart, L. 2008. 'Interpreting and Limiting the Basic Socio-economic Rights of Children in Cases where they Overlap with the Socio-economic Rights of Others', *South African Journal on Human Rights*, 24: 472–94.

—— and D. Horsten, 2009. 'The Role of Sustainability in the Adjudication of the Right to Access to Adequate Water', *SA Public Law*, 24(2): 486–505.

Van Marle, K. 2003. 'Revisiting the Politics of Post-apartheid Constitutional Interpretation', *Journal of South African Law*, 1: 550–57.

—— 2009. 'Transformative Constitutionalism as/and Critique', *Stellenbosch Law Review*, 20(2): 286–301.

Cases

City of Johannesburg v Mazibuko (Centre on Housing Rights and Evictions as amicus curiae) 2009 (3) SA 592 (SCA).
Glenister v President of the Republic of South Africa 2011 (3) SA 347 (CC).
Governing Body of the Juma Musjid Primary School v Essay 2011 (8) BCLR 761 (CC).
Government of the Republic of South Africa v Grootboom 2000 (11) BCLR 1169 (CC).
In re Certification of the Constitution of the Republic of South Africa 1996 (4) SA 744 (CC).
Mazibuko v City of Johannesburg 2010 (4) SA 1 (CC).
Mazibuko v The City of Johannesburg (Centre on Housing Rights and Evictions as amicus curiae) 2008 JOL 21829 (W).
Minister of Health v Treatment Action Campaign 2002 (5) SA 72 (CC).
Occupiers of 51 Olivia Road, Berea Township v City of Johannesburg 2008 (5) BCLR 475 (CC).
Soobramoney v Minister of Health (KwaZulu-Natal) 1997 (12) BCLR 1696 (CC).

Chapter 7

Dignity and Disgrace – Moral Citizenship and Constitutional Protection[1]

Edwin Cameron

Introduction and Summary: Explaining the Role of Dignity

Why has dignity taken such a central place in South Africa's constitutional jurisprudence? And what does it tell us about the fact that South Africa's Constitution was the first anywhere that expressly outlawed discrimination based on sexual orientation, and one of the first to extend equal rights to marry to lesbian and gay couples? The puzzle is worth unravelling.

On a visit to the Constitutional Court (CC) of South Africa in February 2010, Professor Catharine MacKinnon, who described herself as the pioneer of the 'substantive equality' approach to rights, forcefully expressed her bemusement that the Court's equality jurisprudence centred on the right to dignity. In a personal communication, she declared, 'As the pioneer of the substantive equality approach, I just don't get why anyone thinks dignity has to do the work.' MacKinnon has recognised that 'deprivation of dignity is often a powerful dimension of the substance of inequality and does some of its work.' But she has also asserted that ascribing dignity to humans, particularly when employed in the Kantian sense of their unconditional and incomparable worth (Kant 1785), is simply inadequate to address certain social practices or relationships that undermine it, or instances where individuals willingly relinquish it (MacKinnon 2011).

Yet there is sound reason why dignity, for all its indeterminacy, has taken so central a place in the formative jurisprudence of the Court. It is to be found in South Africa's past of racial indignity – where racial subordination was both premised on and enacted shamefulness and disgrace. Apartheid laws deprived black South Africans of their citizenship, gave them education that was inferior to whites', segregated and confined them on land both urban and rural, and relegated them to poorer jobs and economic roles.

But those laws represented, and did, more. They derived from the view that black South Africans were subordinate and inferior humans, and treated them

1 This chapter draws extensively on, but is a truncated version of, my contribution to Christopher McCrudden, ed., 2013. *Understanding Human Dignity*. London: British Academy. Both the editor and publisher have authorised this re-publication.

accordingly. They enunciated and practised the condition of 'non-whiteness' as legally shameful.

I grew up in apartheid South Africa in a desperately poor and fractured white family. But I was glad not to be black. At home, at school and on the street, my daily consciousness was imbued with a sense and gratitude that, at least, I was white. The shame of being black, not only with the legal impediments and subordinations that marked it, but with the stigmatised condition those impediments implied, was not mine. My humanness was superior: unshamefully white.

In this way, apartheid laws damaged both white and black, by stigmatising black people, placing a mark of shame on their race, and by injuring white people with an award of a false conception of superiority (Masango 2012). This legacy re-emerges vividly in persisting, acrid controversy about race in South African society.

But, like other, less racist, societies, apartheid created a further category of subordination and shame: that of deviant sexuality. There, too, the law stigmatised and persecuted a condition that was seen as undesirably shameful: homosexuality and same-sex sexual conduct.

To that category I shamefully belonged. I was gay in an otherwise heterosexual world, a world that would accommodate me only to the extent that I managed to pretend that I was straight.

When it came to determining the ambit of constitutional protection, those negotiating for gays and lesbians could plausibly contend that including sexual orientation as a protected condition was analogous to including race – both conditions had been harshly stigmatised under apartheid, and both had been subjected to severe indignity. By this path, the generous embrace of equality and non-discrimination was extended to sexual orientation.

That same spirit has been evident in the CC's jurisprudence, as will be seen below.

In this chapter, I argue that the inclusion of sexual orientation as a protected ground in South Africa's Constitution, and the Court's vigorous assertion of sexual orientation equality, can be fully understood only by understanding the indignity inflicted by apartheid's racialised assault on black South Africans. That this protection has been based so centrally on asserting the inherent dignity of all reflects the continuing palpability of a past of indignity and shame.

Legal Stigma and Moral Citizenship

In 1963, in a justly famous analysis, the sociologist Erving Goffman identified the 'structural preconditions' of stigma as consisting in a trait or attribute that amounts to an 'undesired differentness' – one that contravenes society's expectations or the standards upon which collective identity is predicated (Goffman 1986: 5–6). Stigma arises because society, through its social settings, laws, cultural practices and policies, creates a structure and language for categorising people and hence for identifying qualities that are regarded as ordinary or 'natural' (ibid.: 2). These take on a normative meaning, which entails that those who cannot meet them are 'discredited' (ibid.: 2, Herek et al 2007: 1).

Discrediting confers an inferior social status, and concomitantly, less power and access to resources (Herek et al. 2007: 2). This is the essence of social stigma, and it takes little imagination to see that apartheid's legal institutions systematically 'discredited' black people.

At its most brutal, the legal apparatus of apartheid denied black South Africans the vote, land, freedom of movement, jobs, public office, educational opportunity, the capacity to learn in their own languages and the liberty to choose their sexual partners and spouses. It deprived them even of their South African citizenship.

The process of degradation of civic status started with the European settlement of South Africa in the seventeenth century (Schlemmer 1970: 20–21, Worden 2000). Over time, successive white governments made laws that regulated both the public and the most intimate aspects of people's lives, and in particular, placed the onerous restrictions on the movements, relationships and economic choices of black people. (Unless I mention otherwise, specifically when I quote Stephen Bantu Biko, I use 'black' to refer to people characterised as 'bantu' or 'African' by the apartheid government.)

Perhaps the most oppressive embodiment of this control was the pass system (Horrell 1978: 171), which required black people at all times to carry a document that denoted permission to be in a particular city or location for a specific purpose. The 'pass' came to symbolise the viciousness and pettiness of apartheid. To be caught without a pass was a crime. Many hundreds of thousands of black South Africans were arrested every year for violating these laws (Burns 1978), and sentenced to jail terms, generally short, but often repeated. The very spectre of arrest dominated black urban life. In this way, apartheid made criminals of a large proportion of South Africa's adult population.

The system of discrimination, constraint and denial required black people to collide, at every turn, with an omnipresent legal machinery that regulated their lives. The laws sought to erect and entrench 'separateness'. Necessarily, they embodied a pervasive strategy of repression and domination (Coleman 1998).

But they did more than this. They branded black South Africans as inferior.

The effect of apartheid's laws in 'discrediting' black people in this way was fiercely contested: indeed, it was the cause of an externally based liberation struggle and a massive internal rebellion.

But the legal meaning of apartheid was to subordinate, discredit and stigmatise blackness. That meaning inflicted injury on all who lived under it, black and white.

The injury was also subsumed internally. The American W.E.B. Du Bois articulated how this may happen. He spoke of a world that yielded an African-American descendant of slaves 'no true self-consciousness, but only lets him see himself through the revelation of the other world', thus creating a sense of 'measuring one's soul by the tape of a world that looks on in amused contempt and pity' (Du Bois 1903).

But whose 'tape' is to be used in this measurement? This question was taken up fiercely and eloquently by Stephen Bantu Biko, the young activist beaten to death in police detention in September 1977. He saw black (here used as encompassing all South Africans of colour, including 'Africans', 'Indians' and 'Coloureds') people's struggle against racial categorisation, restriction and control as being against 'forces that seek to use your blackness as a stamp that marks you out as a subservient being' (Biko 1978: 52).

He asserted a counter-consciousness, an assertive black consciousness, that sought 'to infuse the black community with a new-found pride in themselves, their efforts, their value systems, their culture, their religion, and their outlook to life' (ibid.: 53). His vision recognised the psychic scarring of legal stigma, as well as the internal dimension necessary to true liberation: 'The interrelationship between the consciousness of the self and the emancipatory programme is of paramount importance' (ibid.).

Biko proclaimed that the fundamental tenet of black consciousness was 'that the black man must reject all value systems that seek to make him a foreigner in the country of his birth and reduce his basic human dignity' (*S v Cooper* 1976).

Biko rightly saw that the primary impact of apartheid was a systematised affront to racial dignity, and that its reclamation was a task both public and private, both external and internal. This is so because the effect of systematic degradation persists even after legalised racial (Williams et al. 2008), and other, stigmas are abolished (Steele 1997). They burden even without being internalised, merely because the perceptions might be applicable (ibid.: 617).

But the apartheid state assailed not only race. It also demeaned on the basis of sexual identity.

Sexual expression was severely policed. In 1927, Parliament passed the Immorality Act, forbidding extra-marital sexual relations between white and African people. This was amended after 1948 to prohibit sex between whites and any other race. And further, in 1949 the Prohibition of Mixed Marriages Act was enacted, which not only prohibited marriage between white people and members of all other races, but also declared illegitimate any children born of a marriage later deemed invalid.

What was more:

> Apartheid South Africa exhibited a well-developed tradition of legally-sanctioned discrimination against gays and lesbians. South Africa had gathered anti-homosexuality laws from each of its several legal traditions – all of which condemned homosexuality. The legal situation in pre-liberation South Africa was more harsh (*de jure* at least) than many of its neighbors. Whereas many sub-Saharan nations have no explicit provisions related to homosexuality, South Africa has had condemnatory laws since colonization. (Christiansen 2000: 14)

All sexual expression between men was proscribed. Laws against sodomy and 'unnatural offences' were fiercely enforced. In 1969, the apartheid Parliament expanded the common law and legislative prohibitions on sex between men, by criminalising private conduct 'at a party' (Immorality Act of 1957, s 20A). Right until the lag-years of apartheid, the apartheid Parliament was considering further expansions of these crimes (Gevisser and Cameron 1995).

The symbolic effect of these laws was immense. In *Khumalo v Holomisa* 2002, O'Regan J stated the following at para 27:

> The value of human dignity in our Constitution is not only concerned with an individual's sense of self-worth, but constitutes an affirmation of the worth of human beings shared by all people as well as the individual reputation of each person built on his or her own individual achievements. The value of human dignity in our Constitution therefore values both the personal sense of self-worth as well as the public's estimation of the worth or value of an individual.

As the CC later noted, their meaning was 'that in the eyes of our legal system all gay men are criminals' (*National Coalition* 1999, para 28). The resonance with the way the pass laws made most black South Africans criminals is intense.

In my adolescent and early adult years, I experienced the debilitating effect of this criminality. I felt shame at what I was: a gay man with intense yearning for same-sex companionship and expression. And I felt fear that its expression would lead to a life-ruining confrontation with the criminal law.

Sexual stigma stems from social discomfort or disregard for non-heterosexual behaviour, identity, relationships or communities (Herek et al. 2007). It is oppressive and pervasive, and, as with race laws, it is exacerbated when the law brands the condition as inferior: when the law discredits it.

As with the effects of racial subordination, the reparatory project is both private and public, both internal and external. And here the law is of immense importance. The capacity to function fully within the legal sphere, and to be viewed as a fully legal citizen, helps diminish internalisation of dignity and shame.

Biko's ideas were a premonitory articulation of what dignity has come to mean in South African constitutional jurisprudence: a rejection of any value system that reduces human worth. They also explain the central role of dignity in the South African constitutional order. Dignity-based jurisprudence has helped to foster the notion of an inclusive moral citizenship in South Africa, unburdened by the humiliating exclusions and degradations of the past.

That the equal protection of the laws should have been extended so fulsomely to gays and lesbians, no less than to South Africans oppressed by apartheid's suffocating racial codes, is one of the truly remarkable aspects of our transition.

The explanation lies in the degrading experience of indignity under apartheid, which was in significant respects common to black South Africans and gays and lesbians. This argument could be advanced plausibly because gays and lesbians were deeply involved in fighting apartheid. These included Cecil Williams, who was driving Mr Mandela when he was arrested in 1962, Simon Nkoli, the gay and AIDS activist who died tragically in 1998, and Sheila Lapinsky, founder of the Cape Town-based Organisation of Lesbians and Gays (OLGA) (Gevisser and Cameron, 1995: 75), which initiated discussions with the ANC about sexual orientation as a constitutionally protected condition after 1990.

Dignity as Both a Foundational Value and a Fundamental Right

In the Constitution of South Africa, human dignity is both a founding value (s 1(a)) and a discrete right in the Bill of Rights (s 10). In the interim Constitution under which South Africa's transition to democracy took place, dignity was listed only as a fundamental right (s 10), and it was the CC that declared, in its decision outlawing the death penalty, that dignity played a larger role than merely as a right: it was also the value on which the new democracy was founded (*S v Makwanyane* 1995, paras 58 and 328). As a direct response to the *Makwanyane* decision (as related by Justice Yacoob who was at the time an adviser to the constitution-making process), the Constitutional Assembly, drafting South Africa's final Constitution, listed dignity not only as a fundamental right, but also at the start of the Constitution, as a founding value. It also provided that dignity was one of only two rights – alongside the right to life – that is entirely non-derogable (s 37; in states of emergency, other rights are partially derogable).

Dignity thus operates in the jurisprudence of the Court in two ways: as a foundational value that informs the interpretation of all other rights; and as a fully justiciable right (Currie and De Waal 2005: 275, relying on O'Regan J in *Dawood*). Dignity is relatively rarely invoked as a right in itself (Woolman 2006: 36–19). More often, it operates as a value infusing other rights, most particularly, perhaps, the right to equality.

Dignity has an important public dimension, and is given a unique flavour in South African jurisprudence by imbuing it with *ubuntu* (More 2006: 149 and 156–7). This is embodied in the status and protection that legal, social and political institutions confer. These enable us, without fear of abuse, discrimination or constraint, to engage out in the world in the commitments and activities that embody who we are and what we wish to become – to attain self-actualisation, despite the accidents of our birth and notwithstanding any incidents of lifestyle.

The Court has thus held that the anti-discrimination provisions of the Constitution provide 'a bulwark against invasions which impair human dignity' and that the commitment to dignity underpins the commitment to avoid discrimination (*Harksen v Lane* 1997, para 49). In this way, dignity is the basis of the Court's anti-discrimination jurisprudence.

As is evident, this in many ways follows other societies that have vested dignity as a fundamental constitutional or jurisprudential value (Chaskalson 2000). The German Constitution (Basic Law, article 1), in many ways a product of the Second World War, established the 'inviolability' of human dignity and obliged state institutions to 'respect and protect' it.

Although Canada's Charter of Rights and Freedoms does not specifically mention dignity, the jurisprudence of its Supreme Court has invoked 'respect for the inherent dignity of every human person' to ascribe meaning to those rights and freedoms (*R v Oakes* 1986: 334–5).

The dignity and equality jurisprudence of the South African Constitutional Court has derived much of its formal and conceptual structure from that of the Supreme Court of Canada (*President of the RSA v Hugo* 1997, para 41). But the evolution of dignity as a constitutional value in South Africa has deeper roots, and it is wrong to think it was simply appropriated from elsewhere (Philp 2012). It is best understood through the indignity that apartheid inflicted on most South Africans (Brink 1970, who noted that 'I believe that apartheid is a denial of everything that is basic to human dignity and to the concept of love … ').

Dignity is intrinsic to each person (and may inhere in all beings). It comprises the deeply personal understandings we have of ourselves and our worth as individuals and in our material and social context. No law or social practice can strip dignity, in this sense, away (Waldron 2011). Apartheid was an assault on black South Africans' dignity, but its laws could not deprive them of their intrinsic human worth.

The systematic humiliation and degradation that apartheid's legal structures inflicted on black people may not have detracted from their intrinsic human dignity. But apartheid stemmed from an ideology of racial superiority that imputed a high value to white skin colour and European culture, while regarding black skin colour and African culture as inferior. This left a residue of indignity which was perceived and experienced as shameful. It is from this that the conception of apartheid's racism as 'disgraceful' stems: that it sought to inflict a state of disgrace on people for no morally sound or rational reason.

In one of its earliest judgments, the Constitutional Court distinguished the South African Constitution from others by noting that it marks a 'decisive break from, and a ringing rejection of, that part of the past which is disgracefully racist, authoritarian, insular, and repressive' (*S v Makwanyane* 1995, para 262).

South African constitutional jurisprudence has thus sought to abolish the impediments of the past by ensuring that self-worth is recognised and protected by the formal institutions of the state and its law. Those who suffered from a disgraceful past would be restored to grace.

We have neither forgotten nor fully healed from our oppressive past. But our Constitution has given full recognition to those previously shamed and disgraced by an oppressive system. It has created a legal framework to permit rights-assertions that have enabled people to express their anger, to demand recognition. And in doing so, it has provided the means for overcoming that past, and for asserting, at an individual and collective level, a sense of dignity.

The experience of the shameful effects of racial and gender subordination impelled those envisioning the new constitutional order to include protection for a wide array of conditions that were disabling under apartheid. Over the last decade and a half, South African law has invoked dignity to proscribe the criminal inhibitions on same-sex conduct, and to allow the recognition of same-sex partnerships, adoption, procreation and marriage.

Dignity has also enabled the Court's jurisprudence to advance individual personhood and to erase the residues of shame by bringing differences in sexual functioning out of the hidden realm of the private sphere. The Court's decisions have thus subverted the notion that, to avoid shameful disparagement, individuals' activities and relationships must subscribe to uniformity.

The Court's jurisprudence has sought not merely to abolish the impediments of the past by ensuring that self-worth is recognised and protected by the State and its institutions. It has sought to create a normative framework in which South Africans can assert their personhood without the shameful stigmata of past subordination.

In short, the function of dignity in South African constitutionalism has been to repair indignity, to renounce humiliation and degradation and to vest full moral citizenship in those who were denied it in the past.

Arriving at Same-Sex Marriage

The earliest judgments of the CC saw an inextricable link between dignity and equality. In finding that the death penalty was an unlawful violation of the Constitution, the Court found that the rights to life and dignity are the 'most important of all human rights' as well as 'the source of all other personal rights' set out in the Bill of Rights. As a result, the South African State's commitment to these two fundamental rights had to be evidenced in all of its actions, including the punishments it imposes on wrongdoers (*S v Makwanyane* 1995, para 144). In a concurring opinion that articulated the important historical basis for the emphasis on these fundamental rights, Ackermann J noted that the new constitutional order created a right to life that, unlike in other jurisdictions, is not a qualified one (para 154). To that end, he emphasised that South Africa's past was characterised by the imposition of laws that were 'arbitrary and unequal'. In a separate concurrence, Langa J noted that:

> The history of the past decades has been such that the value of life and human dignity have been demeaned. Political, social and other factors created a climate of violence resulting in a culture of retaliation and vengeance. In the process, respect for life and for the inherent dignity of every person became the main casualties. (Para 218)

Further striking examples of the Court's reliance on dignity as a fundamental right and constitutional value can be seen in a number of leading cases decided early in the life of the CC, such as *President of the RSA v Hugo* 1997, *Brink v Kitshoff* 1996, *Harksen v Lane* 1997 and *Dawood v Minister of Home Affairs* 1997.

But the role of dignity is evidenced most strikingly in the jurisprudence on the equality of gays and lesbians. Over the last thirteen years, our law has invoked dignity to proscribe the criminalisation of sodomy as well as to allow for the recognition of same-sex partnerships, adoptions and, most recently, marriages.

The pronouncements on same-sex relationships and marriage cannot be fully appreciated without understanding the impact of apartheid's expansive racialised assault on the dignity of the majority of South Africa's people. More tellingly, the same-sex rulings may not have been possible had courts relied exclusively upon the rights of privacy and equality. The experience in this field of the United States Supreme Court demonstrates the possible difficulties that may have been encountered had this route been followed (*Bowers v Hardwick* 1986 and *Lawrence v Texas* 2003 being prime examples). Dignity, both as a right and as a foundational value, has enabled our jurisprudence to bring people's differences out of the hidden realm of the private sphere, by undercutting the notion that individuals' activities and relationships must correspond with uniform norms.

In some ways, the cases that led to constitutional recognition of same-sex marriage were themselves the product of a past that treated most South Africans as outcasts in their own country. Instead, the jurisprudence sought to affirm each individual's intrinsic worth, regardless of social station or public disapproval. So, in *National Coalition for Gay and Lesbian Equality v Minister of Justice* 1998, the CC concluded that the effects of the criminalisation of sodomy served as a fundamental assault on the dignity of gay men, and that the constant threat of arrest, prosecution and conviction for sexual activity resulted in stigma that directly impinged on their dignity. Similarly, in *Satchwell v President of the Republic of South Africa* 2000 and in *Du Toit v Minister for Welfare and Population Development* 2002, the Court relied heavily on the right to dignity as well as to equality in according a greater degree of recognition through the law to long-standing same-sex relationships, in both instances between women.

Bringing to a seemingly logical end discrimination based on sexual orientation, the CC held in *Minister of Home Affairs v Fourie* that exclusion of same-sex couples from the right to marry contravened constitutional values and constituted unfair discrimination. In reaching its conclusion, the Court emphasised the evolution of its equality jurisprudence, and particularly the significant role played by the values of human dignity, equality and freedom.

Against the backdrop of preceding cases, the Court highlighted 'four unambiguous features of the context in which the prohibition against unfair discrimination on grounds of sexual orientation must be analysed.' These are (para 59):

- i) the inappropriateness of entrenching a particular family form as the social and legal norm, given the constantly changing nature of familial formation;
- ii) the need to recognise the past persecution of gays and lesbians;
- iii) the fact that no comprehensive legal regulation of gay and lesbian family law rights existed; and
- iv) the fact that our Constitution represents a 'radical rupture' with a past based on intolerance and exclusion.

These considerations stand in stark contrast to the views advanced by Professor Robert P. George and others (Girgis, George and Anderson 2010). Professor George seeks to defend what he calls a 'conjugal' understanding of marriage – which defines marriage as 'the distinctive type of relationship that is ordered to, and would be naturally fulfilled by, the spouses having and rearing children together'. This necessarily excludes from marriage those in same-sex relationships. While he claims that marriage has intrinsic rather than merely instrumental value, he regards its orientation to having children as a necessary element.

In my view, the impermissibility of same-sex marriage seems as difficult to propound on coherent and rational moral grounds as the impermissibility of interracial marriage.

Prof George's argument rests on the 'principle' of joint procreation which is flawed because it is over-inclusive and is arbitrarily stipulative.

It is difficult to see why, given that procreation is no less biologically impossible in cases of infertility than in those of homosexuality, heterosexual intercourse by infertile couples is any more 'oriented' towards bearing children than that by same-sex couples. The only distinction, where procreation is impossible, is that heterosexual sex involves a penis in a vagina. It is ludicrous to suggest that this is an essential element of marriage.

And hence Professor George is constrained to invoke arguments concerning the 'potential' and 'orientation' of opposite-sex coupling – because no other rational basis exists on which to make peno-vaginal coupling, as opposed to any other form of coupling, a matter of distinctive moment in marriage.

But all of this exposes a much deeper flaw in Professor George's posture. This is his attempt to impose rigid preconceptions on forms of human commitment, loving, sexual conjunction and partnership. This rigidity is precisely the evil that afflicted South Africa under apartheid, and which the dignity jurisprudence of the CC has in its first two decades addressed. It is a like evil that this paper addresses. In South Africa, a history of state-controlled racial rigidity had a mutilating impact on black and white alike.

It is in part through understanding the pernicious effects of that rigidity that the Court has so fully embraced the positive assertion of sexual orientation equality and diversity today. Today's arguments opposing same-sex marriage invoke the same rigidities, the same illogicalities, and the same absurdities of racism in South Africa's discredited past. They deserve the same moral opprobrium.

The Limits of Dignity

There is substantial criticism of dignity as a basis on which to adjudicate rights. A main concern has been that dignity is fuzzy – often rife with ambiguity, and hence difficult to give a concrete meaning or effect as a realisable right (Hennette-Vauchez 2011, Ackermann 2006, Khaitan 2011).

One criticism is that using dignity can involve imposing a normative or ethical value onto individual behaviour or choice (O'Connell 2008). This has happened in South Africa. In a case about sex work, *S v Jordan* 2002, the majority of the CC upheld the criminal prohibition, rejecting all grounds of invalidity. But the minority would have overturned the criminal ban on narrow gender-discrimination grounds. That judgment also rejected dignity as a basis. The minority said this was because it was not the criminalisation of sex work, but the commodification of a sex worker's body – that is, the work itself – that undermines her dignity (para 74): 'The very character of the work they [sex workers] undertake devalues the respect that the Constitution regards as inherent in the human body.'

The judgment has been heavily criticised for making an unsustainable distinction between sexual activity that is subject to criminal sanction, and therefore subject to intervention by the State, and that which properly merits sanctuary in the private realm (Currie and De Waal 2005: 444).

Indeed, dignity's rhetorical and conceptual power may be inadequate to challenge narrow conceptions of naturalness or normalness. It has justly been said that *Fourie* idealises marriage as the most appropriate way for two people to garner public recognition and legitimation of their relationship (Barnard-Naudé and De Vos 2010).

And there may be a danger that institutionalising same-sex marriage may replace one set of dangerous repressive social norms for another – the legal sanction of sexual sameness or conformity. In *Le Roux v Dey* 2011, the Court certainly frowned upon sexual 'otherness'. In that case, two schoolboys manipulated an image of two men involved in a 'sexually suggestive' pose, graphically superimposing the faces of their principal and vice-principal onto the bodies. Importantly, the Court held (at para 181) that the mere portrayal of someone as gay was not sufficient to render it defamatory, despite the stigma that still surrounds being gay. It is the constitutional framework that has enabled us to advance from criminalising homosexuality to holding that referring to someone as gay cannot on its own be defamatory.

However, the majority described the image (at para 98) as being of 'two promiscuous men who allowed themselves to be photographed in what can only be described as a situation of sexual immorality, which would be embarrassing and disgraceful to the ordinary members of society'. The boys were thus held liable for defamation.

A minority, of which I was part, found in favour of the plaintiff on the much narrower basis of affront to feelings, or *iniuria*, invoking infringement of dignity. We held that the plaintiff had suffered an affront to his subjectively experienced, personal dignity, and that the children had acted both wrongfully and with intent.

Taken together, *Jordan* and *Le Roux* may be offered as evidence of judicial conservatism about how we express ourselves sexually. This may justly be contrasted with the assertions in the rest of the Court's jurisprudence that no particular social norm for adult, consensual sexual expression should be entrenched, as stated by Justice Sachs in *Fourie* (para 47).

The Possibilities of Dignity

Notwithstanding this approach, dignity has enabled the Court to secure a significant break from the past. As a value and as a right, dignity has affirmed and de-stigmatised those previously excluded. Crucially, it has also provided a framework and tools for future proscription of other forms of discrimination – for instance, against non-citizens – and for recognition of sexual expressiveness.

It is against this backdrop, characterised by the internalisation of stigma and disgrace for the majority of people in South Africa, that constitutionalism has sought to create a reparative legal framework – one in which injury to dignity can be repaired, and in which humanhood can be asserted.

To this end, the Constitution functions as a simple statement and thus an assertion of the dignity of all South Africans. In addition, its provisions provide symbolic affirmation, reinstatement and reparation to those previously excluded, recognising and affirming their diversity.

And it provides a practical framework for the more difficult task of attaining internal dignity, and asserting it externally, by disclaiming stigma and disgrace, and affirming moral citizenship and worth.

The law cannot, on its own, create internal dignity or repair a history of degradation. Nor can the law by itself remove stigma or stop hatred. But it can reject branding people as subordinate and inferior and thus making them objects of shame.

The Court's jurisprudence on the equality of gays and lesbians has, therefore, both addressed social and legal equality, and sought to rectify the subordination of the past by enabling gays and lesbians to assert themselves as equal moral citizens who can fulfil their capacities as humans without shame.

Dignity thus enables not conformity, but rather the advancement of those aspects of our lives that have the potential to be distinct and extraordinary: traversing public spaces fearlessly, developing our minds and speaking freely, and perhaps finding love and generativity.

References

Books, book chapters and articles

Ackermann, L. 2006. 'Equality and Non-Discrimination: Some Analytical Thoughts', *South African Journal on Human Rights*, 22: 597–99.

Barnard-Naudé, J. and P. de Vos, 2010. 'Disturbing heteronormativity: The "queer" jurisprudence of Albie Sachs', *SA Publiekreg/Public Law*, 25: 209–22.

Biko, S. 1978. *I Write What I Like*. London: Heinemann.

Brink, A. 1970. 'Some Aspects of Culture and Apartheid', in ed. P. Randall, *Anatomy of Apartheid*. Johannesburg: Study Project on Christianity in Apartheid Society, pp. 31–2.

Burns, J.F. 1978. '"Pass" Laws, Aspect of Apartheid Blacks Hate Most, Bring Despair and Pent-Up Fury', *New York Times*, 24 May.

Chaskalson, A. 2000. 'Human Dignity as a Foundational Value of Our Constitutional Order, The Third Bram Fischer Lecture', *South African Journal on Human Rights*, 16(193): 196–8.

Christiansen, E.C. 2000. 'Ending the Apartheid of the Closet: Sexual Orientation in the South African Constitutional Process', *NYU Journal of International Law & Politics*, 32: 997.

Coleman, M. ed. 1998. *A Crime Against Humanity: Analysing the Repression of the Apartheid State*. Johannesburg: Human Rights Committee.

Currie, I. and J. de Waal, 2005. *The Bill of Rights Handbook*, 5th edn. Lansdowne: Juta.

Du Bois, W.E.B. 1903. *The Souls of Black Folk*. Chicago: A. C. McClurg & Co.

Gevisser, M. and E. Cameron, 1995. *Defiant Desire: Gay and Lesbian Lives in South Africa*. New York: Routledge.

Girgis, R. R. George and R. Anderson. 2010. ' What is marriage', *Harward Journal of Law and Public Policy*, 34 (1): 245–87

Goffman I. 1986. *Stigma: Notes on the Management of Spoiled Identity*. New York: Simon and Schuster.

Hennette-Vauchez, S. 2011. 'A Human Dignitas? Remnants of the Ancient Legal Concept in Contemporary Dignity Jurisprudence', *I-CON*, 9(1): 32–57.

Herek, G.M. et al. 2007. 'Sexual Stigma: Putting Sexual Minority Health Issues in Context', in eds I. Meyer and M. Northridge, *The Health of Sexual Minorities: Public Health Perspectives on Lesbian, Gay, Bisexual, and Transgender Populations*. New York: Springer.

Kant, E. 1785. *Fundamental Principles of the Metaphysic of Morals*, trans. Thomas Kingsmill Abbott <http://www.gutenberg.org/ebooks/5682> [accessed 30 June 2014].

Khaitan, T. 2011. 'Dignity as an Expressive Norm: Neither Vacuous nor a Panacea', *Oxford Journal of Legal Studies*, 32(1): 1–19.

MacKinnon, C. 2011. 'Substantive Equality: A Perspective', *Minnesota Law Review*, 1: 10.

Masango, A. 2012. 'Constructive Criticism: If We Can't Give It Who Can?' *Daily Maverick*, 2 October.

Moon, G. and R. Allen, 2006. 'Dignity Discourse in Discrimination Law: A Better Route to Equality?' *European Human Rights Law Rev*iew, 6: 610–49.

More, M. 2006. 'South Africa under and after Apartheid', in ed. K. Wiredu, *A Companion to African Philosophy*. Oxford: Blackwell Publishing.

O'Connell, R. 2008. 'The Role of Dignity in Equality Law: Lessons from Canada and South Africa', *International Journal of Constitutional Law*, 6: 272.

Philp, R. 2012. 'In Love with SA's Constitution', *Mail & Guardian*, 24 February.

Schlemmer. L. 1970. 'The Factors Underlying Apartheid', in ed. P. Randall, *Anatomy of Apartheid*. Johannesburg: Study Project on Christianity in Apartheid Society.

Steele. C.M. 1997. 'A Threat in the Air: How Stereotypes Shape Intellectual Identity and Performance', *American Psychologist* 52(613): 616–18.

Toobin, J. 2012a. 'Comment: Learning from Gay Marriage', *New Yorker*, 8 February.

——. 2012b. 'Same-Sex Marriage, Civil Unions, and Domestic Partnerships', *New York Times*, 8 February.

Waldron, J. 2011. 'Dignity and Defamation: The Visibility of Hate', *Harvard Law Review*, 123: 1596–1612.

Williams, D.R. et al. 2008. 'Perceived Discrimination, Race and Health in South Africa', *Social Science Medicine*, 67(3): 441–52.

Woolman, S. 2006. *Dignity in Constitutional Law of South Africa*, 2nd edn. Cape Town: Juta.

Worden, N. 2000. *The Making of Modern South Africa: Conquest, Apartheid, and Democracy*, 3rd edn. Oxford: Blackwell Publishers.

Cases

Bowers v Hardwick, 478 U.S. 186 (1986).

Brink v Kitshoff [1996] ZACC 9; 1996 (4) SA 197 (CC); 1996 (6) BCLR 752 (CC).

Dawood and Another v Minister of Home Affairs and Others [2000] ZACC 8; 2000 (3) SA 936 (CC); 2000 (9) BCLR 837 (CC).

Du Toit and Another v Minister for Welfare and Population Development and Others [2002] ZACC 20; 2003 (2) SA 198 (CC); 2002 (10) BCLR 1006 (CC).

Harksen v Lane NO and Others [1997] ZACC 12; 1998 (1) SA 300 (CC); 1997 (11) BCLR 1489 (CC).

Khumalo and Others v Holomisa [2002] ZACC 12; 2002 (5) SA 401 (CC); 2002 (8) BCLR 771 (CC).

Lawrence v Texas, 539 U.S. 558 (2003).

Le Roux and Others v Dey [2011] ZACC 4; 2011 (3) SA 274 (CC); 2011 (6) BCLR 577 (CC).

Minister of Home Affairs and Another v Fourie and Another [2005] ZACC 19; 2006 (1) SA 524 (CC); 2006 (3) BCLR 355 (CC).

National Coalition for Gay and Lesbian Equality and Others v Minister of Home Affairs and Others [1999] ZACC 17; 2000 (2) SA 1 (CC); 2000 1 BCLR 39 (CC).

R v Oakes, (1986) 19 CRR 308.

S v Cooper and Others 1976 (2) SA 875 (T) (the SASO/BCP trial).

S v Jordan and Others (Sex Workers Education and Advocacy Task Force and Others as Amici Curiae) [2002] ZACC 22; 2002 (6) SA 642 (CC); 2002 (11) BCLR 1117 (CC).

S v Makwanyane and Another [1995] ZACC 3; 1995 (3) SA 391 (CC); 1995 (6) BCLR 665 (CC).

Satchwell v President of the Republic of South Africa and Another [2002] ZACC 18; 2002 (6) SA 1 (CC); 2002 (9) BCLR 986 (CC).

President of the Republic of South Africa and Another v Hugo [1997] ZACC 4; 1997 (4) SA 1 (CC); 1997 (6) BCLR 708 (CC).

Legislation

Constitution of the Republic of South Africa, 1996.
Constitution of the Republic of South Africa, Act 200 of 1993.
Deutscher Bundestag – Basic Law for the Federal Republic of Germany.
Immorality Act 5 of 1927.
Immorality Act 23 of 1957.
Immorality Amendment Act 21 of 1950.
Prohibition of Mixed Marriages Act 55 of 1949.
Prohibition of Mixed Marriages Amendment Act 21 of 1968.

Chapter 8

HIV and the Constitution: Campaigning for Constitutionalism and the Keeping of Constitutional Promises

Mark Heywood and Tim Fish Hodgson

The Global HIV Epidemic and the Law

The HIV epidemic is now well into its fourth decade. The prognosis for people living with HIV has improved dramatically as the epidemic's shape and character have changed. Our understanding of the virus and the means available to lessen its devastating effect has increased dramatically during this time. It has evolved from a mystery illness which was an effective death sentence to what is now a manageable chronic disease (Geffen 2010: 34–9). The willingness amongst politicians, judges, international humanitarian organisations, civil society and even corporations to address the epidemic has also increased substantially. Yet the ubiquity of stigma surrounding HIV remains, with some evidence of countries increasingly resorting to invasive, ineffective, stigma-perpetuating criminal laws to try and stem the transmission of HIV (Jurgens et al. 2009). Whilst the medical and social response to HIV is now universally acknowledged as a human rights issue, violations of the rights of people living with HIV remain common.

Globally, there is now near-unanimous acceptance of the importance of the role of law in protecting the rights of people living with HIV. The Office of the High Commissioner for Human Rights and UNAIDS have produced a comprehensive set of International Guidelines on HIV/AIDS and Human Rights (International Guidelines on HIV/AIDS and Human Rights 2006). The Foreword to the Guidelines notes that lessons learned from the epidemic indicate that 'the protection of human rights in the context of HIV reduces suffering, saves lives, protects the public health, and provides for an effective response to HIV.' Eminent judges from fifteen sub-Saharan African countries have described the disease as 'fundamentally a human rights issue' and have emphasised the importance of law and the responsibilities of judges in combating the epidemic (UNAIDS Statement of Principles on HIV 2009). The hefty report of the Global Commission on HIV and the Law also attempts to create awareness and public dialogue about human rights and other legal issues relating to HIV (Global Commission Report 2012). Finally, an extensive and ever-expanding body of jurisprudence cognisant of the human rights implications and context of the HIV epidemic is being developed by international and domestic courts and tribunals (United Nations Development Programme 2013).

Far from being an exception to this trend, South Africa has become a leader in the field of HIV and the law. This is, in part, a consequence of South Africa's progressive Constitution which aims to 'establish a society based on democratic values, social justice and fundamental rights '(Preamble) and entrenches 'human dignity, the achievement of equality and the advancement of human rights and freedoms'as founding values (s 1). It is also due to a dedicated civil society which remains deeply committed to ensuring that both public and private power are held accountable to the Constitution. This has been underpinned by the work of the Constitutional Court (CC), which has earned respect internationally for its dedication to the Constitution's project of transformation, and for remaining sensitive to social justice considerations in its first two decades of jurisprudence.

The Constitution has had a profound impact on the struggle of people living with HIV in post-apartheid South Africa. It has been leveraged by activists and lawyers to demand rationality of a government which for almost a decade went out of its way to turn its back on widely accepted scientific facts, with devastating consequences. By design, it pervades each and every battle – in the courts, on the streets, or on the pages of newspapers and policy documents – of people living with HIV for equal and dignified lives in keeping with the Bill of Rights. To understand the impact of the Constitution and the law more broadly, a brief political and historical account of the epidemic in South Africa is necessary.

Background and Introduction to HIV and the Constitution

> To understand the role that law can play in the fight against HIV and AIDS, it is necessary to recall what the history of HIV and AIDS has been about. It has been a struggle for the normalisation of the disease; a struggle to have it treated as any other disease. It has also been a struggle against stigma; a struggle for equality and justice; a struggle against discrimination against people living with HIV and AIDS; and a struggle for access to treatment for those dying of AIDS. Perhaps, most importantly, it has been a struggle for rationality against irrationality in the public response to the disease. (Chief Justice Ngcobo, 2011)

The first reported cases of AIDS-related deaths in South Africa in the 1980s fell upon the gay community exclusively. Perhaps in part because of the belief that it was a 'gay disease' and later because it was considered to be a disease emanating from East Africa, the apartheid government's response was minimal at best, and included retrogressive measures such as the detention and deportation of HIV-positive foreign workers (Geffen 2010: 18). As the AIDS epidemic began to grow and spread beyond populations with an especial vulnerability to HIV infection, South Africa charged headlong into a constitutional democracy in the early 1990s. Perhaps because he was preoccupied by the political and legal transition, and focused on political transformation and reconciliation, HIV remained 'low on the radar' during President Mandela's term of office between 1994 and 1999. However, Mandela, who became increasingly outspoken about HIV after leaving office (Berger 2011: 4), subsequently expressed deep regret about failing to do more to combat the epidemic when at the helm (Geffen 2010: 19).

From his appointment in 1999, the response of President Mbeki's government to HIV deteriorated rapidly from one which initially appeared to promise cooperation in combating the epidemic to one of denial, neglect and indifference in the face of suffering. The policies of President Mbeki and the then-Health Minister, Dr Tshabalala-Msimang, hid behind the thin and scientifically inaccurate veil of the views of a fringe group of 'AIDS dissidents' or denialists (Heywood 2003: 281). Although the arguments of denialists vary, the general thrust of President Mbeki's well-documented denialism was that AIDS in Africa was caused not by HIV, but rather by poverty. The emphasis on HIV as the cause of AIDS was therefore berated as an attempt to create a market for drugs – particularly anti-retrovirals (ARVs) – sold by first-world companies (ibid.: 282).

People of all political persuasions and socio-economic backgrounds rallied against the Mbeki government's HIV policies, exercising their democratic rights to hold the government accountable for its failure to provide potentially lifesaving ARVs to tens of thousands of people living with HIV. Spearheading this relentless opposition was a grassroots social movement and activist organisation known as the Treatment Action Campaign (TAC). Formed in 1998, the TAC's activities included campaigning for access to medical treatment, including ARVs, for people living with HIV. The TAC employed various tactics including litigation, threats of litigation, protest and civil disobedience whilst continuously engaging in community-based treatment literacy work in an attempt to educate people on the science of HIV prevention and treatment (Kapczynski and Berger 2008: 45).

It should be remembered that the TAC's campaign for treatment, and the overall thrust of resistance against the government's denialism, was also more broadly 'a campaign for Constitutionalism and the keeping of Constitutional Promises ' (Heywood 2005: 205).

The Impact of the Constitution on HIV

This section will investigate HIV-related litigation which spans the constitutional rights to dignity (s 10), privacy (s 14), equality (s 9), access to healthcare services (s 27), prisoners' rights to medical treatment (s 35(2)(e)), freedom of expression (s 16), freedom of conscience (s 15) and life (s 11). Since the Constitution requires courts to consider the rights in the Bill of Rights when developing common law and when interpreting legislation (s 39(2)), some cases that only involve the Constitution indirectly will be analysed.

HIV and the right to dignity

The struggle for dignity of people living with HIV has been foundational to the response to the HIV epidemic. The CC has made it clear that living with HIV itself is not undignified because 'there is nothing shameful about suffering from HIV' which 'is a disease like any other' (*NM v Smith* 2007). Although often not the focal right in the HIV-related jurisprudence, a respect for the human dignity of people living with HIV appropriately underlies many of these decisions.

HIV and the right to privacy

The stigma associated with HIV in South Africa and elsewhere in the world, highlights the importance of respecting the right to keep one's HIV status private. The plethora of irrational and misleading information that was disseminated to the public during Mbeki's denialist era by the government only exacerbated this stigma and magnified the importance of providing people with detailed accurate information upon which to make informed decisions about issues such as HIV testing, disclosure and treatment. Both informed consent to an HIV test and confidentiality of status are now constitutionally protected rights.

Confidentiality

Near the end of the pre-constitutional era, the Appellate Division (then South Africa's highest court) in 1993 held that the disclosure of a patient's HIV status by his doctor infringed his privacy rights for the purposes of delictual liability. Taking a rational and scientific approach to HIV, contrary to prevailing myths and misunderstandings, the Court held that the doctor's disclosure was not warranted medically or in terms of risk of occupational exposure. Indeed occupational exposure was found to be more likely if there was reason for the patient to conceal his HIV status. Moreover, it concluded that permitting disclosure was a threat to public health because future patients would not come forward for care if they thought their doctors would 'squeal on them '(*Jansen Van Vuuren v Kruger* 1993).

The principles established in *Jansen Van Vuuren* had become a largely accepted part of policy and practice before they were tested before the CC in a very different factual and legal context – the right to privacy having been constitutionally entrenched. In *NM v Smith*, three poor and socially disadvantaged women sued a prominent Member of Parliament, Patricia de Lille, her authorised biographer and her publisher for publishing their names and revealing their HIV status in her biography. The women argued that the publication of their names accompanied by their HIV status was a violation of their rights to privacy and dignity. The various defences raised included the argument that because these women's names had been published in a medical report pertaining to a voluntary clinical trial, which had been reported in the media, the further publication of their names in De Lille's biography was not unconstitutional because the information was already in the public domain (*NM v Smith*: 15–16).

The Court's departure point was that although the claims of the applicants arose under the common law principles of delict, these principles must be informed by the Constitution (ibid.: 13). A majority of the Court held that none of the applicant's prior actions gave 'blanket consent to the publication of their status' and that re-publication amounted, particularly in the 'negative social context of the disease"', to a violation of the applicants' rights to privacy and dignity. The Court noted that the affirmation of confidentiality of HIV status may encourage people to seek treatment, free from the fear of stigmatisation and may result in the improvement of public health policies on HIV/AIDS (ibid.: 17). A 'pressing social need' or a 'compelling public interest' would need to exist to justify infringing upon the right to privacy in this context.

Informed consent

As early as 1996, the High Court found that a prisoner could only agree to an HIV test if pre-test counselling enables them to provide 'informed consent'. This required an understanding of what the purpose of the test is, what an HIV positive result entails and what the probability of AIDS resulting would be (*C v Minister of Correctional Services* 1996). Furthermore, time must be afforded to reflect on whether to exercise the right to refuse to submit to such a test. This judgment was based on common law concepts of privacy and was predicated on an existing Department of Correctional Services policy requiring informed consent prior to testing.

In a similar vein, the Employment Equity Act prohibits HIV testing in the workplace, unless the Labour Court has determined such test to be justifiable (s 7(2)). It then empowers the Labour Court (LC), if it determines that such testing is justifiable, to impose conditions including the provision of counselling and the maintenance of confidentiality (s 50(4)). The LC has held that it is not the purpose of these provisions to prevent anonymous and 'truly voluntary' testing (*Irvin and Johnson v Trawler and Line Fishing* 2002). It therefore concluded that such testing does not require the prior approval of the LC.

Today, The National HIV Counselling and Testing (HCT) Policy Guidelines require testing to be 'ethical' and 'based on human rights'(Guidelines 2010: 21). The Guidelines go even further than the case law, requiring detailed explanations and information to be provided in order for the informed consent requirement to be met.

HIV and the right to equality

South African Airways (SAA), an organ of state, had a policy of not employing HIV-positive persons as cabin attendants. Hoffman, an SAA cabin attendant, challenged the constitutionality of the policy, arguing that it violated his right to equality. SAA argued that the policy promoted passenger health and safety and that people living with HIV were a bad training investment because of limited life expectancy. The right to equality includes a prohibition of unfair discrimination and proceeds to list grounds for which discrimination will be presumed to be unfair (s 9(3)). Although HIV status does not appear as such a 'listed ground', the CC concluded that SAA's policy was clearly discrimination based on HIV status, which was unfair because though 'some people who are HIV positive may, under certain circumstances, be unsuitable for employment as cabin attendants [this] does not justify a blanket exclusion' of all people living with HIV (*Hoffman* v *SAA* 2000). In coming to this conclusion, the Court importantly showed an early willingness to embrace expert scientific evidence on HIV. Acknowledging people living with HIV/AIDS as 'one of the most vulnerable groups in our society', the Court spoke out emphatically against the prevalent stigma against and marginalisation of people with HIV, imploring that they ought to be treated with 'compassion and understanding'. The Court made it clear that people with HIV 'must not be condemned to economic death'.

Subsequent cases relating to discrimination based on HIV status bear the mark of *Hoffman*'s clear, principled and scientific approach to HIV. The LC has held that in terms of s 187(1)(f) of the Labour Relations Act (LRA), where the real or dominant reason for dismissal is an employee's HIV status, it constitutes an automatically unfair dismissal which is therefore legally actionable (*Allpass v Mooikloof Estate* 2011). It came to this conclusion despite the fact that the relevant provision of the LRA did not specifically mention HIV. In doing so, the LC extended *Hoffman*'s reasoning and treatment of HIV to an employment relationship involving a small private employer.

Hoffman's clarity also contributed to the South African National Defence Force (SANDF) settling a similar case initiated in 2008 by the AIDS Law Project (ALP), a long-term partner organisation of the TAC, which has now re-launched as SECTION27 with a broader human rights mandate. From the first days of democracy, the SANDF's HIV testing policy had provided that no HIV-positive person could be recruited, deployed externally, or promoted within in the SANDF. Since soldiers are not covered by the LRA, the ALP relied directly on the Constitution to advance its argument that this policy was unconstitutional. The settlement agreement, which was made a court order, includes an acknowledgement by the SANDF that the policy violated aspirant and current employees' rights to equality, privacy, dignity, fair labour practices and administrative justice (*SA Security Forces Union v Surgeon General AO* 2008). Unfortunately, as late as 2013, the SANDF's lack of commitment to implementing this order has resulted in SECTION27 filing papers in the High Court to ensure compliance with the SANDF's own policy adapted in accordance with the Court's order.

HIV and the right to access to health-care services

The Constitution obliges the State to take 'reasonable, legislative and other measures' to progressively realise the right to access to health-care services within the government's 'available resources' (s 27(2)). This means that the right 'must be made more accessible not only to a larger number of people but to a wider range of people as time progresses'. The measures taken must be reasonable both in conception and implementation. Finally, a plan that ignores those who are in most urgent need of protection will not be reasonable (*Government of RSA v Grootboom* 2000). This right was central to the TAC's entire campaign to get the government to provide ARVs to HIV-positive mothers and their newborn children.

Access to anti-retrovirals

In 2001, after repeated efforts to persuade the government to amend its denialism-inspired policy had failed, the TAC filed a lawsuit seeking an order declaring the government's failure to develop and implement an effective, comprehensive Prevention of Mother to Child Transmission (PMTCT) programme unconstitutional. The government's policy at the time restricted the provision of Nevirapine (an ARV) to pregnant women to a small number of 'pilot sites'. The TAC's primary argument was that this was a breach of the government's positive obligations in terms of s 27 of the Constitution. This litigation culminated in a unanimous CC judgment significantly authored by 'The Court', which ordered the Minister of Health and the representatives of the nine provincial governments to lift restrictions on the availability of Nevirapine to pregnant women 'without delay' and to develop its PMTCT policy to ensure it met the constitutionally prescribed standard of reasonableness. In reaching this conclusion, the Court, after surveying expert evidence which included scientific information about the effectiveness of Nevirapine, declared both government's 'inflexible' policy of restricting access of an affordable, potentially lifesaving drug to limited sites and government's existing PMTCT policy to be unreasonable (*Minister of Health v TAC* 2002).

The *TAC* judgment was not the end of the matter. Before the Court gave its judgment, the Minister of Health publicly denounced the Court's involvement and, at a point, suggested that the Court's order would not be complied with. Even after it had been clarified that the government would comply with the judgment, its actual compliance was grudging and minimal. It took serious cajoling by the TAC, threats of further litigation against individual provinces and initiation of contempt proceedings with regard to one province, to ensure the extensive roll-out of PMTCT services (Heywood 2003: 314–15).

Eventually, however, as a direct result of this litigation and continued pressure, by 2008 PMTCT was almost 'universally applicable 'and it was estimated that 95 per cent coverage of ARV treatment in public-sector ante-natal service sites had been achieved (UNAIDS Report 2010: 35). As of 2012, mother-to-child transmission of HIV had decreased dramatically from its high of nearly 20 per cent of pregnancies to 2.7 per cent (Heywood 2012).

Additionally, the judgment 'dealt a decisive blow against AIDS denialism'. Read with *Hoffman*, it confirmed that the CC would approach HIV-related matters through a rational, scientific lens. It was clear that the Court was open to activists as a forum of principle and rationality to escape from the 'political circus of irrationality ' (Heywood 2003: 309).

With this in mind, through an intensified campaign, the TAC increased pressure on the government to develop and implement a comprehensive ARV programme. By the end of 2003, Cabinet had adopted a plan which committed government to providing ARV treatment through the public health-care system (Kapczynski and Berger 2008: 75). Today, South Africa boasts the largest ARV programme of any country in the world, with over 2 million people receiving life-saving medication on a daily basis from government health-care institutions.

Prisoners' access to ARVs

The constitutional right to health appears at various places in the Constitution including in relation to the right generally (s 27), but also with regard to rights of children (s 28(1)(c)) and prisoners (s 35(2)(e)). In 2006, the TAC once more found itself in the High Court in an attempt to compel the government to ensure that prisoners at Westville Correctional Centre living with HIV/AIDS acquired access to ARVs. The Court expressed regret that the Operational Plan and Guidelines for ARV treatment made only passing reference to prisoners, who, being a class of people extremely vulnerable to infection, ought to have been given 'special consideration'. Seemingly relying on a combination of the right to access to health-care services (s 27) and the equally applicable right of prisoners to medical treatment (s 35(2)(e)), the Court also found government's implementation to be unreasonable because, with one notable exception, there was a 'singular lack of commitment to appreciate the seriousness and urgency of the situation'. It condemned the existing plan as 'patently unworkable' and the steps taken as 'not in the least bit adequate', emphasising the absence of any rational time frames (*EN v Government of RSA* (No. 1) 2006). Apparently still oblivious or indifferent to the seriousness of its failures and the urgency of compliance, the government failed to meet the deadline set by the Court and instead bizarrely applied for leave to appeal against the interim execution order (Hassim 2006: 159). A second judgment of the High Court contained scathing criticism of the government's conduct and warned that if it did not correct its delinquency, a 'grave constitutional crisis involv[ing] a serious threat to the doctrine of separation of powers' would ensue (*EN v Government of RSA* (No. 2) 2006). In the years after this judgment, there has been a progressive expansion in prisoners' access to ARV treatment.

However, reports from prisons and prisoners' groups to civil society organisations such as the TAC, Sonke Gender Justice and SECTION27 reveal that ARV treatment remains unreliable in many prisons. Inconsistent access to treatment often causes prisoners to default from treatment regimens, with the result that many 'natural deaths' reported in prisons are possibly HIV caused or related. Moreover, the response of the Department of Correctional Services has been unsatisfactory, in one instance including the disbanding of an HIV support group for reporting stock outs and shortages in prisons (Keehn 2014).

The Department of Correctional Services' response to five key issues has been severely wanting, these are: testing, treatment, healthcare rights education, ventilation and overcrowding. The Department fails to implement its own policies on testing and treatment for HIV and informing prisoners of their healthcare rights (Judicial Inspectorate for Correctional Services 2012/2013: 51). Overcrowding remains unacceptably high, with Department's most recent statistics pegging it at 34.87 per cent nationwide (Department of Correctional Services 2013: 28). There is moreover a vast difference between overcrowding in individual centres, with some being 'extremely overcrowded and other operating below capacity'. Current plans from the Department indicate it intends to reduce overcrowding at a snails pace of 2 per cent per year (Judicial Inspectorate for Correctional Services 2011/2012: 31).

Coupled with poor ventilation in many prisons, these conditions create a serious danger of exposure to TB, particularly for HIV positive prisoners (Department of Health 2013: 9).

HIV, TB and prisoners' access to medical treatment

There is a growing acceptance of the interconnectedness of the HIV and TB epidemics in South Africa, which has the third highest TB burden in the world. The TB epidemic is exacerbated by the HIV epidemic: 70 per cent of TB patients are also living with HIV (National Strategic Plan 2012–16). It is in this context that litigation surrounding TB infections in one of South Africa's largest prisons culminated in 2012.

Dudley Lee was detained as an awaiting-trial prisoner in Pollsmoor Prison for five years. He contracted TB during this time. He sued the Minister of Correctional Services for damages, contending that his infection was a result of poor health management within the prison. At the time of his incarceration 'TB control measures in the prison were virtually non-existent' (*Dudley Lee v Minister of Correctional Services* 2012). Prisoners and awaiting-trial detainees are to this day often held in cells that have more than double the prescribed occupancy level for long periods of time. They often go without health care. Pollsmoor Prison in particular has had recorded risk rates of infection as high as 90 per cent per annum (Johnstone-Robertson et al. 2011). After succeeding in the High Court, the Supreme Court of Appeal (SCA) ruled against Mr Lee on grounds that it could not be proven that the presence of reasonable, precautionary measures would have 'altogether eliminated' his risk of infection, despite the fact that the SCA found that the prison authorities had negligently failed to maintain reasonable systems to manage the disease.

On appeal, the CC overturned this judgment. The majority of the Court held that the existing common law test for factual causation in delict was sufficiently flexible to avoid the SCA's application of 'rigid deductive logic'. It held that Lee needed to show only that the conditions of his incarceration made it more probable that he was infected than proper systemic measures would have.

In affirming the constitutional norms of accountability and responsiveness by holding prison authorities liable for their clear failures, the judgment should go a long way to encouraging the Department of Correctional Services to be vigilant in fulfilling positive constitutional obligations and scrupulous in its efforts to alleviate the harsh impact that HIV and TB have on the particularly vulnerable prisoner population. This requires the implementation of an effective and comprehensive HIV and TB prevention, diagnosis, treatment, care and support programme.

HIV, the right of access to health-care services and corporate conduct

The South African public and private health-care systems operate in parallel, with the operation of each system affecting the other. The realisation of the right of access to health-care services therefore requires both an efficient public health-care system and an affordable private health-care market (Heywood 2001). The TAC has therefore regularly challenged corporate conduct, yet again using the Bill of Rights' vertical and horizontal applicability as a point of departure (s 8). By intervening as *amicus curiae* in a legal challenge to legislation aimed at making medicines more affordable and reframing the case as a health-care rights matter, it forced the Pharmaceutical Manufacturers Association to withdraw its application. The TAC also mounted an excessive pricing challenge before the Competition Commission, which led to seven voluntary licences being issued to generic drug manufacturers (Heywood 2009: 24–5). The net result of both of these challenges was a significant reduction in the price of drugs, including a range of medicines used to fight HIV and its symptoms.

HIV and the rights of health-care workers to freedom of conscience and expression

Unsurprisingly, given the government's irrational approach to the AIDS epidemic between 1999 and 2007, one of the issues that has arisen frequently is the rights of publicly employed doctors to exercise their freedoms of conscience and expression by objecting to government policy.

In *Gazidis v Minister of Public Services*, Dr Gazidis, employed as a head of department at an Eastern Cape hospital, suggested to a reporter that the then Minister of Health, Dr Dlamini-Zuma, should be charged with manslaughter for the department's PMTCT policy. He was charged for misconduct in terms of the Public Service Act for these comments. The High Court was openly critical of government, finding that 'it is hardly surprising that some members of the medical profession and of the public at large would describe [the policy of "sacrificing the lives of babies" in order to save money] as a murderous one.' Indeed, counsel for the Minister had conceded as much. It therefore held that Dr Gazidis could not validly be convicted for expressing his disquiet with irrational government policy.

The LC was equally severe on the then Mpumalanga MEC for Health in its judgment in *Naude*. The court found that 'the only reason' Naude, a community service medical doctor at a government hospital, had been dismissed was because of his support for an NGO that had been providing ARVs to rape survivors. The MEC had gone as far as opposing doctors prescribing ARVs which would be sourced privately and funded through an NGO (*Naude v MEC for Health* 2008). The Court concluded that Naude's dismissal was directly related to his freedom of conscience and adherence to professional ethics. It was therefore 'arbitrary', 'illegitimate' and automatically unfair in terms of the LRA. The Court rebuked the MEC, describing her as 'tyrannical and dictatorial' and her opposition to the NGO and the provision of ARVs to rape survivors as 'unrelenting', adding that she had misused her powers of appointment to interfere with doctor-patient relationships.

Read together, *Gazidis* and *Naude* clearly indicate that courts will be appropriately sensitive to the importance of the provision of potentially life-saving treatments and critical of lackadaisical, indifferent, or callous government attitudes towards the right of access to life-saving treatment and therefore by inference their right to life. Additionally, courts have shown a strong inclination towards shielding state employees from disciplinary action for exercising their rights to freedom of conscience and opinion (s 15) and expression (s 16).

Emerging Challenges

> We live in a society in which there are great disparities in wealth. Millions of people are living in deplorable conditions and in great poverty. There is a high level of unemployment, inadequate social security, and many do not have access to clean water or to adequate health services. These conditions already existed when the Constitution was adopted and a commitment to address them, and to transform our society into one in which there will be human dignity, freedom and equality, lies at the heart of our new constitutional order. For as long as these conditions continue to exist that aspiration will have a hollow ring.
> (Chief Justice Arthur Chaskalson, in *Soobramoney v Minister of Health* November 1997)

South Africa has come a long way since the days of AIDS denialism. Comprehensive policies are now based on scientific evidence, human rights and meaningful consultation (Heywood 2012). Mother-to-child transmission of HIV is down significantly and its elimination can now realistically be aimed for (Motsoaledi 2012). Approximately 2.4 million people now receive ARV treatment. In 2011 and 2012 alone, 15 million people tested voluntarily for HIV (ASSA 2008). The Minister of Health, far from being in conflict with civil society, works energetically and committedly in partnership with organisations like the TAC to fight the epidemic and revive the public health-care system (Heywood 2012).

The Constitution has played a central role in the attainment of these significant achievements. In most areas, therefore, the problem is no longer – and in some instances never has been – what the law says. Increasingly, this is also true of policy documents that form the core of government and civil society's arsenal to combat the epidemic.

Despite these achievements, it is of grave concern that inefficiency, incapacity, well-documented corruption and a lack of consistently strong, coordinated leadership still frequently determine whether law and policy are implemented and, if so, how effectively and timeously this is done. Drug stock outs are common and cause interruptions of ARV treatment with dire effects. A recent nationwide survey revealed that 21 per cent of health-care facilities surveyed had experienced stock outs and/or shortages of ARV and/or TB medicines in the preceding three months. Over 420,000 patients rely on facilities that were affected by stock outs and shortages during this period (Stop Stock Outs Project 2013). Few patients receive adequate counselling about the importance of strict adherence to their ARV regimen. Accessible information on treatment and prevention literacy is scarce (Heywood 2012).

Moreover, on a systemic level, 'the law is a scarce resource in South Africa': access to justice remains a privilege of the elite (*Permanent Secretary v Ngxuza* 2001). In our view, the right of access to courts (s 34) requires at a minimum for its effectiveness, basic knowledge of human and other legal rights, access to legal assistance and access to courts themselves. The valiant efforts of an increasing number of civil society organisations to provide sorely needed legal and constitutional literacy should not go unassisted by the State, whose ultimate constitutional responsibility it is to 'promote' this right (s 7(2)).The SA Human Rights Commission, which is constitutionally mandated to 'promote respect for human rights and a culture of human rights' (s 184(1)(a)) and is constitutionally empowered 'to educate' (s 184(2)(d)) also has an important role to play. It is quite simply impossible for people to exercise their rights in Court, or anywhere else for that matter, if they do not know and understand them (Heywood and Hassim 2008).

Awareness of rights alone is, however, insufficient because 'access to affordable legal services is not a reality for most South Africans' (Legal Practice Bill 2012). This is especially the case when it comes to civil litigation (Heywood and Hassim 2008). Additionally, further attempts must be made to decrease the exorbitant costs of litigation. The CC has rightly expressed extreme disquiet about the burgeoning of lawyers' fees (*Camps Bay Ratepayers v Harrison* 2012).

It is no longer satisfactory for access to justice to take a backseat upon the benches of the Courts, the seats in Parliament and in the corridors of the Union Buildings, the seat of the National Executive. Access to justice should be a 'core concern', for 'if people in need are not able to bring their cases to court and present them effectively, then the courts cannot satisfactorily perform the function entrusted to them by the Constitution'(Budlender 2004). If the story of HIV and the Constitution teaches us anything, it is that the rule of law, the vitality of our constitutional order, the legitimacy of the Courts and the Constitution, and the realisation of our Constitution's promises depend on it (Heywood and Hassim 2012). Although it is true that part of the TAC's battle for ARVs was 'already won outside of the courts'

(Budlender 2004), if it had not been so determined and successful at getting inside them regularly, this story may have had no happy ending.

References

Books, book chapters and articles

Budlender, G. 2004. 'Access to Courts', *South African Law Journal*, 121: 339–58.

—— 2012. 'A paper dog with real teeth', *Mail and Guardian* <http://www.lrc.org.za/lrc-in-the-news/510-2002-12-07-a-paper-dog-with-real-teeth-mail-and-guardian> [accessed 30 June 2014].

Geffen, N. 2010. 'What we know about AIDS', in idem, *Debunking Delusions: The Inside Story of the Treatment Action Campaign*. Cape Town: Jacana, pp. 12–47.

Hassim, A. 2006. '5 Star Hotel? The Right to Access to ARV Treatment for HIV positive Prisoners in South Africa', *International Journal of Prisoner Health*, 2: 157–71.

Heywood, M. 2001. 'Debunking "Conglomo-talk": A Case Study of the Amicus Curiae as an Instrument for Advocacy, Investigation and Mobilisation', *Law, Democracy and Development*, 5(2): 133–62.

—— 2003. 'Preventing Mother to Child Transmission in SA: Background Strategies and Outcomes of the TAC case against the Minister of Health', *South African Journal of Human Rights*, 19(2): 278–315.

—— 2005. 'Shaping, Making and Breaking the Law in the Campaign for a National HIV/AIDS Treatment Plan', in eds P. Jones and K. Stokke, *Democratising Development: The Politics of Socio-Economic Rights in South Africa*. Leiden: Martinus Nijhoff Publishers, pp. 281–310.

—— 2009. 'South Africa's Treatment Action Campaign: Combining Law and Social Mobilization to Realize the Right to Health', *Journal of Human Rights Practice*, 1(1): 14–36 <http://jhrp.oxfordjournals.org/content/1/1/14.full.pdf+html> [accessed 30 June 2014].

—— 2012. 'Millions of Lives Depend on it', *NSP Review*, Issue 3 <www.nspreview.org/2012/10/03/millions-of-ives-depend-on-it/> [accessed 30 June 2014].

—— and A Hassim, 2008. 'Remedying the maladies of "lesser men or women": the personal political and constitutional imperatives for improved access to justice', *South African Journal on Human Rights*, 24: 263–80.

Johnstone-Robertson, S. et al. 2011. 'Tuberculosis in a South African prison – a transmission modelling analysis', *South African Medical Journal*, 101: 809–13 <http://www.samj.org.za/index.php/samj/article/view/5043/3627> [accessed 30 June 2014].

Jurgens, R. et al. 2009. 'Ten Reasons to Oppose the Criminalization of HIV Exposure or Transmission', *Reproductive Health Matters*, 17(34): 163–72 <http://ssrn.com/abstract=1543808> [accessed 30 June 2014].

Kapczynski, A. and J. Berger, 2008. 'The Story of the TAC Case: the Potential and Limits of Social Justice Litigation in South Africa', in eds Deena Hurwitz et al., *Human Rights Advocacy Stories.* New York: West Academic Press.

Keehn, E. 2014, 'Killing Inmates Softly: HIV Treatment Dysfunction in Prisons', *SA Breaking News*, <http://www.sabreakingnews.co.za/2014/04/30/killling-inmates-softly-hiv-treatment-dysfunction-in-prisons> [accessed 19 August 2014].

Reports

Actuarial Society of South Africa Aids Committee, 2008. 'ASSA 2008 Model' <http://aids.actuarialsociety.org.za/ASSA2008-Model-3480.htm> [accessed 30 June 2014].

Global Commission on HIV and the Law, 2012. 'HIV and the Law: Risks, Rights & Health' <http://www.hivlawcommission.org/index.php/report> [accessed 30 June 2014].

Judicial Inspectorate For Correctional Services, 2012, 'Annual Report for the period of 01 April 2011 to 31 March 2012' <http://judicialinsp.dcs.gov.za/Annualreports/Annual%20Report%202011-2012.pdf> [accessed 19 August 2014].

Judicial Inspectorate For Correctional Services, 2013. 'Annual Report for the period of 01 April 2012 to 31 March 2013' <http://judicialinsp.dcs.gov.za/Annualreports/ANNUAL%20REPORT%202012%20-%202013.pdf> [accessed 19 August 2014].

Stop Stock Outs Project, 2013. 'Stock Outs in South Africa: A National Crisis' <www.health-e.org.za/2013/.../report-stock-outs-south-africa-national-cris...> [accessed 30 June 2014].

UNAIDS Report 2010. 'Republic of South Africa Country Progress Report on the Declaration of Commitment on HIV/AIDS' <http://www.unaids.org/en/dataanalysis/knowyourresponse/countryprogressreports/2010countries/southafrica_2010_country_progress_report_en.pdf> [accessed 7 July 2014].

United Nations Development Programme, 2013 'Compendium of Judgments: Background Material' <http://www.undp.org/content/undp/en/home/librarypage/hiv-aids/compendium-of-judgements--background-material/> [accessed 30 June 2014].

Website and online material

Berger, J. 2011. 'A journey into community involvement in translating HIV research into prevention and treatment programmes: past, present and future struggles in South Africa', 18th Conference on Retroviruses and Opportunistic

Infections <http://www.section27.org.za/section27-senior-researcher-delivers-prestigious-lecture> [accessed 30 June 2014].
Department of Correctional Services, 2013, 'Annual Performance Plan 2012/13' <http://www.dcs.gov.za/Publications/Annual%20Reports/DCS%20Annual%20Performance%20Plan%202012-13.pdf> [accessed 19 August 2014].
Department of Health, 2013, 'Guidelines for the management of Tuberculosis, Human Immunodeficiency Virus and Sexually-Transmitted Infections in Correctional Centres' <http://www.health-e.org.za/wp-content/uploads/2014/06/DCS-TB-HIV-and-STI-Guidelines-2013.pdf> [accessed 19 August 2014].
Motsoaledi, A. 2012. 'Launch of a campaign on accelerated reduction of maternal and child mortality in South Africa' <http://www.gov.za/speech/DynamicAction?pageid=461&sid=27159&tid=66849> [accessed 30 June 2014].
'National Strategic Plan on HIV, STIs and TB 2012–16', 2011 <http://laylacassim.co.za/pdf/National%20Strategic%20Plan%20on%20HIV,%20STIs%20and%20TB.pdf> [accessed 30 June 2014].Ngcobo, Chief Justice S. 2011. 'The problem is us: the role of public policy and the law in the fight against HIV and AIDS', address at the 5th South African National Aids Conference, Durban <www.aidsmap.com/pdf/HATIP-178-July-1st-2011/page/1856368/>.
Ngcobo, S. 'Address by the Chief Justice, at the fifth South Africa HIV and Aids conference', Durban 07/06/2011 <http://uscdn.creamermedia.co.za/assets/articles/attachments/33464_speech_-_5th_sa_aids_conference,_durban.pdf> [accessed 30 June 2014]
Stephens, J. and K. Hardy, 2012. 'Public health, human rights and justice at the heart of case before the Constitutional Court' <www.section27.org.za/press-release-public-health-human-rights-and-justi...> [accessed 30 June 2014].
UNAIDS and OCHCR. 2006. 'International Guidelines on HIV/AIDS and Human Rights' (consolidated version) <http://www.ohchr.org/EN/Issues/HIV/Pages/InternationalGuidelines.aspx> [accessed 30 June 2014].
UNAIDS Statement of Principles on HIV, the Law and the Judiciary in sub-Saharan Africa, 2009 <http://www.unaids.org/en/media/unaids/contentassets/dataimport/pub/agenda/2010/20091212_statementofprincipleshivjudiciary_en.pdf> [accessed 30 June 2014].

Cases

Allpass v Mooikloof Estates (Pty) Ltd t/a Mooikloof Equestrian Centre [2011] ZALCJHB 7;(2011) 32 ILJ 1637 (LC).
C v Minister of Correctional Services 1996 (4) SA 292 (T).
Camps Bay Ratepayers and Residents Association and Another v Harrison and Another [2012] ZACC 17; 2012 (11) BCLR 1143 (CC).
Costa Gazidis v Minister of Public Services Case No: A2050/04 unreported judgment of the Transvaal High Court (24 March 2006).
Dudley Lee v Minister of Correctional Services [2012] ZACC 30; 2013 (2) SA 144 (CC).

EN v Government of the RSA and Others (No. 1) 2006 (6) SA 543 (D).
EN v Government of the RSA and Others (No. 2) 2006 (6) SA 575 (D).
Government of the Republic of South Africa and Others v Grootboom and Others [2000] ZACC 19; 2001 (1) SA 46.
Hoffmann v South African Airways 2001 (1) SA 1 (CC).
Irvin and Johnson Ltd v Trawler and Line Fishing Union and Others [2002] ZALC 105; (2003) 24 ILJ 565 (LC).
Jansen Van Vuuren and Another NNO v Kruger [1993] ZASCA 145; 1993 (4) SA 842 (AD).
Minister of Health and Others v Treatment Action Campaign and Others [2002] ZACC 16; 2002 (5) SA 703.
Naude v MEC for Health Mpumalanga [2008] ZALC 158; (2009) 30 ILJ 910 (LC).
NM and Others v Smith and Others [2007] ZACC 6; 2007 (5) SA 250 (CC).
Permanent Secretary, Department of Welfare, Eastern Cape v Ngxuza [2001] ZASCA 85; 2001 (4) SA 1184 (SCA).
SA Security Forces Union v Surgeon General AO <http://www.saflii.org/za/cases/ZAGPHC/2008/217.pdf> [accessed 30 June 2014].
Soobramoney v Minister of Health (Kwazulu-Natal) [1997] ZACC 17; 1998 (1) SA 765 (CC).

Legislation

Constitution of the Republic of South Africa, Act 108 of 1996.
Employment Equity Act, 55 of 1998.
Labour Relations Act, 66 of 1995.
Legal Practice Bill 2012.
Public Service Act, 103 of 1994.

Chapter 9
Administrative Justice and the Enforcement of the Constitution

Cora Hoexter[1]

Introduction

Principles of good administration have intrinsic value, since requirements such as rationality and procedural fairness may be regarded as meaningful in themselves. But in South Africa today they also have tremendous instrumental value, as they play a fundamental role in the enforcement of the democratic Constitution and of the law more generally.

In the first place, administrative law governs all 'administrative action' as that term is defined. Secondly and more broadly, it governs all exercises of public power – for today, every action involving public power is reviewable on administrative-law principles, at least to some degree; and this is true whether the action takes the form of a decision by a lowly official or by the President of the country when exercising powers derived from the Constitution itself. As O'Regan J put it in *Kaunda v President of the Republic of South Africa* (para 244), 'all exercise of public power is to some extent justiciable under our Constitution'. In its jurisprudence, the Constitutional Court (CC) has ensured that what is not reviewable as 'administrative action' remains reviewable under the rule of law. Using this general constitutional doctrine, the Court has effectively replicated the principles of good administration to govern action that is not strictly administrative action.

Thirdly, and flowing from the first two points, administrative law plays an important role in the implementation and enforcement of certain constitutional rights – particularly those that depend heavily on official action of one kind or another. The prime example of this is socio-economic rights, for the task of public administration is fundamentally concerned with the delivery of social goods. As Nugent JA noted in a case concerning a welfare grant, *MEC, Department of Welfare, Eastern Cape v Kate* (para 22), the realisation of rights usually depends on an administrative process. In that instance, the realisation of the right to social assistance was dependent on lawful and procedurally fair administrative action, and so the denial of administrative justice also amounted to a denial of the right to social assistance. Nugent JA went so far as to describe administrative justice as a procedural right that was essentially ancillary to the realisation of the more

1 This chapter is an abbreviated and revised version of Hoexter 2011.

substantive right to social assistance. This characterisation is controversial, however, to the extent that it suggests that procedural rights are merely instrumental and have no intrinsic value.

During the apartheid era, administrative law had a paradoxical character. Used as a tool by officials, it was a source of oppression for most South Africans – and yet, albeit within the constraints of parliamentary sovereignty, the application of administrative law by the courts was also the citizen's most dependable safeguard against oppression (Budlender 1993: 128). In view of the transformative nature of the South African Constitution (Klare 1998), and given the relevance of administrative law to the constitutional project, it is appropriate that in the democratic era South African administrative law has shed this dual nature and has evolved into an inspiring model of administrative justice. Today, this branch of the law takes a vital part in the more general shift from a culture of authority to a 'culture of justification' (Mureinik 1994), a term that has become emblematic of the transformation of the South African legal order, especially in public law. The culture of justification is advanced not only by constitutional rights and by legislation enacted to give effect to those rights, but also by a number of other constitutional provisions.

But, as Corder has remarked (2002: 7), the 'legislated edifices of administrative justice' are one thing; their translation into reality is another. Gaps are liable to appear between constitutional theory and administrative practice, and initial assumptions about how things will work may turn out to be mistaken. The aim of this chapter is to highlight two significant ways in which administrative justice in South Africa today diverges from what was envisaged under the 1996 Constitution.

Administrative Justice under the 1996 Constitution

Section 33 of the Constitution reads as follows:

> Just administrative action
>
> (1) Everyone has the right to administrative action that is lawful, reasonable and procedurally fair.
>
> (2) Everyone whose rights have been adversely affected by administrative action has the right to be given written reasons.
>
> (3) National legislation must be enacted to give effect to these rights, and must
>
> (a) provide for the review of administrative action by a court or, where appropriate, an independent and impartial tribunal;
>
> (b) impose a duty on the state to give effect to the rights in subsections (1) and (2); and
>
> (c) promote an efficient administration.

Though rights to administrative justice are becoming less of a rarity around the world than they were when this provision was drafted (Jowell 2006, Harlow 2010), the inclusion of these rights in the Constitution is remarkable in itself. In this regard, South Africa benefited particularly from the example of its neighbour, Namibia, which was one of the first countries to include such rights in its Constitution. But more remarkable still is the almost unqualified wording of s 33(1) and its guarantee of not only lawful but also 'reasonable' administrative action. (This bold wording may be contrasted with the more cautious promise of s 24*(d)* of the interim Constitution, which avoided the language of reasonableness and instead conferred a right to administrative action that was 'justifiable in relation to the reasons given for it'.) The very breadth of this constitutional promise was what lay behind the demand in s 33(3) for the enactment of national legislation. The expectation was not merely that the mandated legislation would give effect to s 33(1) and (2) but – as suggested by the reference to an efficient administration – that it would also limit the application of administrative justice to some extent.

The national legislation was enacted in the form of the Promotion of Administrative Justice Act 3 of 2000 (PAJA), most of which came into force in November of that year. It has been described as a piece of 'codification-reform': a legislative restatement, albeit a fairly laconic one, of the common-law principles of administrative law with a view to reforming them (Currie 2007: para 1.5). Amongst other things, this statute defines 'administrative action' (s 1), sets out the ingredients of procedural fairness (ss 3 and 4) and gives substance to the right to reasons (s 5). Sections 3, 4 and 5 have been fleshed out further in a set of Regulations on Fair Administrative Procedures promulgated in 2002. Section 6 essentially codifies the common-law grounds of review, and s 8 contains a non-exhaustive list of remedies that may be awarded by a court.

While the rights in s 33 and their associated legislation are the most important features of the administrative-justice system, it is enhanced by certain other fundamental rights contained in Chapter 2 of the Constitution. The most relevant ones are s 32, the right of access to information (and the national legislation that gives effect to this right); s 34, the right to have disputes settled by a court or other independent forum or tribunal; and s 38, which gives the courts flexible remedial power and confers on litigants wide *locus standi* or standing to enforce the Chapter 2 rights.

Moving beyond the Bill of Rights itself, there are a number of other constitutional provisions of significance to administrative justice. A crucial provision is s 1, which lists the founding values, and especially s 1*(c)*, which identifies the rule of law as a founding value of the South African State. While not in the nature of enforceable rights, the founding values nevertheless 'inform the interpretation of the Constitution and other law, and set positive standards with which all law must comply in order to be valid' (*United Democratic Movement v President of the Republic of South Africa* (No 2), para 19). The doctrine of the rule of law, and more particularly the principle of legality contained within it, may be regarded as the general constitutional counterpart of the specific rights to administrative justice in the Bill of Rights (*Fedsure Life Assurance Ltd v Greater Johannesburg Transitional Metropolitan Council*, para 59). As already mentioned, the CC has developed the principle of legality in a series of cases so as to replicate the principles of good administration for the realm of non-administrative action. Initially, the principle was found to encompass lawfulness (*Fedsure* 1999, para 58; *President of the Republic of South Africa v South African Rugby Football Union* 2000, para 148), then rationality (*Pharmaceutical Manufacturers Association of SA: In re Ex parte President of the Republic of South Africa* 2000, para 85), and eventually procedural fairness as a requirement of rationality (*Albutt v Centre for the Study of Violence and Reconciliation* 2010, paras 68–9). In a judgment handed down in 2012, *Judicial Service Commission v Cape Bar Council* (paras 44–5), the Supreme Court of Appeal held that rationality may, in turn, require reasons to be given for a decision involving the use of public power.

Comparable to the founding values are the values and principles listed in s 195 of the Constitution to govern the public administration. This provision, too, seems to impose duties without conferring enforceable rights, and is again a useful aid to interpretation (*Chirwa v Transnet Ltd*, para 75). Amongst other things, s 195 exhorts the administration to use resources efficiently, to provide services equitably and impartially, to respond to people's needs, to be accountable and to foster transparency.

Another noteworthy part of the Constitution is Chapter 9 and its various institutions that support constitutional democracy, such as the South African Human Rights Commission and the Gender Commission. Of special relevance to the maintenance of administrative justice are two institutions – the Public Protector (a general ombudsman) and the Auditor-General (a watchdog over the use of government finances) – created respectively by ss 182 and 188 of the Constitution and governed by legislation: the Public Protector Act 23 of 1994 and the Public Audit Act 25 of 2004.

Administrative Justice Today

As suggested by the legal framework outlined above, a tremendous amount has been achieved in the promotion of administrative justice; more, perhaps, than the most optimistic reformer could have hoped for. The entrenchment of constitutional rights to administrative justice has both justified and guaranteed the institution of judicial review (Hoexter 2010: 43). The rules of standing have been revolutionised, and access to judicial remedies is well protected by rights including s 34. Furthermore, the enactment of national legislation to give effect to s 33 has brought a number of benefits. For instance, it has made the law clearer and more accessible to prospective litigants and has expanded the old common-law grounds of review.

Perhaps inevitably, however, the constitutional and legal model is an ideal that is not fully matched by reality. In what follows, I examine two of the most important ways in which administrative justice today deviates from the plan of the 1996 Constitution, and from the expectations of administrative lawyers concerning that plan.

Administrators and the Courts

Section 7(2) of the 1996 Constitution requires the state to 'respect, protect, promote and fulfil' the rights in Chapter 2; and s 237 says that all constitutional obligations must be performed 'diligently and without delay'. Section 165(4) requires organs of state to assist and protect the courts, the guardians of the Constitution and the Bill of Rights, and s 165(5) makes all court orders binding on organs of state. In addition to this are the duties imposed on administrators by s 195 of the Constitution, already mentioned above.

Constitutional statements such as these are an official acknowledgement of what common sense tells us: that a transformative project requires the cooperation of all concerned, and that it can succeed only if every functionary performs the task assigned to it. Indeed, to a large extent, the transformative South African Constitution rests on the broader assumption that State organs and functionaries will *want* to do their jobs: that they will share more or less enthusiastically in the Constitution's vision of a society based on social justice and have some degree of commitment to its aim of improving the lives of South Africa's people. At the start of the democratic era, this assumption was shared, I think, by many South Africans, including administrative lawyers – for, as already noted, public administration is fundamentally concerned with the delivery of social goods.

In those days, a fairly pervasive fear amongst progressive lawyers was that courts (which then consisted mostly of 'untransformed' white male judges) could not necessarily be trusted with the project of social transformation, and that reactionary judges might actually use their powers of judicial review to block or hinder the transformative aims of the Constitution. This concern was raised at the Breakwater Workshop in February 1993 – surely the most seminal administrative-law conference ever convened in this country, and one that strongly informed the reform that ultimately took place. The Breakwater Declaration (1993: 19), a sort of manifesto that emerged from the workshop, refers tellingly to 'the potential for abuse of mechanisms of administrative review, especially in order to block social reconstruction by a future government'. Similar concerns lay behind the strictly 'non-constitutional' jurisdiction of the Supreme Court of Appeal (SCA, formerly the Appellate Division of the Supreme Court) under the interim Constitution, and the creation of the CC as a completely new entity untainted by associations with apartheid. Judges, especially elderly white male ones, were perceived to be the problem. There would seem to have been less concern about administrators who might not share in the transformative aspirations of the Constitution or who might be more interested in self-enrichment than in uplifting the poor.

In fact, it is the courts, old-order judges included, that have proved crucial to the enforcement of social transformation, and it is new-order administrators who have most often proved to be the hindrance. The administration of social welfare grants in the Eastern Cape provides distressing examples of the cynical mindset of many officials, of their contemptuous behaviour towards vulnerable people, and of their uncooperative and even recalcitrant attitude towards the courts. Nor is it possible to dismiss these as isolated instances. The law reports are replete with similar examples from this and other provinces, some of which have reached the highest courts.

For several years, the method used by provincial welfare authorities to root out 'ghost pensioners' and other fraudulent claimants was simply to cancel thousands of welfare benefits at a time, the idea being that legitimate claimants would then reapply for their grants and have them reinstated – a process that could take months or even years. The method was, of course, unlawful, and was declared so more than once. As the SCA put it in one case – *Permanent Secretary, Department of Welfare, Eastern Cape v Ngxuza* – the method was also 'extreme' and its consequences 'savage' (para 7), as those who were not ghosts were often left destitute. The same case illustrates unrepentant and obstructive conduct on the part of the administrator in the course of the litigation and, worse, derision shown to its victims. In the words of Cameron JA, the province conducted the case 'as though it were at war with its own citizens' (para 15).

In a similar case that reached the CC – *Njongi v MEC, Department of Welfare, Eastern Cape* – the applicant claimed arrear payments under a disability grant that had been terminated a few years earlier, together with thousands of others, without any explanation. This action was described by the Court as 'unthinkably cruel and utterly at odds with the constitutional vision' to which the province ought to have been committed (paras 17–18). Part of the arrears had been paid but an amount was still clearly outstanding. Far from paying this to Mrs Njongi, however, the administrator resisted her claim on the basis of prescription. The Court rejected this cynical argument and awarded punitive costs against the province for its unconscionable conduct in opposing the application.

Administrative non-compliance with court orders is another troubling trend. In *Nyathi v MEC for Department of Health, Gauteng (Nyathi I)*, the CC acknowledged that from about 2002 there had been a flood of cases in which court orders had been flouted by state functionaries (para 60). In this particular case, the applicant had been left paralysed by the negligent medical treatment he had received at two state hospitals. Liability was admitted and, following a dispute about the amount payable, a High Court ordered the administrator to make an interim payment – which order was not complied with. Sadly, the applicant died before the matter reached the CC. The Court's frustration with the phenomenon of non-compliance is apparent in the following passage from the majority judgment of Madala J (para 63):

> In my view there can be no greater carelessness, dilatoriness or negligence than to ignore a court order sounding in money, even more so when the matter emanates from a destitute person who has no means of pursuing his or her claim in a court of law. But we now have some officials who have become a law unto themselves and openly violate people's rights in a manner that shows disdain for the law, in the belief that as state officials they cannot be held responsible for their actions or inaction.

In this case, the majority declared unconstitutional the portion of s 3 of the State Liability Act of 1957 which prevented execution or attachment against the State for the satisfaction of judgment debts; it suspended its order of invalidity for a year in order to give Parliament time to enact legislation providing for the effective enforcement of court orders. Ironically, the State also failed to comply with this obligation. In *Minister for Justice and Constitutional Development v Nyathi (Nyathi II)*, the State was given a further two years' grace, and the Court devised a scheme for the enforcement of judgment debts against the State in the interim.

The cases mentioned so far may be examples of abnormally bad official behaviour. The depressing reality, however, is that in some areas of the administration incompetence, inefficiency and corruption seem almost to have become the norm. For example, in *Thusi v Minister of Home Affairs and 71 Other Cases*, which concerned the administration of identity documents in KwaZulu-Natal, the court noted that bureaucratic problems bedevilling the Department of Home Affairs included lack of capacity, incompetence, inefficiency, fraud and corruption (para 1).

The picture is even more alarming when it comes to local government. In a report on the financial affairs of municipalities for 2010–11, the Auditor-General revealed that only 13 of 283 municipalities (a mere 5 per cent) had received clean audits (*Consolidated General Report on the Audit Outcomes of Local Government 2010–11).* The rest were characterised by unauthorised, irregular, wasteful, or fruitless expenditure. Other depressing findings were that a vast number of officials lacked the skills and competence to perform their jobs, that many municipalities had paid consultants to do the jobs of their salaried employees, and that there were few or no consequences for poor performance and corruption (for comment, see Marrian 2012, Parker 2012).

Sadly, corruption is not confined to local government. It has become endemic in public administration and is widely regarded as the greatest challenge currently facing the country as a whole. Its growth has been encouraged by a number of factors, including the apartheid legacy; the bad example set by certain public figures such as a former Commissioner of Police, Jackie Selebi, who was sentenced to prison for corruption, and the dominant party's disastrous policy of 'deployment' of its members to government (Gumede 2011, South African Press Association 2012a). Corruption, the CC acknowledged in *Glenister v President of the Republic of South Africa*, is a 'pernicious threat to our collective enterprise to entrench a just and democratic society' (para 172). It has even been suggested that corruption be declared a national emergency so as to end the government's defensiveness on the subject and, in some instances, its denialism (Gumede 2011: 21).

The various problems outlined above are all rooted in a proposition that was expressed by Madala J in *Nyathi I*: that 'public officials seem not to understand the integral role they play in our constitutional State' (para 60). Until they do, it is not only administrative justice that is at risk but the entire constitutional project.

Non-judicial Safeguards and Remedies

A major weakness of South African administrative law in the pre-democratic era was its preoccupation with judicial review and court-based remedies for maladministration. Because the courts were the citizen's best chance of challenging executive high-handedness during apartheid, a general tendency developed of focusing on judicial review and neglecting other ways of checking and disciplining administrative power. This tendency was so strong that in 1992, when an investigation by the South African Law Commission exposed the incoherent nature of the existing system of administrative appeals, the Commission sidestepped the reform of the appeal system and simply recommended an extension of the grounds of review (South African Law Commission 1992: 50, 106).

The following year, the Breakwater Declaration acknowledged both the over-reliance on judicial remedies and the urgent need to develop a broader range of procedures and safeguards in the administrative system. Certain institutions associated with good governance, such as access to information, were virtually unknown to South Africans at the time. Others, such as parliamentary scrutiny of delegated legislation, existed only in a rudimentary form or, like the haphazard collection of administrative appeals, were best known for their deficiencies. The Advocate-General, an ombudsman-type office created in 1979, fell into this category, for its effectiveness was reduced by its inaccessibility to the people and its limited jurisdiction, which was essentially restricted to the dishonest use of public money (see further, Baxter 1984: 288.) The Breakwater Declaration (1993: 18) thus called for a more prospective focus for administrative justice, and a wider range of 'procedures and safeguards which will foster good decision-making'.

The constitutional era ushered in a number of innovations in this regard. One of the most significant is the constitutional right of access to information (s 32 of the 1996 Constitution) and the legislation that gives effect to it, the Promotion of Access to Information Act 2 of 2000. According to the Deputy CEO of the Human Rights Commission, however, it would appear that only half of South Africa's government departments comply with the Act in practice (Unknown 2011, reporting on an address by Naledzani Mukwevho to a national information officers' forum). Furthermore, the openness and transparency it seeks to achieve are currently under threat from the Protection of State Information Bill, a piece of draft legislation that allows for the classification of information on security grounds by a wide range of organs of State and creates broadly defined criminal offences that carry very heavy penalties.

Several other safeguards provided for in the Constitution have proved to be disappointingly weak in practice. Individual ministerial responsibility, always feeble under apartheid, remains so. Cabinet Ministers simply do not feel pressure to resign, no matter how poorly they or their departments have performed. Parliamentary oversight of the executive and the administration, a potentially valuable adjunct to judicial review, is another example. The system of reporting to Parliament on the activities of the executive branch has generally been ineffective for various reasons, including the late submission of reports and the absence of an official procedure for responding to reports (Corder, Jagwanth and Soltau 1999: para 5.2–3).

Parliamentary scrutiny of delegated legislation has been another disappointment. While s 101(4) of the Constitution contemplates that ministerial regulations and other such instruments will be tabled and/or approved by Parliament, the current legislation perpetuates the pre-democratic position. In terms of s 17 of the Interpretation Act 33 of 1957, all that must be tabled is a list of delegated legislation, and not the legislation itself. On the more positive side, some statutes (the PAJA included) specifically require regulations made under them to be submitted to or approved by Parliament before publication in the *Government Gazette*. Moreover, the province of Gauteng has enacted a Scrutiny of Subordinate Legislation Act 5 of 2008. The statute provides for the tabling of legislation as well as its scrutiny by a standing committee. The national Parliament is currently investigating ways of improving oversight and accountability mechanisms more generally (see *Oversight and Accountability Model: Asserting Parliament's Oversight Role in Enhancing Democracy*).

Two watchdog institutions with huge potential are the Auditor-General and the Public Protector, already mentioned above. The Auditor-General has been described as the most likely of all the Chapter 9 institutions to retain its independence and discharge its constitutional responsibilities (Woolman and Schutte 2005: 2). In practice, however, the effectiveness of the office of Auditor-General is reduced by 'persistent disregard' of its recommendations by government departments and other public institutions – a finding of the *Asmal Report* (2007: 78). Another, perhaps less pressing problem identified in this report is insufficient cooperation between the Auditor-General and the Public Protector.

In theory, the Public Protector is the perfect complement to judicial review of administrative decision-making. The use of the service is free and, unlike the courts, the Public Protector is well placed to handle large numbers of relatively minor complaints. Until recently, however, the office has suffered from persistent doubts about its independence – fuelled by the office's reliance on funding from the executive (ibid.: 106–7) and by statistics suggesting that members of the dominant party, the African National Congress, were very likely to be cleared of wrongdoing by the 'ANC Protector'. This description gained currency from late 2006, when it was reported that the Public Protector had made negative findings in only three of sixteen investigations into the activities of ANC members since 2003 (see, for example, O'Grady 2006). In particular, great scepticism was expressed about the anodyne 2005 report produced by the Public Protector of the day, Lawrence Mushwana, on the infamous 'Oilgate' investigation.

This investigation was prompted by allegations about the transfer of huge sums of public money from a parastatal, PetroSA, to a private company that was acting as a front for the ANC. The Public Protector's report was widely regarded as a 'whitewash' and subsequently became the subject of a court challenge. Upholding the judgment of the court *a quo*, the SCA found that Mushwana's investigation had been so selective and so superficial as to be no real investigation at all (*Public*

Protector v Mail & Guardian Ltd, paras 140–45). Meanwhile, Mushwana had become chair of the Human Rights Commission. He declined to step down from this position after the Court's ruling, pointing out that the SCA had not actually recommended his resignation (see Faull 2010).

On a more edifying note, the current Public Protector is known and respected for her qualities of independence and courage. In her first four years in office, Thuli Madonsela had already published a number of damning reports on maladministration involving senior government officials.

Finally, it is worth pointing out that the enactment of the PAJA offered a valuable opportunity to enhance existing non-judicial safeguards associated with administrative justice and to create new ones. Innovations proposed by the South African Law Reform Commission in its draft Bill (South African Law Commission 1999) included an Administrative Review Council that would have driven further specified reforms, from improving the system of internal appeals (which remains as deficient as ever) to programmes for educating administrators and the public. Sadly, this and other draft provisions were jettisoned by the legislature, and today s 10(2) of the PAJA merely enables the Minister to establish such a council to advise him or her on such reforms. The power has not been exercised and may never be.

Conclusion

This chapter has sought to describe two significant ways in which administrative justice in South Africa today diverges from the noble transformative scheme of the 1996 Constitution, or from what was envisaged or assumed to be its scheme. As has been shown, initial ideas about the respective roles of administrators and the courts in the enforcement of administrative justice have been challenged over time. Notwithstanding what has been achieved in theory, problems such as endemic corruption and non-compliance with court orders are placing the entire constitutional project at risk. Furthermore, several non-judicial safeguards and remedies have proved less effective in practice than they may seem on paper.

References

Books, book chapters and articles

Baxter, L. 1984. *Administrative Law.* Cape Town: Juta.

Breakwater Workshop Participants. 1993. 'The Breakwater Declaration: Administrative law for a future South Africa', *Acta Juridica*, 1993: 17–20.

Budlender, G. 1993. 'The accessibility of administrative justice', *Acta Juridica*, 1993: 128–37.

Corder, H. 2002. 'Reviewing review: Much achieved, much more to do', in eds H. Corder and L. van de Vijver, *Realising Administrative Justice*. Cape Town: Siber Ink, pp. 1–19.

Currie, I. 2007. *The Promotion of Administrative Justice Act: A Commentary*, 2nd edn. Cape Town: Siber Ink.

Faull, L. 2010. 'Mushwana unmoved by Oilgate ruling', *Mail & Guardian* <http://www.mg.co.za> [accessed on 10 June 2010].

Gumede, W. 2011. 'Tackling corruption', *Focus (Journal of the Helen Suzman Foundation)*, 60: 15–23.

Harlow, C. 2010. 'Judicial review and administrative justice', in eds C. Forsyth et al., *Effective Judicial Review: A Cornerstone of Good Governance*. Oxford: Oxford University Press, pp. 85–100.

Hoexter, C. 2010. 'The constitutionalization and codification of judicial review in South Africa', in eds C. Forsyth et al., *Effective Judicial Review: A Cornerstone of Good Governance*. Oxford: Oxford University Press, pp. 43–60.

—— 2011. 'Administrative justice: Not entirely according to plan', *Diritto Pubblico Comparato ed Europeo*, IV: 1428–41.

Jowell, J. 2006. 'The democratic necessity of administrative justice', *Acta Juridica*, 2006: 13–22.

Klare, K.E. 1998. 'Legal culture and transformative constitutionalism', *South African Journal on Human Rights*, 14(1): 146–88.

Marrian, N. 2012. 'Audit chief says R11bn misspent by councils', *Business Day* <http://www.businessday.co.za/> [accessed on 24 July 2012].

Masombuka, S. 2012. 'Selebi "not gravely ill", *Times Live* <http://www.timeslive.co.za/> [accessed on 23 July 2012].

Mureinik, E. 1994. 'A bridge to where? Introducing the interim Bill of Rights', *South African Journal on Human Rights*, 10(1): 31–48.

O'Grady, K. 2006. 'Mushwana letting ANC petticoat show', *The Weekender*, 11–12 November: 3.

Parker, F. 2012. 'Gordhan's war on incompetence and impunity', *Mail & Guardian* <http://www.mg.co.za/> [accessed on 27 July 2012].

South African Press Association. 2012a. 'Cadre deployment causes poor performance', *The Citizen* <http://www.citizen.co.za/> [accessed on 25 July 2012].

—— 2012b. 'Parties divided over Selebi parole', *News24* <http://www.news24.com/> [accessed on 20 July 2012].

Unknown. 2011. 'Government fails to inform the people', *Business Day* <http://www.bdlive.co.za/> [accessed on 28 September 2011].

Woolman, S. and Y. Schutte, 2005. 'Auditor-General', in eds S. Woolman et al., *Constitutional Law of South Africa*, 2nd edn. Cape Town: Juta, Chapter 24, B1–16.

Reports

Ad Hoc Committee on the Review of Chapter 9 and Associated Institutions. 2007. *Report of the Ad Hoc Committee on the Review of Chapter 9 and Associated Institutions* ('*Asmal Report*').

Auditor-General of South Africa. 2012. *Consolidated General Report on the Audit Outcomes of Local Government 2010–11* <www.agsa.co.za> [accessed on 15 November 2012].

Corder, H., S. Jagwanth and F. Soltau, 1999. *Report on Parliamentary Oversight and Accountability*. Cape Town: Faculty of Law, University of Cape Town.

Parliament of South Africa. n.d. *Oversight and Accountability Model: Asserting Parliament's Oversight Role in Enhancing Democracy* <www.parliament.gov.za> [accessed on 10 October 2011].

Public Protector. 2005. *Report on an Investigation into an Allegation of Misappropriation of Public Funds by the Petroleum Oil and Gas Corporation of South Africa, Trading as PetroSA, and Matters Allegedly Related Thereto.*

South African Law Commission. 1992. *Report* (Project 24).

—— 1999. *Report on Administrative Justice* (Project 115).

Cases

Albutt v Centre for the Study of Violence and Reconciliation 2010 (3) SA 293 (CC).

Chirwa v Transnet Ltd 2008 (4) SA 367 (CC).

Fedsure Life Assurance Ltd v Greater Johannesburg Transitional Metropolitan Council 1999 (1) SA 374 (CC).

Glenister v President of the Republic of South Africa 2011 (3) SA 347 (CC).

Judicial Service Commission v Cape Bar Council 2012 (11) BCLR 1239 (SCA).

Kaunda v President of the Republic of South Africa 2005 (4) SA 235 (CC).

MEC, Department of Welfare, Eastern Cape v Kate 2006 (4) SA 478 (SCA).

Minister for Justice and Constitutional Development v Nyathi (Nyathi II) 2010 (4) SA 567 (CC).

Njongi v MEC, Department of Welfare, Eastern Cape 2008 (4) SA 237 (CC).

Nyathi v MEC for Department of Health, Gauteng (Nyathi I) 2008 (5) SA 94 (CC).

Permanent Secretary, Department of Welfare, Eastern Cape v Ngxuza 2001 (4) SA 1184 (SCA).

Pharmaceutical Manufacturers Association of SA: In re Ex parte President of the Republic of South Africa 2000 (2) SA 674 (CC).

President of the Republic of South Africa v South African Rugby Football Union 2000 (1) SA 1 (CC).

Public Protector v Mail & Guardian Ltd 2011 (4) SA 420 (SCA).

Thusi v Minister of Home Affairs and 71 Other Cases 2011 (2) SA 567 (KZP).

United Democratic Movement v President of the Republic of South Africa (No 2) 2003 (1) SA 495 (CC).

Legislation

Constitution of the Republic of South Africa, Act 200 of 1993.
Constitution of the Republic of South Africa, 1996.
Constitution of the Republic of Namibia.
Gauteng Scrutiny of Subordinate Legislation Act 5 of 2008.
Interpretation Act 33 of 1957.
Promotion of Access to Information Act 2 of 2000.
Promotion of Administrative Justice Act 3 of 2000.
Protection of State Information Bill (B 6B-2010).
Public Audit Act 25 of 2004.
Public Protector Act 23 of 1994.
Regulations on Fair Administrative Procedures GN R1022 *GG* 23674 of 31 July 2002.
State Liability Act 20 of 1957.

PART III
Citizenship, Political Rights and the Party System

Chapter 10

From Disenfranchisement to Enfranchisement: The Right to Vote in South Africa

Francesca Romana Dau

Introduction

The first free, equal and democratic elections held in South Africa between 26 and 29 April 1994 have been recognised as a rare historical moment in which the whole of humanity took a significant step forward (Southall 1998: 443–69). As Andrew Reynolds (1994) notes, midnight on 26–27 April 1994 witnessed the lowering of the last colonial flag in Africa, marking the end of 300 years of colonialism and four decades of the apartheid regime. Until 1994, the demographics of the relationship among the social groups inhabiting South Africa necessitated the denial of universal enfranchisement by the white minority if they were to maintain their political rule and economic privileges. This led to the complete disenfranchisement of the 'non-Whites' (Ranchod 1978: 43–51). In fact, from an historical perspective, the granting of universal suffrage and the recognition of the majoritarian principle might have led to a homogeneous majority from an ethnic point of view. The majority resulting from an arithmetical calculus would have prevailed in South Africa, through the sheer strength of numbers; thus, black people over the minority white people (Sachs 1995: 55–67).

The British constitutional scholar Ian Loveland (1999) has dedicated an entire book to those topics, analysing the legal and socio-economic basis of disenfranchisement in South Africa between 1855 and 1960. It is widely acknowledged that part of the constitutional history of South Africa is intimately entwined with its British equivalent. Indeed, the majority of British constitutional-law students are aware of the main case law that codified racial discrimination and the total removal of the voting rights of non-whites in South Africa, such as *Harris v Minister of the Interior* (1951). For all these reasons and more, the right to vote occupies a special place in the framework of the South African Bill of Rights.

Section 19 of the 1996 Constitution reads as follows:

Political rights

(1) Every citizen is free to make political choices, which includes the right
  (a) to form a political party;
  (b) to participate in the activities of, or recruit members for, a political party; and
  (c) to campaign for a political party or cause.

(2) Every citizen has the right to free, fair and regular elections for any legislative body established in terms of the Constitution.

(3) Every citizen has the right to free, fair and regular elections for any legislative body established in terms of the Constitution.

(4) Every adult citizen has the right –
  (a) to vote in elections for any legislative body established in terms of the Constitution, and to so in secret; and
  (b) to stand for public office and, if elected, to hold office.

Therefore, we see that franchise rights are listed in the broader category of political rights, including freedom to organise political parties, and the right to free and fair elections. Moreover, the right to vote will be a shell devoid of meaning if it is not combined with the right to free and fair elections (Steytler 1993: 3).

A deeper analysis will therefore assist in understanding not only the letter of the Constitution and of the law, but also the social and political consequences of certain dispositions. The Constitution of 1996 (s 1(d)) inserts 'universal suffrage' among the fundamental values of the new order showing how this right is closely related to the building of a unique South African citizenship. Thus, the vote becomes a symbol of the nation-building process, in effect to say that beyond socio-economic differences, the people of South Africa belong to the same political community.

In this chapter, the 'law on the books' will be combined with the 'law in action' with the aim of highlighting the procedural and the substantive meaning of these rights in the particular historical experience of South Africa. Rather than moving directly on to a description of s 19 of the Constitution, it will prove more beneficial to focus on the significant and revolutionary approach pursued by the Constitutional Assembly in incorporating it in the new constitutional order. The fact that the provisions concerning the right to free, fair and regular elections were put before the right to vote, while in one sense being a simple drafting technique, is also a meaningful demonstration of the role occupied by the procedural aspects of suffrage in this new order. This assists us in distinguishing between the procedural and the substantive approach.

This chapter is divided into two main parts. The first focuses on the procedural approach in the interpretation of the right to vote. The second part concerns the substantive aspect hidden behind the provisions of s. 19(3) of the Constitution. The analysis of the constitutional provisions is placed side by side with those groundbreaking judgments of the Constitutional Court (CC) that have assigned increasing significance to its legal terms.

The Right to Free, Fair and Regular Elections in s 19(2): The Procedural Approach

As indicated previously, the right to vote is considered an empty shell if not connected to the right to free, equal and regular elections. The latter right, in the interpretation of scholars of international law, consists of an inseparable triad of rights – the right to take part in the conduct of public affairs, directly or through freely chosen representatives, the right to vote and to be elected in the context of free elections by universal suffrage, and the right of access to public office in your country. This forms the foundation of the legitimacy and the legality of political power (Sudre 2008: 522–8).

The CC, in para 12 of its judgment in *New National Party v Government of Republic of RSA* (1999), stressed that:

> The right to vote is of course indispensable to, and empty without, the right to free and fair elections; the latter gives content and meaning to the former. The right to free and fair elections underlines the importance of the exercise of the right to vote and the requirement that every election should be fair has implications for the way in which the right to vote can be given more substantive content and legitimately exercised.

It is widely known that this right has subsequently been inserted in article 3 of Protocol no. 1 of the European Convention on Human Rights (Pinelli 2001: 845–61).

However, defining its effect within a national legal order involves practical and tangible problems that are not easy to resolve. On the one hand, according to the reasoning of the CC in its *New National Party* decision, the interpretation of this right would imply the existence of an independent administrative body in charge of organising the elections and supervising the procedure in accordance with national and international legislation, such as the African Charter on Democracy, Elections and Governance, which entered into force in 2012. On the other hand, the material effect of this right is connected with the attribution to each citizen of one (and only one) vote, and with the constant verification of the legal requirements for access to voting. South African scholars, moreover, have stated that one of the fundamental techniques to give effect to that right is the establishment of an independent institution in charge of regulating and administering the electoral process, which is very common in African countries (Harms 2005: 456).

The Independent Electoral Commission (IEC) of South Africa is a constitutional body presided over by a judge and conceived within the framework of the so-called 'State Institutions Supporting Constitutional Democracy', in Chapter 9 of the Constitution. It is equipped with extensive functions and has the task of organising and supervising the entire electoral process, from the preparatory phase until the proclamation of the results. The same institution plays a vital role in relation to political parties, with the task of compiling and keeping a public register of political parties and watching over the fund for the public financing of these parties. The idea that the management of the electoral process had been entirely devolved from the Ministry of Home Affairs to a body conceived as independent from executive power did not immediately find favour with the South African Government. In fact, in 1997, it attempted to introduce a Bill to transfer control of the spending power of the Commission to the Ministry itself, but this did not result in any real shifting of authority (Lodge 1999: 24). As confirmed by the Constitutional Court in *New National Party v Government of South Africa* (paras 98–9), the independent status of the Electoral Commission is embodied with the full right to autonomy and self-regulation, with the possibility of having access to reasonable financial funds to conduct their business, as well as being placed exclusively under the monitoring and auditing of the Parliament and not of the Government.

While the establishment of an IEC was truly an 'institutional fashion' of the African constitutionalism of the 1990s (Gazibo 2006: 611), a set of legal and political elements has clearly marked the destiny of those institutions. What has made the Electoral Commission of South Africa one of the most authoritative institutions in electoral management on the African continent is the definition of its legal status and the political stature it has been able to acquire in the institutional arena. The Commission could be regarded as one of the most virtuous and authoritative institutions in the panorama of the electoral institutions in Africa, considering that the political will to make these institutions work is more influential than the rules and procedures which design them (Faure 1996).

This notwithstanding, in the South African constitutional order, the existence of an independent institution is a necessary but not sufficient condition to give effect to that right (Harms 2005: 458, Cheadle et al. 2002, Fick 2002: 2–3). As a corollary of the equity (*fairness*) of the election, the CC raised two further principles in *NNP of SA v The Government of the RSA and Others* (para 12). The first states that no citizen is allowed to vote more than once during a single election, and the second that any person who is not qualified to vote cannot effectively vote.

The Right to Vote in s 19(3): The Substantive Approach

On the one hand, as we have seen, the right to vote is intimately linked with the guarantee of a fair administration of the electoral procedure. On the other hand, nevertheless, behind the provisions of s 19(3) of the Constitution one can discover the true conceptualisation of the right to vote connected with the historical and socio-political aspects that have characterised South Africa's past.

The Constitution states clearly and unequivocally a number of fundamental principles relating to the understanding of suffrage: the individual ownership of voting rights, the extension of universal suffrage, the equality of representation and the secrecy of the ballot (Philippe 2003: 76). However, the innovation of the South African Constitution is demonstrated by the revolutionary concept of the right to vote through the definition of legal ownership in an exclusively individual, rather than collective, manner, as opposed to that which had been misused during the discrimination of the apartheid era.

The constitutional framework must be combined with the constitutional jurisprudence which has attributed the right to vote to the value of human dignity, and with statutes that have implemented the constitutional provision (Electoral Act of 1998, as amended by the Local Government: Municipal Electoral Act of 2000 and by the Electoral Laws Amendment Act of 2003).

In its judgment in *August and Another v Electoral Commission and Others* (1999: para 17), which has circulated in common-law countries and has been considered an authoritative precedent by the Canadian Supreme Court in *Sauvé v Canada (Directeur général des elections:* paras 35–43), the CC developed a remarkable approach to political rights. Justice Sachs, interpreting s 19, states that 'The universality of the franchise is important not only for nationhood and democracy. The vote of each and every citizen is a badge of dignity and of personhood. Quite literally, it says that everybody counts.' The achievement of universal suffrage, says Sachs, was a milestone for both the acquisition of the right to a full and effective citizenship extended to all South Africans regardless of race, and for the realisation of an 'inclusive nationality', a truly 'all-embracing nationhood'. The nation-building process started, indeed, from the recognition of the right to vote of the entire people of South Africa, reversing the historical and social inequalities into the arithmetical equation of 'one person, one vote'.

Extending the right to vote regardless of race, sex, or religion is not just a means of allowing the community of citizens to participate in political life and to effectively address the policies of the government. It also has an intrinsic purpose, to manifest the equality of citizens in the political community. The CC, considering the historical abuse of the right to vote as an instrument of domination of one group over another, has linked in an indissoluble way the justification of the ownership of voting rights to human dignity, so that the right to vote has become '*a badge of dignity and of personhood*'.

According to this concept of suffrage, the substantial and socio-economic inequality of South African citizens is symbolically resolved by the assignment of an equal political weight to each elector, through the instrument of the vote.

The issue of discrimination and the legitimacy of differential treatment were addressed in *Democratic Party v. Minister of Home Affairs* 1999, in which the Court was required to rule upon the constitutionality of the Electoral Act of 1998. The catalyst for the applications related to the prescription of the Act that required the possession of a bar-coded identity document to register on the electoral roll.

The legal representative of the Democratic Party had opposed the argument that, although seemingly neutral, this provision had the effect of introducing an indirect discrimination against vulnerable groups of citizens on the grounds of race, age, residence, religious and political beliefs, and political belonging. In particular, the appeal was based upon the fact that a large section of white potential voters, residing in rural areas and of a young age, was not in possession of the 'green bar-coded identity card'. The applicant concluded that the Electoral Act, although not directly and intentionally, violated the right to vote and introduced a restriction to certain categories of citizens that could not be justified on the basis of the general clause on limitation of rights, in s 36 of the Constitution. The CC, nevertheless, dismissed the appeal, admitting the possibility that the electoral laws and regulations of the right to vote can have potentially restrictive consequences, for only regulatory purposes, on certain categories of people *(The Democratic Party v The Minister of Home Affairs and the Electoral Commission*, paras 11–13).

These consequences may also vary depending on the place of residence, the level of education, and political affiliation, and yet this is not considered to be within the terms of indirect and unlawful discrimination as the Court stated in the same case at paras 18–19. The only differential measurements allowed in the discipline of political rights, in derogation from the principle of formal equality of representation, are set out in s 33(1) of the Electoral Act of 1998 which lists the classes of citizens eligible to apply for access to special measures, as follows:

> 33. Special votes.
> (1) The Commission-
> *(a)* must allow a person to apply for a special vote if that person cannot vote at a voting station in the voting district in which the person is registered as a voter, due to that person's-
> (i) physical infirmity or disability, or pregnancy;
> (ii) absence from the Republic on Government service or membership of the household of the person so being absent; or
> (iii) absence from that voting district while serving as an officer in the election concerned, or while on duty as a member of the security services in connection with the election;
> *(b)* may prescribe other categories of persons who may apply for special votes.

A further constitutional prescription, with a revolutionary impact, was the inclusion of the requirement to draw up a common single national register, the so-called 'national common voters roll', as one of the fundamental values of the Republic included in s 1(d) of the Constitution. Even though it can be justified within the political theory of liberal democracy and can be found among the instruments of positive discrimination in electoral matters (Kymlicka 1995: 229–63, Reynolds 2006: 3), the technique of compiling separate electoral rolls for groups and minorities was particularly despised by the South African Constitutional Assembly and indeed throughout public opinion, due to the unlawful differential treatment perpetrated historically through this instrument. The first common electoral register, on non-racial grounds, was introduced in South Africa in 1999, with the provision of a single qualification for voting, the legal age of eighteen years (De Ville and Steytler 1996: 1). There had been no voters' roll in the first democratic elections of 1994, because logistical difficulties made this impossible (Booysen and Masterson 2009).

The Exclusion from the Right to Vote

As mentioned above, South Africa is extremely sensitive to the disenfranchisement discourse and 'legislation dealing with the franchise must be interpreted in favour of enfranchisement rather than disenfranchisement' (*August and Another v Electoral Commission and Others*, para 17). Therefore, the cases of exclusion from the right to vote must be sufficiently justified.

The criteria of age and citizenship, as stated in s 1 of the Electoral Act, excluded access to the vote of people under the age of eighteen, as well as foreigners with legal permission to stay or permanently resident in the territory of the State. Also, people with mental illness, and prisoners are excluded from the right to vote. Although the exclusion of the first two categories did not appear controversial, what proved to be the most problematic was the exclusion from suffrage of people with mental illnesses and prisoners. In fact, those who have been declared to be suffering from mental disorders by a High Court and detained under the Mental Health Act of 1973 are explicitly excluded from the right to vote.

Section 8(2) concerning registration in the National Common Voters Roll reads as follows:

> The chief electoral officer may not register a person as a voter if that person:
>
> …
>
> *(c)* has been declared by the High Court to be of unsound mind or mentally disordered;
>
> *(d)* is detained under the Mental Health Act n. 18 of 1973.

In Harms's view, the exclusion of this category of citizens declared 'incapable of discernment' by reason of insanity is a form of direct discrimination on the ground of disability that must be considered unconstitutional because most of the persons concerned are considered to be perfectly capable of casting a vote (Harms 2005 at 460). Nevertheless, this criterion of exclusion is still part of the South African constitutional order.

The question of the right of prisoners to vote is worthy of deeper analysis. At the time of the approval of the Electoral Act of 1993, the problem of extending the suffrage to prisoners had remained unresolved (ibid. at 461). In contrast, the Electoral Act of 1998, by failing to provide explicit limits, should have been interpreted as a granting of voting rights to prisoners. However, the IEC decided to preclude the registration of prisoners from the electoral rolls, citing financial and administrative reasons (Fatin-Rouge Stefanini 2007: 617–43).

The legal reasons for the prisoners' enfranchisement are highlighted by the CC in the judgment in *August v The Electoral Commission and Others*: the legislative silence should not have been interpreted as a means to exclude prisoners from the suffrage. This Court, in fact, ordered (in para 42) the IEC to 'take all reasonable steps' to make possible the participation of prisoners in elections and to implement positive measures in the framework of the 'special vote' as provided for in s 33 of the Electoral Act 1998.

After the Court's ruling, Parliament has intervened to modify the electoral law of 1998, with the integration of prisoners into the category of those entitled to vote (Schedule 2 of the Municipal Electoral Act of 2000). Following the same legal arguments – that the Constitution states that every adult citizen has the right to vote – attempts to exclude yet another category of prisoners were declared unconstitutional by the Court, in *Minister of Home Affairs v National Institute for Crime Prevention and Re-Integration of Offenders (NICRO)*.

A further extension of the suffrage was carried out by the Electoral Laws Second Amendment Act of 2003 which amended s 33 of the 1998 Act with the addition of a new group of citizens eligible to apply for the special vote: South African citizens temporarily residing abroad. This issue was decided by the Court during the campaign for the general election of April 2009.

In the case of *Richter v The Minister for Home Affairs and Others*, the Court considered confirmation of an order of constitutional invalidity concerning s 33 of the Electoral Act of 1998, on the electoral capacity of South African citizens permanently resident abroad. What was at stake was the fact that this section contained no provision for the exercise of the franchise by citizens resident abroad. Justice O'Regan, author of a unanimous judgment, embraced the foundations of the concept of suffrage, referring to the case of *August*, and reiterated the importance of the right to vote in a constitutional democracy.

Here the Judge stressed furthermore that the vote is not only laden with strong symbolic value, but also with civic duty which gives direct responsibility to each citizen to choose the government, serving as a pillar of a functioning democratic regime. Even in this judgment, the Court reiterated that the right to vote gives the State a positive obligation to take all necessary measures to ensure that this right can be exercised, while the electoral system is an instrument that gives effect to the right to vote. Section 33 of the 1998 Act, which allows the possibility to request a 'special vote' for only certain categories of persons, is here configured as a limit on the right to vote.

To assess the reasonableness of such a limit, the Court also considered other 'open and democratic societies' in which mechanisms are in place to ensure the participation of foreign nationals in the vote, based upon the report compiled by the International Institute for Democracy and Electoral Assistance (IDEA). In this judgment, the value of citizens living abroad for study or work reasons, maintaining an interest in their own country and contributing to its welfare and material wealth in a society symbolically conceived without geographical boundaries, was emphatically recognised (*Richter v The Minister for Home Affairs and Others* 2009: para 69). For these reasons, the Court confirmed the ruling of constitutional invalidity of s 33, indicating that the effects of the order involved all registered South African citizens who would have been abroad on the day of the election, 22 April 2009, and thus proceeding to extend the right to vote to all citizens residing abroad and regularly recorded in the national electoral roll.

The extension of voting rights to South African citizens living abroad, given the course of South African history, represents a true act of reconciliation with the white community, many of whom emigrated in the days after the collapse of the apartheid regime. This step also endorses the acquisition of a concept of citizenship in which people are released from territory, resulting in a virtual extension of the boundaries of the State, towards a broader definition of the political community.

Conclusion

This chapter has attempted to describe some of the most salient aspects of the right to vote in the new South African constitutional order, distinguishing the procedural and the substantive aspects of this right. As we have seen, the right to vote occupies a special place in the framework of the Bill of Rights for historical reasons, and the CC has pushed towards a wide enfranchisement rather than disenfranchisement. The achievement of universal suffrage and the constitutionalisation of the principle of 'one person, one vote' was the means to build up the South African nation on the basis of formal equality rather than on substantive equality. The nation-building process, in fact, rested on the recognition of formal equality in the political field and on the participation of all the citizens in the political community (Seedorf 2001: 1857). A common citizenship, as described in s 3 of the Constitution, was the first instrument that introduced an equal juridical identity, becoming the cornerstone of the building of the 'rainbow nation'. The importance of introducing a common citizenship for all South Africans also ended the practice of recognising different categories of persons with a different set of rights in the socio-economic and cultural sphere as well as in the political one (Maharaj 1999, Bentley and Habib 2008). Nation building and citizenship, in fact, are intimately linked with the South African constitutional narration and are crucial topics in our discourse (Federico 2003).

This notwithstanding, there are still some problematic categories of citizens excluded from the vote, such as people with mental illness, and this appears not to be fully in line with the constitutional intention.

References

Books, book chapters and articles

Bentley, K. and A. Habib, 2008. *Racial Redress and Citizenship in South Africa*. Cape Town: HRSC Press.

Booysen, S. and G. Masterson, 2009. 'South Africa', in eds S. Kadima S. et al., *Compendium of Elections in Southern Africa 1989–2009: 20 Years of Multiparty Democracy*. Johannesburg: EISA.

Cheadle, H., D. Davis and N. Haysom, eds, 2002. *South African Constitutional Law. The Bill of Rights*. Durban: Butterworths, 272 ss.

De Ville, J. and N. Steytler, eds, 1996. *Voting in 1999: Choosing an Electoral System*. Durban: Butterworths.

Fatin-Rouge Stefanini, M. 2007. 'Le droit de vote des détenus en droits canadien, sud-africain et conventionnel européen', *Revue internationale de droit comparé*, 3: 617–43.

Faure, M. 1996. 'The Electoral System', *Journal of Theoretical Politics*, 8(2): 133–57.

Federico, V. 2003. 'La cittadinanza nell'esperienza sudafricana', *Quaderni Costituzionali*, 1: 113–43.

Fick, G. 2002. 'Elections', in eds S. Woolman et al., *Constitutional Law of South Africa*, 2nd edn. Cape Town: Juta, pp. 2–3.

Gazibo, M. 2006. 'The Forging of Institutional Autonomy. A Comparative Study of Electoral Management Commissions in Africa', *Canadian Journal of Political Science*, 39(3): 611–33.

Harms, I. 2005. 'Political Rights', in eds I. Currie et al., *The Bill of Rights Handbook*, 5th edn. Lansdowne: Juta.

Kymlicka, W. 1995. *La cittadinanza multiculturale*. Bologna: Il Mulino, pp. 229–63.

Lanchester, F. 2006. *La rappresentanza in campo politico e le sue trasformazioni*. Milano: Giuffré, pp. 44–57.

Lodge, T. 1999. *Consolidating Democracy. South Africa's Second Popular Election*. Johannesburg: Witwatersrand University Press.

Loveland, I. 1999. *By Due Process of Law. Racial Discrimination and the Right to Vote in South Africa 1855–1960*. Portland: Hart Publishing.

Maharaj, G. 1999. *Between Unity and Diversity. Essay on Nation-building in Post-apartheid South Africa*. Claremont: Idasa/David Philip Publishers.

Philippe, X. 2003 'Afrique du Sud, Constitution et élections', in *Annuaire Internationale de Justice Constitutionnelle*. Aix-en-Provence: Presses Universitaires d'Aix-Marseille, p. 76.

Pinelli, C. 2001. Art. 3. 'Diritto a libere elezioni', in eds S. Bartole et al., *Commentario alla Convenzione europea per la tutela dei diritti dell'uomo e delle libertà fondamentali*. Padova: Cedam, pp. 845–61.

Ranchod, B.G. 1978. 'Constitutions and Political Rights', in ed. J. Benyon, *Constitutional Change in South Africa. Proceeding of a Conference on Constitutional Models and Constitutional Change in South Africa, University of Pietermaritzburg, 14–16 February 1978*. Pietermaritzburg: University of Natal Press, pp. 43–51.

Reynolds, A. 1994. *South Africa. Electoral System Design and Conflict Management in Africa*, Paper ACE Project, Electoral Knowledge Network ,www.aceproject.org>.

—— 2006. *Electoral Systems and the Protection and Participation of Minorities*. London: Minority Rights Group International.

Sachs, A. 1995. 'Règle majoritaire et droits des minorités', in eds G. Conac et al., *L'Afrique du Sud en transition. Réconciliation et coopération en Afrique Australe*, Paris: Economica, pp. 55–67.
Seedorf, S. 2001. 'La garanzia costituzionale delle minoranze in Sud Africa', in *Giurisprudenza Costituzionale*, Vol. 3.
Southall, R. 1998. 'The Centralisation and Fragmentation of South Africa's Dominant Party System', *African Affairs*, 97: 443–69.
Steytler, N. 1993. *Free and Fair Elections*. Cape Town: Juta.
Sudre, F. 2008. *Droit européen et international des droits de l'homme*. Paris: Presses Universitaires de France, pp. 522–8.

Cases

August and Another v Electoral Commission and Others 1999(3) SA 1 (CC).
Minister of Home Affairs v National Institute for Crime Prevention and Re-Integration of Offenders (NICRO) 2005 (3) SA 280 (CC).
New National Party v Government of South Africa 1999 (3) SA 191 (CC).
Richter v The Minister for Home Affairs and Others 2009 (3) SA 615 (CC).
The Democratic Party v The Minister of Home Affairs and the Electoral Commission 1999 (3) SA 254 (CC).
Sauvé c. Canada (Directeur général des élections), [2002] 3 R.C.S., 519, CSC (Canada).

Legislation

Constitution of the Republic of South Africa, 1996.
Electoral Act 203 of 1993
Electoral Act 73 of 1998
Electoral Laws Amendment Act 3 of 2003
Electoral Laws Amendment Act 34 of 2003
Electoral Laws Second Amendment Act 40 of 2003
Local Government: Municipal Electoral Act 27 of 2000
Mental Health Act 18 of 1973

Chapter 11
The Contradictions of Party Dominance in South Africa

Roger Southall

The lifting by State President FW de Klerk of bans on the African National Congress (ANC), South African Communist Party (SACP), Pan-Africanist Congress (PAC) and other parties on 2 February 1990 led to a remarkable process of negotiation between contending actors culminating in the democratic elections of April 1994. The adoption of the interim Constitution in late 1993 reflected a broad consensus around liberal democratic principles (free elections, a Bill of Rights, the independence of the judiciary and so on). This was a product of the defensive powers retained by the government (control of the state, military and policing apparatus plus significant support from among demographic minorities, notably whites) in contrast to the offensive powers enjoyed by the ANC (ability to contest state control in both township and rural areas based on majority support amongst the mass of the population alongside extensive African and wider international backing).

Adoption of a party list Proportional Representation (PR) system provided for maximum representation of all shades of opinion, with the transitional election also involving elections on the same basis for nine newly created provinces. The outcome of the election was regarded by substantial minorities as peculiarly beneficent, for while the ANC secured an indisputable victory, it fell short of the two-thirds majority which, in terms of the interim constitution, would have enabled it to drive the finalisation of the constitution-making process without the support of other political parties. Thus although the ANC was able to secure some changes to its liking during the negotiation of the final Constitution by the Constitutional Assembly during 1996, the resulting document was largely bound by the terms hammered out during the transitional process of 1990–1994.

Although it increased its proportion of electoral support during the course of the first three post-transitional elections, the ANC has consistently faced significant levels of opposition, even though the parties of opposition have remained very fragmented, with potential for their unity constrained by race, ethnicity, style, ideology, regional affiliation and their leaderships' personal ambitions. Nonetheless, the ANC's domination of the electoral arena has led to the marginalisation of smaller parties and the emergence of the liberal Democratic Alliance (DA) as the major force of opposition.

For all that the ANC itself dislikes the label, it has established itself as a 'dominant party': in other words, it has established electoral dominance for a prolonged period; as a result, it has enjoyed dominance in the formation of governments; and furthermore, its domination of the governmental machinery has allowed it to determine the public agenda. This chapter will explore the electoral basis of the ANC's domination and the impact this has made on the party system.

The Electoral Basis of ANC Dominance

The outcome of the five democratic general elections is illustrated in Table 11.1. These elections have all been administered by the Independent Electoral Commission (IEC). All elections were declared by electoral observers as substantially free and fair, and there is no reason to believe that the election results distort the views of 'the people' (February 2009).

The President is elected by Parliament rather than directly by the people. Perhaps because this has been no bar to a considerable centralisation of power under the presidency (notably during the era of Thabo Mbeki, who served as President 1999–2008), there has been no concerted move by the ANC to change the system. Meanwhile, ANC dominance has been largely replicated in the upper chamber of parliament (initially a Senate, subsequently the National Council of Provinces under the final Constitution, both elected by provincial legislative assemblies) and rather more by its continuous electoral hold over seven or more of the nine provinces. The principal provincial outliers have been the Western Cape (where whites, Coloureds and Indians taken together outnumber Africans) and KwaZulu-Natal, where the ANC has had to confront the predominantly Zulu-ethnically based Inkatha Freedom Party (IFP) of Chief Mangosutho Buthelezi.

In the Western Cape, following a series of provincial electoral outcomes which saw first, the ANC playing second fiddle within a coalition to the formerly ruling National Party (NP) from 1994, and second losing out to a (now 'New') National Party (NNP)-Democratic Party (DP) coalition in 1999, the ANC was enabled to take control of the province in coalition with the NNP in 2002 (following a controversial process of floor-crossing by members of political parties) and to confirm this via a coalition victory in 2004. However, rampant divisions within the provincial ANC along largely African versus Coloured lines led in 2009 to its loss of the province to the DA, the latter a product of a merger between the DP and NNP in 2000 (Daniel and Southall 2009). The DA's hold on the province was to be confirmed when five years later it increased its share of the provincial vote from 51 per cent in 2004 to 59 per cent in 2014.

In KwaZulu-Natal the IFP assumed leadership of the provincial government from 1994, when it obtained a bare 50.5 per cent popular majority in the provincial election, through to 2004. The IFP's provincial predominance built upon the largely chiefly-led, rural, ethnic and patronage-based support it had established as the government of the pre-1994 KwaZulu bantustan and its violent clashes with the

Table 11.1 South African National Assembly Elections 1994–2014

Party	Valid Votes	% Valid Votes	Elected Seats
1994 Election			
ANC	12,237,655	62.65	252
NP	3,983,690	20.39	82
IFP	2,058,294	10.54	43
DP	338,426	1.73	7
Other	915,433	4.68	16
Total	19,533,498	100	400
1999 Election			
ANC	10,601,330	66.35	266
DA	1,527,337	9.56	38
IFP	1,088,664	8.58	34
NNP	1,098,215	6.87	28
Others	1,378,783	8.62	34
Total	15,977,142	100	400
2004 Election			
ANC	10,880,915	69.69	279
DA	1,931,201	12.37	50
IFP	1,088,664	6.97	28
NNP	257,824	1.65	7
Others	1,454,067	9.3	36
Total	15,612,671	100	400
2009 Election			
ANC	11,650,748	65.90	264
DA	2,945,829	16.66	67
CoPe	1,311,027	7.42	30
IFP	804,260	4.55	18
Others	968,865	5.49	21
Total	17,680,729	100	400
2014 Election			
ANC	11,436,921	62.2	249
DA	4,091,584	22.2	89
EFF	1,169,259	6.4	25
Others	1,704,733	9.26	37
Total	18,402,497	100	400

Source: Daniel and Southall 2009: 234; Schulz Herzenberg and Southall 2014: 106.

United Democratic Front during the latter 1980s, which was informally allied to the ANC when the latter was still in exile, before foregoing its independence (and eventually dissolving itself) once the ANC returned to South Africa after 1990. However, the level of support for the ANC (32 per cent in 1994 improving to 39 per cent in 1999) was such that the IFP was forced to rule in uneasy coalition with it. This lasted until 2004, when the ANC, via steady erosion of the IFP's capacity to extend patronage in key areas, became the leading party in the province with 48 per cent of the vote. Subsequently, the IFP's remaining grip on the province was shattered by a 63 per cent victory for the ANC in 2009. This was generally ascribed to the elevation of Jacob Zuma, a Zulu, to the leadership of the ANC, which then indulged in its own particular brand of ethnic mobilisation and its further erosion of the IFP's traditional base in rural areas (Butler 2009). Subsequently shaken by an internal revolt against the authoritarian octogenarian leadership of Buthelezi which had spawned the birth of a rival National Freedom Party, the IFP's share of the provincial vote fell to just 11 per cent in 2014, allowing the DA with 13 per cent to claim the status of the province's official opposition (Schulz-Herzenberg 2014a: 212–14).

ANC dominance was initially contained by the requirement of the interim Constitution that the post-transitional government should be one of national unity (this replicated at provincial level) wherein parties gaining 10 per cent or more of the vote could choose to be represented in the cabinet. This resulted initially in a Government of National Unity (GNU) which united the formerly ruling NP and IFP under Nelson Mandela's leadership, symbolised by former State President De Klerk serving as a co-Deputy President alongside Thabo Mbeki of the ANC. However, following the withdrawal of the NNP from the coalition after the promulgation of the final constitution in 1996 (De Klerk's objecting to what he deemed to be the ANC's marginalisation of the NNP in cabinet), the ANC has been in effective total control of the government, notwithstanding its continuing inclusion of a handful of ministers from minority parties, notably the IFP, until the latter withdrew after the 2009 election.

The ANC has found the list PR system much to its liking. Not only does it consistently translate its support into proportional majorities in Parliament and the majority of provincial assemblies, but it has also enabled it to manipulate party lists so as to ensure that its legislative representation includes members of demographic minorities, this formally expressive of the party's commitment to non-racialism and gender equality. While this is praiseworthy, vocal critics have complained that the PR system has strengthened party bosses versus individual party representatives in legislatures, and has facilitated the ANC's domination over parliament and provincial legislatures. The elimination of parliamentary constituencies (used before 1994), argue the critics, has embodied the loss of accountability of MPs and Members of Provincial Legislatures (MPLs), as rather than being responsible towards local voters, they are responsible to their party superiors, not least because, under the Constitution, parties are able to move ('redeploy') their representatives in and out of legislatures at will. Thus, despite survey evidence that a substantial majority of voters would prefer a Mixed Member Proportional electoral system (MMP) whereby MPs would be elected from regionally demarcated multiple member constituencies, the ANC has consistently chosen to ignore the majority recommendations of an Electoral Task Team, established in 2002, to review the electoral system, claiming that list PR ensures reflection of national concerns (Mattes and Southall 2004).

In contrast, the ANC proved rather less than concerned with the ideal of representativeness when, in 2002, the government opportunistically passed legislation to allow for floor-crossing in national and provincial legislatures, this practice hitherto barred by the Constitution. The move had its origins in a crisis in the ranks of the opposition. The NNP, having moved out of the GNU, had sought to arrest its decline by merging with the DP to form the DA, only for its leading elements to become uncomfortable in opposition. Offered a lifeline in the form of a return to collaboration with the ANC, the NNP under new leader Marthinus van Schalwyk returned to coalition with the ANC in the Western Cape. As noted above, this enabled an ANC-NNP coalition to wrest control of the provincial and Cape Town municipal governments away from the DA. Indeed, over subsequent years, floor-crossing – albeit allowed only during two annual windows – worked overwhelmingly in favour of the ANC, as members of small parties sought to feather their nest by ensconcing themselves in the ruling party. However, so blatant was the process, and so cynically regarded by the public, that the legislative provision was reversed in 2007 (the NNP by then having folded itself completely into the ANC in 2005, although ironically leaving the bulk of its support base behind with the DA).

Notwithstanding its overall dominance, careful assessment of voting behaviour poses questions for the ANC. For all that the ANC's proportion of the vote has remained consistently high (increasing from just under 63 per cent in 1994 to a high of just under 70 per cent in 2004 before falling back to a low of 62 per cent in 2014), the nature of its later victories have been qualified by various factors.

- Firstly, the absolute number of votes which the ANC received in 2014 (11.44 million) was significantly below what it had obtained in 1994 (12.37 million). To some extent the reduction can be explained by the fact that whereas in 1994 voters merely had to show their Identity Documents to vote, by 2014 there had been long installed a system of voter registration. Nonetheless, the propensity to register and to vote has fallen since 1999. The percentage of registered voters relative to the estimated voting-age population (which has increased from 22.6 million in 1999 to 32.69 million in 2014) fell from 80.4 per cent in 1999 to 77.4 per cent in the latter year. Meanwhile, although the level of voter turnout remains high by international standards, it fell from 89.3 per cent in 1999 to 73.5 per cent in 2014. Furthermore, whereas some 86 per cent of the voting-age population cast a vote in 1994, this figure was down to just 57.1 per cent in 2009 (Schulz-Herzenberg 2014a: 195–6).

- Secondly, the enthusiasm of those who vote for the ANC has decreased over time. According to Schulz-Herzenberg (2009), 60 per cent of the electorate in 1994 were 'ANC partisans', but thereafter this figure fluctuated between 34 per cent and 60 per cent, before settling at 48 per cent some months prior to the 2009 election. In short, core ANC support is lower than initially supposed and many African voters support the party at election time, not because they are partisans but because they do not regard opposition parties as feasible alternatives. Correspondingly, although the ANC has shed 'partisans' at a slower rate than opposition parties, the proportion of 'independents' amongst the electorate has continued to grow. These trends continued in 2014 (Schulz Herzenberg 2014b).
- Thirdly, the ANC's hold on minority populations is declining. The suggestion that a South African election is little more than a racial census has been comprehensively discredited. Certainly, 'race matters', but Schultz-Herzenberg (2009: 37; 2014b: 32–7) argues cogently that this relates to party images of whether or not parties are seen as inclusive or exclusive. Thus any opposition party wanting to attract African voters, who constitute the large majority, have to work hard to promote an image of inclusiveness. That hitherto significant opposition parties, notably the DA, have enjoyed only limited success in doing so constitutes a major barrier to their electoral expansion. On the other hand, internal tensions within the ANC (notably within the Western Cape) which have increasingly set Coloureds against Africans have rendered the party significantly less 'non-racial'. Although during 2009 new ANC party leader Jacob Zuma sought to promote the ruling party as 'a home for all', the election of that year saw a major shift of the Coloured community away from the ANC into the arms of the DA and the newly formed Congress of the People (Cope). Unwittingly, the ANC 'is becoming a party with an increasingly African identity' (Daniel and Southall 2009: 237).

Despite these nuances, the ANC continues to demonstrate a remarkable ability to 'regenerate itself in power'. Booysen (2011), who examines this phenomenon in extensive detail, argues that massive political protest on the ground (widely dubbed service delivery protests') fails to translate into ultimate alienation from the ANC. She notes how the ANC continues to promote its image as the party of liberation from apartheid, and does so largely successfully, even while its performance in government is characterised by evident failures in such areas as education, health, sanitation and job-creation at the same time as it is becoming increasingly mired in corruption. Yet she observes that 'the brick' supplements 'the ballot', and protest is far more likely to reflect poor South Africans' rejection of individual ANC politicians and local governments, as failing to implement ANC policy, than rejection of the ANC itself. However, whether or not the ANC will continue to be able to continue to regenerate itself in power may well depend upon whether it is able to contain rampant factionalism.

From 2005, the ANC was rent by a bitter power struggle between Jacob Zuma and Thabo Mbeki. Zuma was dismissed from his post as Deputy President by Mbeki following revelations in the High Court that he had received regular covert payments from Schabir Shaik, one of his close advisers, who was convicted of corruption related to the 1998 arms deal. Thereafter Zuma became a lightning rod for anti-Mbeki sentiment, much of it emanating from the alienation felt by the ANC's partners, the Congress of South African Trade Unions (Cosatu) and the SACP at the Mbeki government's market-oriented economic policy. Despite Zuma's dubious credentials, he gathered a sufficient anti-Mbeki momentum behind him to displace Mbeki when the latter, despite having to stand down as national president in terms of the Constitution following the next general election, rashly sought a third term as president of the ANC at the party's Congress in Polokwane in December 2007. Although defeated by Zuma, Mbeki retained considerable minority support within the party, and remained President of the country. However, when in September 2008 a High Court judge ruled that Zuma's prosecution through the courts for corruption had been politically motivated, the ANC summarily forced Mbeki's resignation, leading to an interim presidency of Kgalema Motlanthe, who had replaced Zuma as Deputy President. Subsequently, after Zuma became President following the 2009 election, the Acting National Director of Public Prosecutions controversially announced that criminal proceedings against him would be dropped.

ANC political hegemony was severely undermined by the bitter contest between Mbeki and Zuma at Polokwane. It led to vicious blood-letting, as Mbeki supporters were purged from positions at all levels of the party, and as Zuma supporters scrambled for positions of power which granted them access to state resources. Corruption, present yet more contained under Mbeki, has become ever more blatant, with the friends and family of Zuma being particular beneficiaries. Concerned above all to secure himself a second term in office, Zuma presided over a fracturing of the coalition which had brought him to power. Most notably, this involved a long-running battle with Julius Malema, president of the ANC Youth League, who was eventually expelled from the party in early 2012. This culminated in his formation of a new party, the Economic Freedom Fighters (EFF) in 2013, which adopted a radical-nationalist programme designed to appeal to workers and the poor. Building upon the platform provided by the tragic deaths of some 44 miners when police opened fire upon striking workers at platinum mines in North West province in August 2013, the new party posed a radical threat to the left of the ANC during the election campaign in 2014, eventually securing third place (behind the DA) with some 6.4 per cent of the vote. Meanwhile, having been alienated by what they portrayed as the ANC's continuing adherence to 'neo-liberal' fiscal policies and by the blatant pursuit of private accumulation by ANC elites, the National Union of Metalworkers of South Africa (NUMSA), Cosatu's largest union, was threatening to break from the tripartite alliance (which bound the labour federation to the ANC and SACP) and to form a radical socialist movement in league with social movements after the 2014 election. Thus although

Zuma's enhanced domination of the party machinery allowed him to secure re-election as ANC president at the party's Mangaung conference in December 2012, his leadership was not unchallenged, and indeed he was recognised as something of a political liability during the course of the 2014 election campaign. Although the ANC recovered sufficiently from its difficulties to secure a solid victory, it was widely predicted that the electoral landscape was changing, allowing increased opportunity for parties of opposition (Southall 2014).

The Consolidation and Fragmentation of Opposition

Ultimately, the choice of party list PR (without a threshold dictating a minimum proportion of votes in order to obtain representation) as the electoral system was made during the constitution-making process prior to 1994 in order to maximise the representativeness of the 400 member National Assembly and provincial legislatures. This sought to combine the advantages of majority rule with appropriate representation for opposition parties expressive of South Africa's diverse population along lines of race, ethnic affiliation, class, religion and other identity. This certainly worked to encourage participation, with some 19 parties contesting the founding democratic election in 1994, although most were so small that they failed to secure sufficient votes for even a single seat in the National Assembly. In that particular election, some 6 opposition parties gained 148 seats and 37.4 per cent of the vote. Subsequently, the breadth of opposition in the National Assembly widened with a larger number of opposition parties sharing a smaller proportion of the vote. So that in 2009, 12 parties secured 136 seats and 34.3 per cent of the vote. Although subsequently some 15 parties gained representation in the National Assembly with 151 seats with a larger, 40 per cent of the vote, in 2014, these gross figures obscure a very significant simultaneous process of the consolidation and fragmentation of the political opposition. The overriding characteristics of this, apart from the decline of the IFP, have been the terminal decline of the NNP; the rise to predominance of the DA; and the fragmentation of the remainder of the opposition into a clutch of minor parties, of which the EFF seems potentially the most threatening to the ruling party. The immediate focus here is on the rise to predominance in opposition circles of the DA.

The Demise of the NNP

As the former ruling party, the NP had enormous difficulties in adjusting to life within a democracy. In its initial post-apartheid role, as a junior partner in the ANC-led GNU, it exuded uncertainty. Led by former State President (and subsequently, under Mandela, Deputy President) FW de Klerk, it sought to consolidate the democratic settlement by giving voice to minority concerns within government. However, the NNP remained an uneasy partner to the ANC, and deeply distrustful of a party which represented a largely impoverished black majority. Once the 1996 Constitution had been promulgated, De Klerk's reaction to his perceived marginalisation by the ANC led to his leading the NNP out of the GNU and into unambiguous opposition. He proceeded to resign as leader in September 1997, making way for Marthinus van Schalkwyk, who although the party's Gauteng provincial leader, was generally regarded as a political lightweight.

Van Schalkwyk was left with a largely conservative rump in Parliament which had previously been glued together by its position in government. Now that it was in opposition, it wavered uncertainly between shoring up its reputation as a protector of (racial) minority rights, or moving towards the political centre in order to attract conservative support more widely. In the event, Van Schalkwyk's widely derided leadership was a significant factor in the NNP's disastrous performance in the 1999 election and provided the backdrop to the formation of an alliance of convenience between the DP and the NNP to contest the municipal elections in 2000. This was formalised as the DA under the leadership of the DP's Tony Leon, with Van Schalkwyk becoming Deputy Leader, this signalling the NNP as the junior partner. For the moment, however, merger of the two parties was obstructed by the prohibition on floor-crossing, meaning that the DP and NNP were compelled to retain their separate identities until they could fight as a combined party at the next general election.

The alliance proved extremely unhappy. Van Schalkwyk rapidly found himself playing second fiddle to Leon, and soon he engaged in covert negotiations with the ANC. In November 2001 he took his party out of the DA and back into a loose coalition with the ruling party. Facilitated by the floor-crossing saga of 2002–2003, this enabled the ANC-NNP to take control of both the Western Cape and the Cape Town City Council. However, a significant bloc of representatives had stayed behind in the DA, for in linking up with the ANC, Van Schalkwyk had lost considerable support, taking with him only those elements who were desperate for a return to office. After a totally dismal showing in the 2004 general election, Van Schalkwyk agreed in 2005 to collapse the NNP into the ANC, where he earned his reward by appointment to the Cabinet. However, as demonstrated by the results of the 2009 provincial election in the Western Cape, Van Schalkwyk left the large proportion of the NNP's supporters behind him (Southall and Daniel 2005).

The Rise of the DA

The DA is the successor to the liberal tradition in South African politics. Although a significant actor during the constitutional negotiations, punching well above its weight in favour of liberal principles, the DP fared poorly in the 1994 elections, as apprehensive minority populations clustered behind the NP. However, thereafter the DA's electoral performance registered a steadily upward trajectory: from the DP's mere 1.7 per cent of the vote in 1994, to the DA's 22.2 per cent of the national vote in 2009. After the 1999 election, when it shoved the NNP into third place, it became the Official Opposition in Parliament, providing it with privileges for calling government to account beyond those shared by other opposition parties in Parliament.

The factors behind the rise of the DP/DA are various. Prominent among them has been the ability of the party to articulate a vigorous message of opposition to the ANC. Although it was extremely difficult to compete against a triumphal ANC basking in the glory of liberation, it became progressively easier for the DA to campaign on the need for government accountability. Second, the DP/DA has proved adroit at outpacing its competitors, with particular attention having been paid to the capture of white (notably Afrikaner) and Coloured support which in 1994 had gone to the NNP. While deeply conservative white support has peeled off to minor parties, most former NNP voters have pragmatically opted to throw their weight behind the DA as the de facto protector of minority interests. While the implosion of the NNP had seen a significant proportion of Coloured voters lining up behind the Independent Democrats (ID) in 2004, a party formed by the former Pan-Africanist Congress MP Patricia De Lille in 2003, their numbers were much reduced in 2009. Following the ID's entering a coalition with the DA at provincial level and municipal level in Cape Town, the DA took provincial power in 2009. Subsequently, the ID merged itself fully into the DA, with De Lille becoming Mayor of Cape Town.

The subsequent performance of the DA has been remarkable. In 2009 it exceeded its own expectations, increasing its share of the national vote by 4.3 from 12.4 per cent in 2004. Its campaign clearly consolidated opposition support, benefiting from the poor performance of other parties which appealed only to small minority interests, and, as noted, it capitalised on the declining fortunes of the ID in the Western Cape. Significantly too it outran the challenge of COPE which, founded in the wake of Thabo Mbeki's ejection from the Presidency in September 2008, for a period threatened to split the ANC and form the core vehicle of opposition spanning racial lines. However, COPE polled 1.6 million fewer votes than the DA, which became the only party in the National Assembly to record significant growth, with all other parties, the ANC included, losing support (Jolobe 2009). By 2014, with COPE having imploded, the DA continued its rise in the polls, securing over 22 per cent of the vote.

Despite the considerable presence of minor parties in the National Assembly, the DA's rise has threatened to transform South African politics into a de facto two party system. This has been underlined by its capture of power in the Western Cape, with the new DA leader, Helen Zille, leaving Parliament in 2009 to take office as provincial premier, determined to combine the image of the party as an effective opposition with one whose performance as a government will outshine that of the ANC. However, notwithstanding its continuing rise in the polls, it may be that DA support is approaching its ceiling.

Above all, the DA is finding difficulties rising above the accusations of the ANC that it has become the successor to the NNP as the embodiment of white interests, and those of property and wealth. Thus Pallo Jordan (2014), a leading

ANC intellectual, has argued that in effect the DA has done little more than capture the 20 per cent of the vote which the NNP managed to secure in 1994. However, after the resignation of Leon in 2007 and the succession to the leadership of Helen Zille, the DA has significantly changed its orientation, so that while determinedly hanging on to its minority support and deepening it amongst the Coloured community, it has made major efforts to make inroads amongst Africans.

During the 2009 elections, Zille campaigned vigorously in African areas, taking the battle to the ANC in its heartlands, appropriating much of its style and imagery in song and dance. Subsequently, she quietly backed a young black MP, Lindiwe Mazibuko, in her successful campaign to take over from her as parliamentary leader after her own departure for the Western Cape premiership. In 2014, the appeal to African voters continued, spearheaded by the rise in prominence of the articulate and flamboyant Mmusi Maimane, who drove the DA's campaign in Gauteng, the country's economic heartland. Ultimately, despite black middle class voters continuing to articulate reluctance to vote for the DA, the party laid claim to having received some 760 000 black African votes, a considerable portion (18.6 per cent) of its overall vote.

The DA now proclaims itself as the true vehicle of non-racialism. Even so, for all that the DA continues to defy expectations by picking up increasing its African support, it appears inherently unlikely that it can successfully challenge the ANC on its own turf. Even though the ANC is in internal turmoil, the DA will battle to win over an African population whose condition, overwhelmingly, reflects the legacy of apartheid – poverty, unemployment and social decay. Most within disadvantaged communities, although bitterly disappointed by the ANC's performance in power, see redress as necessarily spearheaded by state intervention. With the ANC itself increasingly adopting an interventionist orientation (and moving away from pro-market strategies adopted under Mbeki), most observers see it as only being seriously threatened from the left (Southern and Southall 2009).

Much speculation has been generated by the vigorous performance of the EFF, which under Malema has sought to pose a revolutionary challenge not merely to the ANC as the ruling party but to the constitutional settlement of 1994 as an embodiment of elite interests. Whether it manages to avoid the fate of COPE, which was to be torn apart by leadership disputes, to use parliament to develop its credibility, and to establish a mass organisation with firm roots remains to be seen. Furthermore, how it will deal with the formation by NUMSA and other elements of a socialist party (which at time of writing seems a highly likely prospect) will determine whether the ANC is to be faced by a significant challenge from its left. A coalition or united force of the EFF and a NUMSA-socialist party could represent a major challenge to ANC hegemony; an internecine battle between competing elements to the left of the ANC could serve to re-enforce it, or indeed to drive more African voters into the arms of the DA. In short, the 2014 election campaign gave strong indications that the electoral landscape may be changing.

The Contradictions of Party Dominance

Successive, impressive election victories have confirmed the ANC's status as a dominant party. The explanation for the ANC's electoral hegemony lies in its legacy as a liberation movement. History is written by the winners, and the ANC today repetitively states a monopoly claim to have brought liberation to the mass of South Africans. In a society still riven by huge disparities of wealth, income, and life opportunity along the lines of race, this claim continues to resonate, even if its purchase will steadily decline amongst voters who were 'born free' after 1994. However, while the massive extent of protest against 'service delivery' failures on the ground indicates severe disillusion with the ANC in government, few impoverished African communities perceive a viable alternative party of government to vote for, a dimension of contemporary politics which the DA is hard pressed to change. Nonetheless, any suggestion that the longevity in power of the ANC is guaranteed is highly questionable, for extended incumbency has brought with it an extent of vicious internal contestation within the ANC which is threatening to destroy its legitimacy, as the scramble for party and state position by ANC elites for state-derived material wealth overwhelms and distorts debates about policy, ideology and performance.

It is in this context that the DA is making determined efforts to make inroads into the ANC's electoral constituency. However, many argue that it is reaching its ceiling in terms of electoral support. Its effective absorption of the main body of the NNP's popular support is proving to be double edged. On the one hand, it has enabled the party to establish itself as the ANC's major electoral rival, and to take control of the Western Cape. But on the other, while the party is working hard to project its image as genuinely non-racial, its victories in the Western Cape are seen as racialised, in the sense that they have been founded upon the successful coalition of the provincial white vote (liberal and conservative), and the large Coloured community which has been alienated by the ANC. The DA is variously portrayed as the party of privilege, of those segments of the electorate which are better off, an image which is solidified by its espousal of pro-business, market-oriented policies which, despite the multiple failures of the ANC in government, do not readily appeal to the African majority. Meanwhile, as demonstrated by the fate of COPE, any rebellion from within the interstices of the ANC will need to be founded upon much more than pique at loss of position and privilege by a defeated faction.

There is, in short, a growing vacuum at the heart of South African party politics, for while the ANC has become a victim of its own dominance, the principal party of opposition, as presently constituted, is constrained by its own legacy, its own constituency, and its chosen ideology. Whether or not the birth of the EFF and the prospective creation of a socialist party at the behest of NUMSA constitutes a new social force, and one which can step into that vacuum to challenge the hegemony of the ANC, constitutes the major question posed to South African democracy.

References

Books, book chapters and articles

Booysen, S. 2011. *The African National Congress and Regeneration of Political Power*. Johannesburg: Wits University Press.

Butler, A. 2009. 'The ANC's National Campaign of 2009: *Siyanqoba!*', in eds R. Southall and J. Daniel, *Zunami! The 2009 South African Elections*. Johannesburg. Jacana Media, pp. 85–113.

Daniel, J. and R. Southall, 2009. 'The National and Provincial Electoral Outcome: Continuity with Change', in eds R. Southall and J. Daniel, *Zunami! The 2009 South African Elections*. Johannesburg: Jacana Media, pp. 215–31.

February, J. 2009. 'The Electoral System and Electoral Administration', in eds R. Southall and J. Daniel, *Zunami! The 2009 South African Elections*. Johannesburg: Jacana Media, pp. 47–64.

Jolobe, Z. 2009. 'The Democratic Alliance: Consolidating the Official Opposition', in eds R. Southall and J. Daniel, *Zunami! The 2009 South African Elections*. Johannesburg: Jacana Media, pp. 131–46.

Jordan, P. 2014. 'Parliament Resembles that of a Stable Democracy', *Business Day*, 22 May.

Mattes, R. and R. Southall, 2004. 'Popular Attitudes towards the South African Electoral System', *Democratization*, 11(1): 51–76.

Schulz-Herzenberg, C. 2009. 'Trends in Party Support and Voter Behaviour, 1994–2009', in eds R. Southall and J. Daniel, *Zunami! The 2009 South African Elections*. Johannesburg: Jacana Media, pp. 23–46.

—— 2014a. 'The 2014 National and Provincial Results', in eds C. Schulz-Herzenberg and R. Southall, *Election 2014 South Africa: The Campaign, Results and Future Prospects*. Johannesburg: Jacana Media, pp. 228–40.

—— 2014b. 'Trends in Electoral Participation, 1994–2014', in eds C. Schulz-Herzenberg and R. Southall, *Election 2014 South Africa: The Campaign, Results and Future Prospects*. Johannesburg: Jacana Media: 20–41.

Southall, R. 2004. 'The State of Party Politics: Struggles within the Tripartite Alliance and the Decline of the Opposition', in eds J. Daniel, A. Habib and R. Southall, *State of the Nation: South Africa 2003–2004*. Cape Town: HSRC Press, pp. 53–77.

—— 2014. 'The Context of the 2014 Election: Prologue to Change?', in eds C. Schulz-Herzenberg and R. Southall, *Election 2014 South Africa: The Campaign, Results and Future Prospects*, Johannesburg: Jacana Media, pp. 1–19.

—— and J. Daniel, 2005. 'The State of Parties Post-election 2004: ANC Dominance and Opposition Enfeeblement, in eds J. Daniel, R. Southall and J. Lutchman, *State of the Nation: South Africa 2004–2005*. Cape Town: HSRC Press, pp. 34–57.

Southern, N. and R. Southall, 2011. 'Dancing like a Monkey: The Democratic Alliance and Opposition Politics in South Africa', in eds J. Daniel et al., *New South African Review 2: New Paths, Old Compromises*. Johannesburg: Witswatersrand University Press, pp. 68–82.

Chapter 12
Freedom of Information: Controversies and Reforms

Iain Currie

The Constitutional Rights

Both of South Africa's post-apartheid constitutions have recognised a right to freedom of information. The interim Constitution confined the scope of the right to information held by the State and required the information seeker to show that it was required for the exercise or protection of their rights. The 1996 Constitution considerably expanded this scope. The text of s 32 is as follows:

> Access to information
> 32.(1) Everyone has the right of access to
> (a) any information held by the state; and
> (b) any information that is held by another person and that is required for the exercise of protection of any rights.
> (2) National legislation must be enacted to give effect to this right, and may provide for reasonable measures to alleviate the administrative and financial burden on the state.

Section 32(1)(a) deals with access to official information, the conventional ambit of the freedom of information principle. The right is unqualified, either by reference to subject matter or by reference to the persons who may exercise the right. But the most bold and progressive innovation was, of course, s 32(1)(b) which expanded the freedom of information principle to encompass information in private hands, subject to the threshold that the information is 'required for the exercise or protection of any rights'.

These rights are intended to be a deliberate reversal of past practice. The apartheid state, like most authoritarian regimes, was obsessed with official secrecy and made good use of a variety of laws that ensured close control of information in the State's hands. The rights, along with other transparency principles in the Constitution, are intended to loosen the State's habits of secrecy and encourage the development of an open and democratic society.

The rationale for the extension of the freedom of information principle to private-sector information is less obvious, and the courts have not ventured to theorise on this question. It is clear that the right in s 32(1)(b) should not be taken to impose general obligations of transparency on private bodies, who remain 'entitled to reasonable protection of privacy and commercial confidentiality' (*Unitas Hospital v Van Wyk* para 55). Instead, the right, controlled as it is by the threshold requirement that its exercise is 'required' to protect other rights, should be seen as justified by (and its scope confined by) the fundamental principle that occasional invasions of the private sphere are justified in order to protect the rights of others (Currie and Klaaren 2002: 65).

In terms of s 32(2), the constitutional right had to be given effect to by legislation before it came into operation. That legislation is the Promotion of Access to Information Act of 2000 ('the PAIA'). The Act came into effect on 9 March 2001. It gives legislative effect to s 32 of the Constitution, elaborating on the constitutional right, limiting it and providing mechanisms and procedures for its protection and enforcement. The right of access to information in South Africa therefore has a statutory basis and the role of the constitutional right is largely confined to the indirect role of informing the interpretation of the Act. The constitutional right remains directly applicable, however, in the adjudication of challenges to the provisions of the PAIA (see, for example, *Brümmer v Minister for Social Development*, a successful challenge to certain time-bar provisions in the PAIA). It will also be directly applicable to constitutional challenges to other legislation limiting the freedom of information rights, such as the official secrets legislation discussed further below. It will also be directly applicable in litigation seeking access to information that is not covered by the PAIA, such as court records (*Independent Newspapers (Pty) Ltd v Minister for Intelligence Services: In re Masetlha v President of the Republic of South Africa* para 23).

At the time of writing, the constitutional right of access to information and the possibility of a court challenge to legislation that is thought to have the effect of unjustifiably limiting has been, and remains front-page news. The cause is the government's attempt to replace South Africa's apartheid-era official secrets legislation. The resultant legislation, the Protection of State Information Bill, has been the subject of determined and largely successful opposition by a civil-society campaign. The campaign opposes what it regards as the Bill's restrictions on freedom of information and media freedom and characterises these as threatening to undermine the considerable progress that has been made in the protection, promotion and realisation of these fundamental principles since the democratic transition in 1994.

After numerous amendments, the Protection of State Information Bill (dubbed the 'Secrecy Bill' by its critics) was finally passed by Parliament in April 2013 and was referred to President Zuma for assent. In terms of s 79 of the Constitution, the President may decline to assent to a Bill and refer the Bill back to Parliament for reconsideration. This power is not a veto and may be used only where the President has reservations about the constitutionality of a Bill. Zuma was reported as saying that in his view 'the Bill would not pass constitutional muster' in the form that it had been presented to him. The President's reservations were however confined to two obscure sections of the Bill that had not hitherto attracted any notice from the Bill's opponents. Despite the limited scope of the referral, civil-society activists expressed the hope that Parliament would use the opportunity of reconsidering the Bill to attend to the other areas in which it was said to be constitutionally defective (Hartley 2013).

The ad hoc committee of Parliament, reconvened to consider the President's referral, ignored the calls of opposition parties and activists, and declined to revisit any aspect of the Bill other than the two particular sections highlighted in the referral. The committee also made certain textual corrections to the Bill before referring it to the plenary Parliament which passed Bill 6H of 2010 on 13 November 2013. As of late June 2014, President Zuma had not yet signed the corrected Bill.

Despite considerable cutting back of some of its more controversial features during the parliamentary process, the Bill's critics argue that it still has numerous constitutional flaws and have threatened court proceedings to challenge its constitutionality should it be enacted in its current form (Evans 2013).

The controversy over the Protection of State Information Bill provides a useful focus for this brief survey of the impact of the constitutional right to freedom of information in the 15 or so years since its first entrenchment. The adventures of the Bill since its introduction have highlighted both the achievements of South Africa's post-1994 freedom of information regime as well as some of its shortcomings. The debate over the Bill, in addition to a simultaneous law-reform process aimed at establishing a data-protection regime for South Africa, has provided a useful opportunity for a review of the PAIA and has permitted the correction of some of the defects that have so far inhibited it from fully achieving its purposes.

Evaluating the Effectiveness of the PAIA

On paper at least, the PAIA grants extensive freedom of information rights. Some ten years since its enactment, anecdotal evidence suggests that the PAIA request mechanism is routinely used by members of the public and by specialist NGOs, researchers and activists to obtain access to public-body information. There is also considerable evidence, however, that the Act is routinely maladministered and that the positive obligations imposed by the Act are widely ignored (Currie 2011).

Section 32 of the PAIA requires public bodies to submit annual reports to the South African Human Rights Commission detailing the number of requests for access to information received and dealt with by the public body concerned. The s 32 reports are therefore potentially an extremely useful source of data on the extent of the usage and implementation of the Act. However, according to the Commission, the obligation is routinely ignored by public bodies, particularly at the provincial and municipal level. The failure of many public bodies to report is frequently attributable to simple maladministration, but in some instances bodies, particularly at local government level, have justified their failure to comply on the basis that they have received no requests for access to information. If correct, this indicates a troubling lack of public awareness of the availability of the access rights (South African Human Rights Commission 2011: 153). Incomplete as they may be, the most recent set of s 32 reports made to the Commission revealed that about 15,000 requests are made annually to national government departments, of which some 700 are refused. A handful of these requests, following the compulsory internal appeal procedure, are referred to court for independent dispute resolution.

There are no comprehensive empirical studies available on the implementation of the Act. In the absence of such studies, much of the evidence available to researchers is anecdotal. Requesters have reported that PAIA requests are often dealt with extremely slowly, or, more troublingly, are simply ignored. There appears to have been little use by requesters of the private-sector provisions of the Act, but the extent to which the Act has had any impact on the private sector is almost impossible to measure (Currie 2011).

Reform of the PAIA's Enforcement Provisions

As noted above, one of the constitutionally mandated tasks of the PAIA is to promote access to information in the sense of providing accessible and user-friendly mechanisms to enforce the constitutional and statutory rights. The Act has, so far, largely failed in this endeavour.

In its draft form, the PAIA (then called the Open Democracy Bill – see Currie and Klaaren 2002: 7:9) envisaged that the rights of access to information would be enforced through a dispute-resolution process by an independent entity with the power of making authoritative and binding decisions. The specific recommendations of the Bill in this regard (entailing the establishment of a specialised division of the High Court and the creation of an Open Democracy Commission) were not accepted by Parliament on financial grounds. In the PAIA as enacted, disputes over access to information requests (after exhaustion of an internal appeal process in the case of public bodies) are to be litigated in the High Courts. The model adopted by many jurisdictions – of having a specialised information commission with duties of promotion and powers of dispute resolution – was not followed.

It is generally accepted that this arrangement is inadequate to ensure the effective achievement of the PAIA's goals. Litigation is self-evidently too inaccessible and cumbersome to be an effective means to enforce the freedom of information rights in the Act and in the Constitution (Ad Hoc Committee on the Review of Chapter 9 and Associated Institutions 2007: 174). For the extensive rights of access to information granted by PAIA to be more than rights on paper, provision must be made for resolution of access disputes by some form of independent tribunal. The tribunal must be easily accessible and it must be able to decide disputes authoritatively, cheaply, quickly and effectively. Because of the expense and inefficiencies associated with litigation in the ordinary courts, most jurisdictions opt for dispute resolution by a specialised information commission or by specialised administrative tribunals.

An opportunity to correct this long-standing problem with the Act has presented itself in the form of important cognate legislation that will create a statutory data-protection regime for South Africa. The proposals have their provenance in a study conducted by the South African Law Reform Commission, which proposed a new information protection authority with enforcement authority over both the PAIA and the data protection legislation (South African Law Reform Commission 2009). The proposals were included in the provisions of draft legislation formulated by the Commission.

That draft legislation was introduced in Parliament in 2009. After an exceptionally lengthy process of consideration by Parliament, it was passed in August 2013. Certain sections of the Protection of Personal Information Act came into effect on 11 April 2014. The remainder of the Act is expected to commence in the first half of 2015.

The Protection of Personal Information Act is general legislation to regulate the processing of personal information by public and private bodies. It follows the European model for data-protection regimes in that it centres on a set of 'conditions for lawful processing of personal information'. The 'conditions' (really, principles) flesh out a higher-level requirement that personal information must be processed lawfully and reasonably. The conditions create a framework of general rules for the processing of personal information, leaving the subsequent development of more detailed regulatory norms to an independent regulator. In what are likely to be its most important provisions, the Act establishes an independent governmental authority named the 'Information Regulator'.

The Information Regulator is intended to have supervisory powers in respect of both the Personal Information Act and the PAIA. In particular, the authority would be specifically empowered to resolve disputes under provisions of both PAIA and privacy legislation. The Information Regulator would be accessible as a dispute-resolution mechanism intermediate between internal appeal against decisions of public or private bodies and recourse to the courts, and would be empowered to make binding orders to resolve disputes. This reform would cure the long-standing deficiency of the PAIA: the absence of a specialised supervision body and the lack of an independent dispute-resolution mechanism intermediate between the internal appeal process and High Court litigation. Moreover, given the considerable degree of overlap between the functions of data protection and access to information, the institutional design of the proposed Regulator – a subject-specialised regulatory authority, necessarily equipped with considerable technical expertise in fields such as information systems and information security – is highly appropriate for supervision of the PAIA.

Limitation of Freedom of Information: The Protection of State Information Bill

The Protection of State Information Bill is the result of a law-reform process that commenced in the mid-2000s. In 2008, the bill was introduced in Parliament by the Ministry of Intelligence. It had as its principal aim the repeal and replacement of the existing state information classification law. It therefore proposed the repeal in its entirety of the Protection of Information Act 84 of 1982. This Act is currently South Africa's official secrets legislation. A tenacious survivor of the old order, it creates broad and absolute prohibitions on the disclosure of information the secrecy of which '[the discloser] knows or reasonably should know to be required by the security or the other interests of the Republic.' There is also a prohibition on the receipt of information in contravention of the Act.

The detailed regulation of the process of classification of information is not found in the 1982 Act but rather in a document known as the 'MISS' – the Minimum Information Security Standards (1996). This is a Cabinet document setting out the 'national information security policy' (Klaaren 2002).

Another principal object of the State Information Bill was to reconcile the necessity for a classification and information security regime with the constitutional principles of transparency and accountability in governance, as well as with individual rights. In regard to the latter, the Bill declared that it was one of its objects to 'harmonise the implementation of this Act with the Promotion of Access to Information Act, 2000'. It gave effect to this object by providing in essence (in clause 28 of the 2008 Bill) that the Bill was subject to the PAIA: 'A request for access to a classified record that is made in terms of the Promotion of Access to Information Act must be dealt with in terms of that Act.'

As drafted, the Bill intended to put into law a government duty to process important information in a secure manner that went far beyond the conventionally narrow protection of national security information. In this sense, the Bill was understood as a statutory mirror of the PAIA, imposing general duties on government to secure information that was identified by the PAIA as meriting protection against disclosure. The PAIA only stipulates rules for information processing by government *after receipt of a request* made in terms of the Act. The Information Bill was therefore intended to be an information-processing law: to provide general rules for the proper treatment and non-disclosure of important (the Bill used the term 'sensitive') government information, consistent with the PAIA.

The 2008 Bill was withdrawn from Parliament towards the end of 2008 after the committee dealing with the Bill had voiced serious difficulties with aspects of it. A revised version of the Bill was introduced into a newly-elected Parliament as the Protection of Information Bill 6 of 2010. The 2010 version of the Bill, which differed in important details from its predecessor, attracted and continues to attract unprecedented criticism. These criticisms, which had received only minimal public attention in 2008, soon generated a level of public concern and outrage that no other legislative development had merited since the democratic transition. The re-introduction of the Bill in 2010 came at a time when relations between the government on the one hand and the press and civil society on the other were at a low point. This has occasioned considerable suspicion about its purpose.

In such an atmosphere, the Bill was bound to be controversial. First, it is a legislative measure of considerable breadth (regulating information security across the whole spectrum of government) and depth (intending to regulate the secure processing of valuable government information, widely defined). Second, it is a Bill emanating from the state security sector and takes the form of an official secrets law with the attendant measures of classification and the criminalisation of espionage. The conclusion drawn by the Bill's opponents was therefore inevitable: that the Bill was intended to make most of the state's information an official secret and to criminalise the possession of such secrets. This would shut down the press, much of civil society and, for good measure, even academic research.

A scan of newspaper headlines from 2010 gives a sense of the tenor of this reaction: 'Assault on democracy', 'Zimbabwe-like', 'War on the press', 'Censorship reminiscent of the apartheid era'. The civil society reaction to the details of the Bill could be characterised as principally concerned with the broad scope of the Bill. The Bill was certainly broad in scope, particularly if compared to official secrets laws in other jurisdictions. But its scope was principally a product of its legislative history and its intention not only to provide for the protection of state secrets in the narrow sense but also to provide for a comprehensive regime of government confidentiality that would replace the existing regime. The Bill was a state information-processing law in the broad sense, in addition to being an official secrets law. But the ambitions of the Bill were difficult to reconcile with its provenance in the intelligence ministry and with its overall categorisation as state security legislation, providing as it did for a classification regime and for the prohibition of offences such as espionage and sabotage. Put another way, an official secrets law seemed a disconcertingly odd place to find provisions relating to the secure treatment of valuable information and general prohibitions on disclosure of sensitive information. The broad scope of the Bill, when combined with widespread suspicion about government's motives in introducing it, made plausible the frightening prospect that any piece of government information, no matter how innocuous, could be treated as if it were the most closely guarded state secret.

The government initially defended the Bill against its opponents. Despite this, the degree of condemnation of the Bill and the mobilisation of a wide range of civil society organisations against it, led the Minister of State Security to intervene. In a public statement released after briefing the parliamentary committee at its meeting of 22 October 2010, the Minister announced that several changes were to be made to the Bill and that a considerably revised version would be placed before Parliament. These changes, the first of many to the Bill, resulted in the deletion of Chapter 5 of the 2008 and 2010 Bills which had provided for the protection against disclosure and, in some cases, the classification of two categories of information: 'sensitive information' and 'commercial information'.

The removal of chapter 5 makes the resultant Act a far more conventional example of official secrets legislation. The principal criterion for classification is 'national security'. The definition of this criterion remains the same as it was in the 2008 and 2010 Bills and is relatively narrowly defined, specifically excluding 'lawful political activity, advocacy, protest or dissent'.

With the fundamental reduction in the scope of application of the Act, much of the original concern about its impact on freedom of information has dissipated.

The opponents of the Act are, at this stage, principally concerned about a perceived chilling effect on media freedom and on whistleblowing created by criminal offences that would punish the publication of classified information without reference to the possibility of a defence that the public interest in publication outweighs the harm to national security.

There is, however, a potential conflict between the Act and the right of access to information created by the deletion, in the last stages of the parliamentary process, of the provisions described above designed to harmonise the Bill with the PAIA. As we saw above, as originally drafted, the State Information Bill was subject to the PAIA. A request for classified information would accordingly have been dealt with in terms of the PAIA, including its grounds for refusal and its dispute-resolution mechanisms. The retention of this provision would have had the implication that the reform of the PAIA's enforcement mechanisms, described above, would have applied also to dispute resolution in terms of the Protection of State Information Bill. But, with the removal of this provision, the Protection of State Information Act now directly limits the PAIA and therefore also the constitutional right of access to information.

Someone making a request for classified information must follow the request procedure in the PAIA. What follows, however, is a separate process of consideration of the request, governed not by the PAIA but by s 19 of the Protection of State Information Act. The key criteria are the enumerated 'principles of state information' which govern the classifiability of information in state hands. Essentially, a request for access to information will trigger a review of the classification by the head of the state body that holds the information. The criteria for this review are the classifiability of the information, rather than, as in previous drafts, the criteria for refusal of access to information in the PAIA.

This problematic and last-minute adjustment to the Bill has made it inevitable that there will be a constitutional challenge based not only on the media freedom right, but also on the right of freedom of information.

Conclusion

An assessment of the implementation of South Africa's freedom of information rights is likely to reach mixed conclusions. On the one hand, the rights have ensured the reversal of the old-order presumption against access to official information. The rights are routinely, though unevenly, invoked and relied upon. In a number of high-profile court decisions, information activists and journalists have secured important victories.

On the other hand, the constitutional right and the PAIA, particularly the proactive obligations of the latter, are frequently ignored or maladministered by public bodies. The recent developments in relation to the Protection of State Information Bill have highlighted some of the vulnerabilities of the current statutory regime. At the same time, however, the controversy that aspects of the

Bill have elicited is an encouraging indication of the willingness of South African citizens to defend their hard-won rights to freedom of information.

References

Books, book chapters and articles

Currie, I. 2011. 'Freedom of information and the constitution', *Diritto Pubblico Comparato ed Europeo*, IV: 1363–74.

—— and J. Klaaren, 2002. *The Promotion of Access to Information Commentary.* Cape Town: Siber Ink.

Evans, S. 'Opposition Hopes for Secrecy Bill Court Review', *Mail & Guardian* <http://www.mg.co.za> [accessed 6 August 2013].

Hartley, W. 2013. 'Zuma Now Has Doubts about ANC's "Secrecy Bill"', *Business Day*, 13 September.

Klaaren, J. 2002. 'National Information Insecurity: Constitutional Issues Regarding the Protection and Disclosure of Information by Public Officials', *South African Law Journal*, 119: 721.

South African Broadcasting Corporation, 2013. 'Zuma's Legal Advisors Check Constitutionality of Info Bill. SABC News' <http://www.sabc.co.za/news> [accessed 6 August 2013].

Reports

Ad Hoc Committee on the Review of Chapter 9 and Associated Institutions. 2007. *Report of the Ad Hoc Committee on the Review of Chapter 9 and Associated Institutions* (*Asmal Report*).

South African Human Rights Commission, *Annual Report 2011.*

South African Law Reform Commission, *Report on Privacy and Data Protection, February 2009.*

Cases

Brümmer v Minister for Social Development and others 2009 (6) SA 323 (CC).

Independent Newspapers (Py) Ltd v Minister for Intelligence Services: In re Masetlha v President of the Republic of South Africa 2008 (5) SA 31 (CC).

Unitas Hospital v Van Wyk 2006 (4) SA 436 (SCA).

Legislation

Constitution of the Republic of South Africa, 1996.

Promotion of Access to Information Act 2 of 2000.

Protection of Information Act 84 of 1982.
Protection of Personal Information Act 4 of 2013.
Protection of State Information Bill (B 6H-2010).

PART IV
Transformative Constitutionalism

Chapter 13

Constitutional Reform in South African History

Hugh Corder

> This Constitution provides a historic bridge between the past of a deeply divided society characterised by strife, conflict, untold suffering and injustice, and a future founded on the recognition of human rights, democracy and peaceful co-existence and development opportunities for all South Africans, irrespective of colour, race, class, belief or sex.
> ('Postamble', National Unity and Reconciliation, 1993 Constitution of South Africa)

The history of public governance in South Africa is overwhelmingly characterised by the imposition of constitutional systems, to suit sectoral needs. Using the rule of law as the organising theme, my intention in this chapter is to sketch the process of constitutional development over the past century, emphasising the enormity of the shift in the basic norm which underlies the current Constitution. I will also review those constitutional amendments which have been adopted since 1996, and speculate on likely pressures for further reform.

As the definition of the rule of law is contested, it is imperative to sketch my understanding of it. Its primary meaning must be that all people and governmental bodies function subject to the law (or 'rule by law'). Secondly, the 'law' must comply with certain formal prerequisites in order to be valid, such as that it must be sufficiently certain in meaning and likely impact, prospective in effect, promulgated and widely publicised, and enacted by the appropriate law-making authority under the constitution. It must possess an 'inner morality' (Fuller 1986: ch 2). Thirdly, it is increasingly required that any legal rule must attain a minimum level of compliance with a number of fundamental human rights, *at least* of the civil-political type (such as equality, dignity and basic freedoms) and even a foundational level of provision of socio-economic rights. This aspect of the definition has become widely accepted after the Second World War, including in South Africa (Mathews 1986: 20).

Using this working definition, I proceed to evaluate the varying fortunes of the South African Constitution over the past century, with the emphasis on the last two decades.

The Development of Constitutional Government in South Africa

The four territories which made up the Union of South Africa in 1910 were British colonies before union, but with contrasting constitutional histories. The Cape Colony had been ruled by the Dutch for the first 150 years of European settlement, and then by the British for just longer than a century. Based on the Westminster system, it had relatively well-developed institutions and processes of responsible government. The Natal government was notionally similar, but the Transvaal and Orange Free State had remarkably different constitutional origins.

Both these 'Afrikaner republics' had adopted written constitutions in the 1850s, which had provided basic rights for their citizens (narrowly defined so as to exclude 'non-Afrikaners' and women), so that the notion of constitutional supremacy has a longer-standing pedigree in South Africa than is often assumed. The superficial similarity, however, hid two 'widely divergent ... constitutional traditions'. In Thompson's view (1954: 73), the Orange Free State had a rigid constitution loosely based on the American model; the judiciary acted independently, and the *Volksraad* (or Parliament) stayed within its legislative powers, whereas the *Zuid Afrikaansche Republiek* had the opposite experience.

South Africa's first Constitution (the South Africa Act) of 1910, mirrored its British parent, establishing legislative sovereignty in Parliament, an executive headed by a Prime Minister and Cabinet who were members of Parliament, a superior court judiciary headed by a Chief Justice in the only court with national appellate jurisdiction, an electoral system based on first-past-the-post constituency representation, and so on. However, it differed from its imperial parent in critical respects, none more so than that the franchise was reserved for those classified as 'European' (later 'white') in most of the country. (No account of the history, or indeed current situation, of South Africa can avoid the use of racial typology. In this chapter, 'black' refers to black Africans, 'coloured' refers to people of mixed race, 'Indian' refers to those who originated in Asia, while 'white' refers to those of European extraction.) The exceptional province was the Cape, which preserved its non-racial franchise when it entered the Union. Of course, the franchise was limited only to men throughout the country, until the Women's Enfranchisement Act of 1930 extended the vote, but only to 'European' women. In addition, Parliament was bound to follow a special process (set out in ss 35, 137 and 152) when amending the South Africa Act in two respects: when altering the status of English and Afrikaans as official languages, and when amending the non-racial character of the franchise in the Cape. This was an effective curb on parliamentary sovereignty and, to a very limited extent, a guarantor of the rule of law, as it acted as a retarding influence on the ease of abolition of the interests entrenched.

The basic structure of constitutional government remained broadly modelled on Westminster until 1983, but this formal adherence was not matched by governmental practice. Crucially, the 'sense of fair play' and the innate respect for the 'rule of law', essential to the *informal limitations* imposed by the legislative and executive bodies on the exercise of their own power, benefited only the electorate. Such limitations were increasingly eroded when the apartheid regime unleashed its massive programme of race-based social engineering in the early 1950s and when Parliament enacted increasingly invasive measures in the name of the preservation of 'state security' later that decade (Dugard 1978). This tendency reached a crescendo of 'state lawlessness' in the second half of the 1980s (Budlender 1988), when emergency powers were invoked by the executive, in what in retrospect were the death-throes of apartheid.

Constitutional amendments were generally not needed to implement the measures which laid the foundations in law of the apartheid policy, as Parliament was authorised to make law for the 'peace, order and good government' of the country (South Africa Act: s 59). It is important to note that the apartheid regime followed a formally legalistic course, save for the last five years of its rule. In other words, race classification and all the injustice which flowed from it were authorised by Acts of Parliament, subordinate legislation, and the formal allocation of discretion to government officials. Some argued that this amounted to compliance with at least 'rule by law', while others (Meierhenrich 2008) argue that this provides some explanation for the fact that an entrenched Constitution and judicial review are the cornerstones of the current Constitution.

However, constitutional amendments were needed to remove the franchise from those not classified 'white'. This occurred in two stages. The National Party government in the 1930s legislated to remove all 'native' voters from the common electoral roll (Representation of Natives Act). Parliament duly observed the procedural strictures of the entrenched clauses in adopting this law, which served formally to emphasise the value of constitutional constraints on unlimited legislative authority.

The second attempt to change the franchise qualifications caused the 'coloured vote constitutional crisis'. In implementing apartheid after 1948, Parliament passed legislation which placed 'coloured' voters on a separate voters' roll. The widespread opposition to this step, both within and outside the electorate, included a series of legal challenges (*Harris I and II* and *Collins*) to the government's failure to follow the entrenched procedures. After six years and an election in which the National Party achieved electoral gains, the highest court eventually succumbed to the cumulative effects of legislative pressure (Forsyth 1985). The resolve of the appellate judges was also affected by the almost doubling of their complement and the elevation to their ranks of those who were unlikely to resist Parliament's perseverance.

This cynical circumvention of constitutional guarantees marks out South Africa's constitutional history, and sets a potentially damaging precedent whereby the popular will trumps the rule of law. While the Appellate Division initially established important 'manner and form' standards to be complied with by all legislatures, its subsequent submission to legislative injustice was both an acknowledgement of the limits of judicial authority under the separation of powers, as well as a telling blow to its independence and stature.

South Africa adopted two further constitutions before the end of apartheid. The first (Constitution Act 1961) was enacted following the country's expulsion from the British Commonwealth, and amounted to a 'domestication' of the South Africa Act. The last constitutional change was a desperate gamble to stave off the inevitable arrival of majority rule, although the government touted it as progressive. This was the 'tricameral' Constitution (1983), which brought adult 'coloured' and Indian citizens into Parliament, but in separate Houses. Unsurprisingly, the proportions of MPs (white, coloured and Indian) were 4:2:1, which meant that the House representing whites would always be able to trump even the combined forces of the other two Houses. The further key consequence of this constitutional arrangement was that almost 80 per cent of the population was effectively excluded from participation in government, the theory being that black South Africans should give expression to their political views through the governing bodies set up in the rural 'homelands' to which they were allocated on 'ethnic' grounds, and through the equally discredited urban local authorities set up to administer the segregated black townships in the major cities.

The fundamental illegitimacy of this monstrous experiment predictably provoked a storm of protest, which culminated in the government losing effective control over many urban areas, necessitating rule by emergency powers from mid-1985. Taken together with the concerted efforts of exile groupings and the anti-apartheid movement in the developed world to force the implementation of trade, financial, cultural and sporting sanctions against South Africa, and with the demise of Soviet hegemony in central and eastern Europe and the disappearance of the 'communist threat' in Southern Africa, the apartheid regime relinquished control over Namibia in 1989 and freed political prisoners and 'normalised' political activity within South Africa in February 1990.

In sum, therefore, constitutional reform in this first stage of South Africa's history was characterised by the *decolonising pull away* from the imperial power until 1960, and by the increasingly devious attempts by successive white minority governments to justify the *exclusion from participation in government and access to basic rights of the vast majority of its citizens*. These were accompanied throughout by a decline in respect for the Constitution as anything more than a manipulable formula for formalising racist power, and by the abandonment of any real pretence at adherence to the core values of the rule of law. The last two decades have been dedicated to attempts to deal with this traumatic history, and to build a governing culture worthy of the values set out in the Constitution.

The Revolution: 1990–96

Constitutional reform was naturally foremost on the political agenda throughout this period, and it amounted to a thoroughgoing revolution of the institutions and manner of public governance in every form. The current task is to reflect critically on the most influential pressures for adopting the model currently in place.

There is no doubt that South Africa benefited from substantial shifts in the balance of world political power around 1990. The fall of the Berlin Wall in 1989 led to a burst of constitution-making in most constituent parts of the former Soviet Union, with a heightened emphasis on limited government under law and the protection of basic rights under an independent judicial authority. This coincided with the thinking of most constitutional scholars concerned with the future of South Africa. For example, the work of the South African Law Commission (1989, 1991) on 'Group and Human Rights', made the protection of individual rather than 'group' human rights acceptable in government circles. Again, the exiled African National Congress (ANC) had a long history of adherence to the idea of charters of rights, chief among them the *African Claims* of 1943, the *Freedom Charter* of 1955, and the *Constitutional Guidelines* of 1988. Several meetings which took place outside South Africa from 1987 to 1989 strengthened common understanding between constitutionalists on all sides of the political divides. In the intense negotiating process which ensued from 1990 to 1993, such individuals were able to bring considerable persuasive influence to bear on the groups which they were advising.

Most commentators agree that the essential elements in the transition from apartheid to democracy were as follows: primarily, that the process was as inclusive as possible and that 34 fundamental principles of constitutional governance, which would be mandatory in any final constitution, were agreed on during negotiations between late 1991 and early 1994, as was the idea that there should be a phased transfer of power and a process of drafting a lasting Constitution, starting in January 1994 and ending in June 1999.

Further essential elements of the transition were: the negotiating process was largely 'closed', which allowed deals to be brokered outside the glare of media attention; a willingness to acknowledge and accommodate the views of others, even if strongly divergent from one's own, prevailed; there was immensely strong leadership from the two main political groupings, assisted by astute strategic thinking and action by hard-working and dedicated negotiators on the ground; disputes which threatened to derail the negotiations were frequently referred to 'technical committees', staffed mainly by lawyers, which usually resulted in a face-saving compromise which the negotiators were relieved to accept as the advice of 'experts'; the drafters and negotiating parties learned many lessons from the constitutional experience of other countries; and the notion of 'sufficient consensus' was used as the basis for determining progress where unanimity could not be achieved.

The first constitutional product of these tense years was the interim Constitution of 1993. While formally a law passed by the tricameral Parliament, thus preserving legislative continuity, it amounted to confirmation of what had been agreed at the negotiations. It was amended twice before the first election in April 1994 to appease parties who were holding out on participation in the elections, and on several occasions during its life, but such changes were immaterial. Perhaps most importantly, in the theme of this chapter, was this Constitution's foundation in the notion of constitutional supremacy, and its unwritten subscription to the rule of law (1993 Constitution: s 4).

Much more could be written about this Constitution, but it is perhaps sufficient to note that it provided the framework for, and a considerable proportion of the substance of, the final Constitution; that, while government was conducted according to its provisions from mid-May 1994 until early February 1997, the newly elected Parliament doubled as a Constitutional Assembly to draft the final Constitution; and that the first text produced within the two-year deadline and submitted to the Constitutional Court was referred to the Constitutional Assembly because it failed in seven important respects to comply with the Constitutional Principles (*Certification of the Constitution I*). The amended text was finally certified as sufficiently compliant (*Certification of the Constitution II*), which allowed President Mandela to sign it into law on 10 December 1996.

The final Constitution (1996) has the following significant features concerning the rule of law and constitutional supremacy. The 'Founding Provisions' in s 1 encapsulate many of the values which underlay the Constitutional Principles. So we see pre-eminence given to human dignity, equality, freedom, non-racialism and non-sexism, *the supremacy of the Constitution and the rule of law*, and the necessity for free and fair elections and a multi-party system of democratic government, 'to ensure accountability, responsiveness and openness'(1996 Constitution: s 1). The importance of these values is emphasised by the fact that any proposed amendment requires a 75 per cent majority in the National Assembly, as well as the approval of six of the nine provincial legislatures, whereas any other provision of the Constitution needs only two-thirds support in the Assembly plus six provincial legislatures (s 74).

The rest of the Constitution further emphasises the rule of law and constitutional supremacy. The Bill of Rights (chapter 2) contains a relative novelty in that the rights of access to information (s 32) and to court (s 34), and to administrative justice (s 33) have been included. The inclusion of such rights was justified by the desire not to allow a resurgence of the gross abuse of discretionary authority by government under apartheid. There can be no doubt that this is one avenue through which the rule of law has gained prominence as a formal requirement of the constitutional system.

A final noteworthy aspect of the Bill of Rights is the set of instructions given to judges who interpret its provisions (s 39). Not only must they 'promote the values that underlie an open and democratic society based on human dignity, equality and freedom', they 'must consider international law', and 'may consider foreign law'. This deliberate placing of the South African Constitution within the vanguard of constitutional good government internationally adds to its stature nationally, and strengthens the hold of the rule of law.

The Constitution further strongly emphasises public consultation and participation in the law-making activities of Parliament (s 59), as well as Parliament's obligation to hold the executive accountable (s 55(2)). In the executive, both individual and collective ministerial responsibility are stressed (s 92(2)), and all executive action is subject to scrutiny according to the provisions of the Constitution, including those presidential powers formerly regarded as 'prerogative' (s 84(2), and *President of the RSA v Hugo*). A united national court system at both superior and magisterial levels is provided for (chapter 8), with the Constitutional Court (CC, headed by the Chief Justice) as the final authority on all matters, both constitutional and common-law in nature, at its discretion. The Supreme Court of Appeal (SCA) and all the High Courts in the country have constitutional as well as 'common-law' jurisdiction. Superior court judges are appointed on recommendation of the Judicial Service Commission (JSC) made up from diverse constituencies. The 'State Institutions Supporting Constitutional Democracy', such as the Public Protector, Auditor General, Electoral Commission, Human Rights Commission, Commission for Gender Equality, and so on, must develop good governance practices consistent with the Constitution (chapter 9).

Finally, the remaining chapters (10 to 14) include express authorisation for the authority of customary international law as part of South African law, unless 'inconsistent with the Constitution or an Act of Parliament' (s 232), and provide for governance subject to the Constitution and the rule of law.

This Constitution has been in place for 17 years, and most observers agree that its objective is to turn a 'culture of authority' into a 'culture of justification' (Mureinik 1994). Indeed, one of its remarkable features is the extent to which non-state actors are expected to comply with its basic principles. However, no matter how well canvassed and drafted, every constitution must be capable of amendment, and the recent origins of the South African Constitution have not shielded it from demands for its alteration.

Continuing Transformation

The Constitution had been amended on 17 occasions by the end of 2013. These amendments fall arguably into three categories: those of a formal nature, those necessitated by practical necessity, and those with substantial effect on the constitutional text. Some of the amending Acts contain elements of more than one of these categories, but there is no readily discernible pattern underlying them all.

The formal amendments (First 1997, Second 1998, Sixth 2001, Eleventh 2003 and Twelfth Amendment 2005) have provided for largely uncontroversial name changes for places and officers, some substantive changes, and for other relatively technical matters. The amendments dictated by practical necessity (Third 1998, Fourth and Fifth Amendment 1999) have concerned common-sense matters such as classifying cross-provincial border municipalities, the timing of the announcement of elections, and how to allocate undistributed delegates in the proportional representation electoral system. None of these amendments threatens the core values of constitutional supremacy and the rule of law; it is the third category which has potential impact on those fundamentals

Let us start with a set of five constitutional amendments which stirred much political emotion, dealing with the constitutionality of 'floor-crossing' at all three levels of government. Given an electoral system based on proportional representation, whether a member of the legislature elected under the banner of one party, or the entire party itself, can lawfully join another party between elections, while retaining their elected status, raises important questions. Political circumstances in 2002 made it acceptable for the ruling party to accept the legitimacy of such floor-crossing, and three acts amending the Constitution (Eighth and Ninth 2002, and Tenth 2003) duly provided for this. The ANC gained most from these arrangements, but the cynical misuse of this practice continued to create unease and the Constitution was amended again twice (Fourteenth 2007 and Fifteenth 2009) to abolish floor-crossing. So the process has come full circle, but not without damage to the integrity and legitimacy of representative government. This also shows a disturbing willingness by most political parties to act against the spirit of the Constitution, when it suited them.

A second and deeply controversial pair of amendments (Twelfth 2006 and Thirteenth 2007) was the result of the determination of the ANC leadership to change the provincial boundaries of four of the provinces so as to eliminate cross-border municipalities. Such changes effectively moved tens of thousands of people from a better-run and wealthier province to a more inefficient and poorer one, and in each case a substantial majority of such residents determinedly resisted such changes. Several court battles at the highest level (*Matatiele* 2006 and *Merafong* 2008) were not ultimately able to resist executive will, with the result that the Constitution was amended to reflect these shifts. Like the floor-crossing saga, however, but for reasons of a change in ANC leadership in late 2007, Merafong was reincorporated into Gauteng (Sixteenth Amendment 2009).

Other substantive matters which have been changed in the Constitution are to be found in the Sixth (2001), Seventh (2001), Eleventh (2003) and Seventeenth (2012) Amendments. These concerned among other things the manner of enacting financial legislation in Parliament; the authority vested in a higher level of government to intervene in the affairs of a dysfunctional governmental authority beneath it; the lengthening of the Constitutional Court justices' terms of office; and far-reaching changes to aspects of the jurisdiction and operations of the judiciary. The most controversial among these were the last two.

First, the changes in terms of judicial office brought about by the Sixth Amendment. When it was decided that a Constitutional Court with final say over the interpretation of constitutional power should be part of the future South Africa, it was accepted that independence and accountability would be best served by appointing its judges for a fixed term of office. The final Constitution (s 176(1)) determined this uncontroversially at twelve years. However, in order mainly to allow the then Chief Justice, the much-respected Arthur Chaskalson, to remain on the Bench for a year or two longer, the government attempted to bring the terms of office of constitutional justices in line with those of all other judges. Regrettably, this happened just before the expiry of his term, and the apparently 'personal' nature of this proposal proved deeply embarrassing to the Chief Justice. The amendment also drew substantial opposition from those who opposed it in principle (see Du Bois 2002). In the end, a compromise was reached at a term of 15 years, with some qualifications, but damage had been done.

Secondly, many necessary changes to the way that the courts were managed and operated required attention in the constitutional era, and discussions between judicial leadership and the executive to achieve a mutually acceptable resolution have taken place for some 15 years or so. These negotiations finally bore fruit in the Superior Courts Act of 2013. In anticipation of the latter, the Constitution Seventeenth Amendment Act was assented to by the President in early 2013, and came into force in August of that year. Besides redesignating the High Court as a single body with 'divisions' in the various regional centres (s 2, amending s 166(c)) and providing that labour and competition law appeals will effectively no longer lie from the specialist appeal courts to the SCA (s 4, amending s 168(3)(a)), the Amendment achieves several significant changes.

First, it provides that the Chief Justice is 'the head of the judiciary' and exercises 'responsibility over the establishment and monitoring of norms and standards for the exercise of the judicial functions of all courts' (s 1, amending s 165). This may be an encouraging sign as far as the rule of law is concerned, as it has been interpreted as giving the judicial branch of government an appropriate degree of managerial and financial independence. Work on providing a framework of governance for the courts has been pursued by the Office of the Chief Justice (proclaimed formally as a department of state) since late 2010. The exact model preferred, and whether the executive branch will be willing to accept a fair degree of autonomy in judicial governance, remain in doubt. This amendment also throws into the spotlight the qualities needed of a Chief Justice in future, given the substantial managerial capacity and political acumen required.

The second important amendment establishes the CC as the highest court for every justiciable issue. The desirability of having an 'apex court' has generated sharp divisions within the judicial and legal community. In the end, a compromise was reached: besides constitutional matters, the CC may hear 'any other matter, if [it] grants leave to appeal on the grounds that the matter raises an arguable point of law of general public importance which ought to be considered by [it]', criteria the application of which are within the jurisdiction of the CC (s 3, amending s 167(3)). The third noteworthy amendment belatedly formalises the appointment of one of the CC justices as Deputy Chief Justice, and of acting CC justices, when there is a vacancy or the incumbent is absent (s 9, amending s 175(1)).

Finally, some constitutional amendments have been triggered by decisions of the Constitutional Court. For example, the Constitution Eighteenth Amendment Bill of 2009 (not yet enacted) proposes to remedy the difficulties identified by the Court in *Nyathi v MEC for Department of Health, Gauteng, and Another* in holding the state liable for its debts.

So it seems that, now that many 'technical problems' have been ironed out and anticipating that subsequent judgments of the Court will necessitate constitutional amendments infrequently, future amendments may signal a desire to change the substance of a constitutional provision, prompting the question of whether the change fits the overall values and logic of the constitutional model.

Constitutional Review

The Constitution (s 45(1)(c)) itself requires Parliament to establish a Constitutional Review Committee to review the working of the Constitution at least annually. A reading of three of this committee's recent reports (2007, 2009, 2011) reveals that the committee discharges its responsibility by advertising annually, calling for public submissions on changes needed to the Constitution. It then refers such submissions (usually about a dozen) to the Legal Services Office of Parliament, and debates them itself. The overwhelming majority of submissions elicit the comment that no amendment to the Constitution is necessitated. Some concerns are referred to a particular government department or local authority for attention, while yet others are referred to the relevant parliamentary committee. Thus there is, at a public level, a continuing engagement by Parliament with the need for amending the Constitution.

Political factors within the dominant majority party, however, are much more likely to lead to pressure for constitutional amendment, and these may from time to time threaten the maintenance of the rule of law and constitutional supremacy. Tensions between the three arms of government according to the doctrine of the separation of powers are bound to arise, even in stable democracies of long standing. If one considers the tortured and divisive history of South Africa, the degree of comity which has existed between the judiciary on the one hand and the executive and legislature on the other is surprising. In my view (Corder 2009), this is a tribute both to the political leadership displayed by President Mandela during the critical first five years of democracy, as well as the political sensitivity of the judicial leadership, particularly in the CC (see also Roux 2009). However, this does not mean that this Court has shied away from political issues. Indeed, the first judgment handed down (*Makwanyane* 1995) controversially declared the death penalty to be unconstitutional. Nor has the Court been afraid to confront other instances of executive and legislative unlawfulness, but it has generally expressed its views in a nuanced and non-offensive manner which has allowed those who needed to remedy their actions to do so without losing face politically.

With the passage of time, however, and as political and judicial leadership have changed, it was perhaps inevitable that tensions would arise and that the executive would be tempted to seek a more pliant judiciary, even while maintaining the essential foundations of judicial independence and impartiality. This area of political life provides a good focus for identifying the pressures which are likely to lead to constitutional changes, and must be closely monitored.

Continuing socio-economic inequalities and the failure by executive government speedily and efficiently to address them also place considerable strain on the supremacy of the Constitution and the rule of law. Whereas the Constitution provides the explicit rationale for the narrowing of the socio-economic disparities in its strong endorsement of socio-economic rights, political frustrations translate paradoxically into impatience with the 'counter-majoritarian' and participative nature of the democracy which is at the heart of the Constitution. The courts are increasingly the target of populist political attacks because they frequently provide the forum for exposing deficient or unlawful (and sometimes unconstitutional) conduct. Twenty years after the advent of freedom, much of the leadership in government (except at the most senior level) was not involved in the struggles for democracy, and even President Zuma has on occasion appeared not to understand the basic nature of the constitutional democracy in place. This has caused subtle shifts in the balance of political power, as the government uses its majority voice on the JSC to ensure that more amenable lawyers are appointed as judges, and as those judges already on the Bench begin to express themselves more cautiously when faced with aberrant conduct by the rest of government. This could even be seen as an unspoken amendment of the interpretation of the Constitution, if not its provisions.

Concern about the maintenance and even strengthening of the rule of law and the supremacy of the Constitution is clearly present, despite frequent assurances from the ANC government that it is committed to the Constitution. This commitment should be there, because the basic principles of the Constitution accord with much in that party's tradition, and as it was the majority party when the Constitution was drafted and adopted. At this stage, there seems to be little reason for pessimism about the future of these core elements of South Africa's constitutional democracy, but a good dose of vigilance would not go amiss.

References

Books, book chapters and articles

Budlender, G. 1988. 'Law and Lawlessness in South Africa', *South African Journal on Human Rights*, 4(2): 139–52.

Corder, H. 2009. 'On Stormy Waters: South Africa's Judges (and Politicians) Test the Limits of Their Authority', Geoffrey Sawer Memorial Lecture, Australian National University, unpublished.

Du Bois, F. 2002. "'Tenure on the Constitutional Court', *South African Law Journal*, 119: 1–17.

Dugard, C.J.R. 1978. *Human Rights and the South African Legal Order*. Princeton, NJ: Princeton University Press.

Forsyth, C. 1985. *In Danger for Their Talents: A Study of the Record of the Appellate Division of the Supreme Court of South Africa 1950–80*. Cape Town: Juta.

Fuller, L.L. 1986. *The Morality of Law*, revised edn. New Haven, CT and London: Yale University Press.
Mathews, A.S. 1986. *Freedom, State Security and the Rule of Law*. Cape Town: Juta.
Meierhenrich, J. 2008. *The Legacies of Law Long-Run Consequences of Legal Development in South Africa, 1652–2000*. Cambridge: Cambridge University Press.
Mureinik, E. 1994. 'A Bridge to Where?: Introducing the interim Bill of Rights', *South African Journal on Human Rights*, 10: 31.
Roux, T. 2009. 'Principle and Pragmatism on the Constitutional Court of South Africa', *International Journal of Constitutional Law*, 7: 106–38.
Thompson, L.M. 1954. 'Constitutionalism in the South African Republics' *Butterworths South African Law Review*: 49–72.

Reports

South African Law Commission (Project on Group and Human Rights) *Working Paper* of 1989 and *Interim Report* of 1991.

Cases

Collins v Minister of the Interior 1957(1) SA 552 (AD).
Harris v Minister of the Interior 1952(2) SA 428 (AD).
In Re Certification of the Constitution of the Republic of South Africa, 1996 1996(4) SA 744 (CC).
In Re Certification of the Amended Text of the Constitution of the Republic of South Africa, 1996 1997(2) SA 97 (CC).
Matatiele Municipality and Others v President of the RSA and Others 2006(5) SA 47 (CC).
Merafong Demarcation Forum v President of the RSA and Others 2008(5) SA 171 (CC).
Minister of the Interior v Harris 1952(4) SA 769 (AD).
Nyathi v MEC for Department of Health, Gauteng, and Another 2008(5) SA 94 (CC).
President of the RSA v Hugo 1997(4) SA 1 (CC).
S v Makwanyane 1995(3) SA 391 (CC).

Legislation

Constitution of the Republic of South Africa, Act 200 of 1993 (Interim Constitution).
Constitution of the Republic of South Africa, Act 108 of 1996 (Final Constitution)
Representation of Natives Act, 12 of 1936.
Republic of South Africa Constitution Act, 32 of 1961.

Republic of South Africa Constitution Act, 110 of 1983.
South Africa Act, 9 Edw VII, ch 9, 1909.
Women's Enfranchisement Act, 18 of 1930.

Chapter 14

The Position of Indigenous Customary Law in South Africa's New Constitutional Order

Tom Bennett

Historical Background

In order to understand the present position of customary law in South Africa's legal system, some idea of the history of this subject is needed. From the mid-nineteenth century, the colonial powers formally recognised the indigenous laws of Southern Africa and the courts applying them. This was done, however, not through any sense of enlightened toleration for cultural difference, but rather because the colonial authorities realised that it would be impossible to enforce alien laws on their subjects. In this way, a de facto system of indirect rule came about, although it was only in the 1920s that it was elevated to an official policy in other parts of Anglophone Africa (Bennett 1985: 46–7).

Recognition of customary law and the chiefly courts was none the less restricted by the overall justification for colonial rule: to assimilate the natives to European notions of Christianity and British civilisation. As a result, certain practices, such as initiation dances and child marriage, were banned, and customary law was subject to a so-called 'repugnancy proviso', which meant that it had to conform to 'the general principles of humanity observed throughout the civilized world' (Peart 1982: 110ff).

In the 1920s, the government of the Union of South Africa instituted a dramatic change of policy. The idea of assimilation was abandoned in favour of segregation. The Native Administration Act of 1927 accordingly made customary law applicable only in a special system of courts constituted by traditional leaders and native commissioners. This regime was given its decidedly racist stamp by a rule that these courts were reserved for blacks only. Hence, when apartheid appeared in 1948, the foundation of segregation had already been laid, and the incoming government had only to elaborate the existing laws and tighten up their enforcement.

The next relevant turning point in South Africa's legal history came with the promulgation of the first democratic Constitution in 1993. Until then, although customary law had been generally recognised, it was still regarded as a minor component of the legal system, subordinate in all respects to the common law. (In South Africa, when this term is used in opposition to customary law, it means the combination of English and Roman-Dutch law, as developed by judicial precedents and legislation.) The new Constitution provided an occasion for carefully rethinking the legal order (Sachs 1990: 24).

At first, there was some talk of 'africanising' the law, but this idea was soon forgotten, and the common law maintained its dominant position. In fact, serious attention was paid to customary law only late in the negotiating process. In August 1993, traditional rulers were admitted to the Multi-Party Negotiating Process, largely as a result of bargains struck with the National Party and the ANC, whereby the chiefs were promised that their traditional system would be maintained in the future legal order (Albertyn 1994: 57–60). This requirement was translated into s 211(3) of the final Constitution: 'The courts must apply customary law when that law is applicable, subject to the Constitution and any legislation that specifically deals with customary law.'

In addition, the final Constitution guaranteed the rights to culture, language and religion:

> Section 30
>
> Everyone has the right to use the language and to participate in the cultural life of their choice, but no one exercising these rights may do so in a manner inconsistent with any provision of the Bill of Rights.
>
> Section 31
>
> (1) Persons belonging to a cultural, religious or linguistic community may not be denied the right, with other members of that community -
> (a) to enjoy their culture, practise their religion and use their language; and
> (b) to form, join and maintain cultural, religious and linguistic associations and other organs of civil society.
>
> (2) The rights in subsection (1) may not be exercised in a manner inconsistent with any provision of the Bill of Rights.

As a result of these provisions, customary law now enjoys a special status in the South African legal system, primarily because it is based on a guaranteed right to culture (unlike the common law). When read in conjunction with other provisions in the Constitution, such as s 39(2), it can no longer be assumed that English and Roman-Dutch law are the 'common law' of the land. Customary law, as the personal law of the great majority of the population, has become its equal *(S v Makwanyane and Another* 1995).

Nevertheless, the application of customary law is subject to three conditions. It must, first of all, be 'applicable', which implies a determination by the courts, in accordance with statutory and judge-made choice of law rules governing conflicts of personal law, that it is appropriate in the circumstances of the case (Bennett 2004: 49–68). In the second place, it is deemed to be repealed to the extent that it is inconsistent with legislation. Thirdly, customary law must always give way to the Bill of Rights in terms of an internal limitation clause in ss 30 and 31.

While the Constitution brought about a radical change to the status of customary law, it had no immediate effect on the system of courts applying that law. Magistrates' courts and the High Court continue to operate primarily in terms of the common law. Only one concession is allowed for the cultural orientation of African litigants: the courts may take judicial notice of customary law, provided that it is sufficiently certain and readily ascertainable (s 1(1) of Act 45 of 1988). If not, it must be proved by calling expert testimony.

Otherwise, those wanting to litigate in accordance with a familiar language, law and procedure can approach one of the courts of the traditional leaders. These tribunals are the hardy survivors of the colonial and apartheid eras, and they were expressly retained in the final Constitution (Schedule 6, sec. 16(1)). Hence, an estimated 1,500 traditional rulers continue to bring affordable justice to the rural population (SA Law Reform Commission 2003: paras 2.1.1–5). While most litigants in these courts are probably in favour of keeping them (SA Law Reform Commission 1999: para 3.4.1), the customary courts have been widely criticised for failure to maintain the judicial standards prescribed by the Constitution (*Bangindawo and others v Head of the Nyanda Regional Authority and Another* 1998, *Mhlekwa and Feni v Head of the Western Tembuland Regional Authority and Another* 2001).

The Bill of Rights and Statutory Reforms

The drafters of the Bill of Rights in the final Constitution were clear that, as an emphatic break with the apartheid order, everyone in the country would henceforth have the benefit of a uniform code of fundamental human rights. In particular, any unfair discrimination on grounds *inter alia* of race, age, sex, or gender would no longer be allowed (s 9).

When negotiations for a democratic constitution began, however, the public assumed that fundamental rights would be applicable only vertically, that is, to relations between citizen and state. The interim Constitution permitted horizontal application (that is, between individuals), but only in certain circumstances – which prompted a burst of speculative litigation. The final Constitution cleared up these ambiguities, and carried horizontality even further: the Bill of Rights was made binding on natural persons 'if, and to the extent that [a right] is applicable, taking into account the nature of the right and the nature of any duty imposed by the right' (s 8(2)). In this regard, equal treatment was given specific mention: s 9(4) provided that no *person* may unfairly discriminate against another person on any of the proscribed grounds, notably sex or gender.

These provisions set the stage for an immediate confrontation between the Constitution and customary law, since traditional African cultures have long been associated with gender discrimination and chiefly rule. The issue was complicated by the fact that the version of customary law used by the courts and administrative officials was out of date. It reflected an idealised notion of traditional African culture that lagged far behind contemporary social practice. Thus, any constitutional challenge could be met by saying that the 'living' law that was actually being observed by the people might be in accord with the Bill of Rights (Himonga and Bosch 2000: 306).

Soon after the interim Constitution came into operation, the legislature set about attempting to resolve these problems. The courts could clearly not institute fundamental reforms on their own. Not only were the issues too many and too complex, but legislation was the function of elected Members of Parliament, not an unelected judiciary.

Through a complex and participatory process led by a Special Project Committee of the Law Reform Commission, the Department of Justice launched a reform programme aimed at the customary law of marriage and divorce, succession and administration of estates, application and ascertainment of customary law, the status of children, and the composition and procedure of traditional courts. The Departments of Constitutional and Land Affairs, respectively, were responsible for separate projects on the powers of traditional leaders and customary land tenure.

Measuring the success of law reform is always an imponderable. Nevertheless, even from a superficial standpoint, few of these projects can be considered successful. The Law Commission's proposals on application and ascertainment of customary law were simply shelved. The Constitutional Court declared the Communal Land Rights Act (11 of 2004) invalid for failing to follow the proper consultation procedures, and the government had to withdraw a Bill on Traditional Courts (B15–2008) because of widespread protest from civil society. Strong objections were made to the fact that the Bill did little other than confirm, in modified terms, the personnel of the courts and their existing civil and criminal jurisdiction. What is more, traditional rulers were given generous powers to enforce customary law within areas of jurisdiction that corresponded to the bantustans of the apartheid era. No provision was made for opting out of the system on the ground that a defendant had no affiliation to the court, or on the grounds that cultural orientation and the nature of the case made litigation before a magistrate's court more suitable (Mnisi-Weeks 2011: 3ff).

The act dealing with the powers of traditional rulers (the Traditional Leadership and Governance Framework Act of 2003) could perhaps be considered as a limited success in that it won the acquiescence of traditional rulers. During the colonial and apartheid eras, indigenous polities had obviously been exploited to meet the demands of the prevailing policy (see, for example, Beinart and Bundy 1987: 7, Van Kessel and Oomen 1997: 563–4), but, apart from the Cape and Transkei – where attempts were made to remodel chieftaincies on the British idea of a local authority – the government accepted what was already there.

In theory, the Traditional Leadership and Governance Framework Act, together with ensuing provincial legislation, was supposed to sweep away all reminders of the past. As it happened, however, the Act did remarkably little to change the boundaries or office holders set in place by the previous regimes. Change was restricted to renaming. Thus, the Act adopted a new nomenclature for officer holders – kings, queens, senior traditional leaders, headmen and headwomen – and it declares that 'tribes' are now 'traditional communities' (s 28(3)).

Such officer holders and communities which had already been recognised by the State remained in place. Henceforth, however, they were required to establish traditional councils 'in line with principles set out in provincial legislation' (s 3(1)), and, presumably, in line with the requirements relating to their composition set out in the national Act itself. These requirements were the most revolutionary in the Act, since they stipulated that one-third of the members of the new councils had to be women and 40 per cent had to be democratically elected for terms of five years (s 3(b) and (c)). Again, in practice, actual changes have been minimal.

A special commission set up under the Act to deal with disputes about leadership and boundaries has been overwhelmed with claims.

One innovation under the final Constitution was the creation of legislative institutions for traditional rulers at both provincial and national levels. The six provinces containing such rulers were required to establish 'houses of traditional leaders', and, at national level, a similar provision obliged Parliament to create a like-named council (now also called a house). While these bodies lack full law-making powers, they can advise and make proposals on matters concerning traditional authority and customary law, and any bills on these topics must be referred to them.

With regard to matters of private law, Parliament passed a Children's Act in 2005 and Child Justice Act in 2008 after a lengthy period of consultation and preparation. The two Acts introduced an ambitious omnibus of reforms, aimed at bringing the common and customary law into line with international norms on the status of children, as well as their proper care and protection. The Child Justice Act, however, introduced a distinctively African idea of restorative justice to trial and sentencing procedures. It will take some years to determine how effectively the State is able to implement these various provisions.

In the case of succession and administration of estates, the Law Reform Commission's investigation was so slow that it was overtaken by a suit in the Constitutional Court. The existing statutory rules requiring application of customary law to succession and administration of African estates were struck down. Until Parliament took remedial action, the Court filled the resulting lacuna by applying the common law. Four years later, the Reform of Customary Law of Succession and Regulation of Related Matters Act of 2009 was promulgated. In effect, this Act simply imposes a common law regime. Some consideration is given to cultural sensibilities through elaborate modifications of the common law of intestate succession to accommodate polygamous marriages, and even the rare cases of women-to-women marriages and unions designed to produce offspring for the house of a barren spouse.

If 'success' can be ascribed to any of the recent reform legislation in South Africa, then the customary law of marriage and divorce must be considered the highlight. The Law Reform Commission placed this project first on its reform agenda, because customary marriages had never enjoyed full recognition in South Africa, due not only to an abiding prejudice against polygyny, but also to the fact that the courts' version of customary law no longer represented the views and practices of those who lived it. The Special Project Committee was instructed to draft a bill that would ensure respect for African cultural traditions, a thoroughgoing reform of marital relations and an alignment of the law with the Bill of Rights. Two years later, the Recognition of Customary Marriages Act of 1998 appeared.

While this Act made a valiant effort to reconcile culture and the Bill of Rights, it could not escape a strongly rooted tradition of patriarchy in customary law. To some extent, however, the Special Project Committee could resolve this issue by recognising that all people engaged in marital and other domestic relations had to confront similar social and economic problems regardless of their cultural orientation. These problems – notably maintenance and custody of children – were felt most acutely by women and children. They had already been the subject of legislative reform in the common law, and the Committee borrowed freely from this source (SA Law Reform Commission 1998: paras 2.1.23–4).

The following examples in the Customary Marriages Act show how the Committee sought to achieve its aims. Under customary law, a marriage is gradually strengthened and confirmed over time. If, during this process, the spouses' relationship is called into question, it can be proved only by reference to the proper performance of wedding rituals, payment of bridewealth and whatever evidence is available from members of the community. In order to simplify proof, the Committee proposed that couples could, if they wished, have their unions registered. After consulting the public, however, it appeared that most people – women in particular – wanted registration to be mandatory, in the belief that it would make customary unions as binding as their civil or Christian counterparts (SA Law Reform Commission 1998: para 4.5.14).

Largely in response to this request, the Act makes registration of marriage compulsory. Unfortunately, past experience had shown that people seldom comply with such state-imposed formalities, not least because they have little or no access to the necessary officials, and there are no appropriate sanctions to induce compliance. As a result, the Act contains an anomalous provision that failure to register has no effect on the validity of marriage.

An even more contentious issue was the husband's right to take as many wives as he wishes. Long condemned by mainstream churches and colonial administrations, polygyny was now under attack for discriminating against women. This was the predominant view of the public, and, although the Project Committee sympathised, it felt that polygyny on its own was not the cause of the subordinate status of women. Rather, it was only one factor contributing to the patriarchal nature of gender relations.

For this and other reasons – the impossibility of enforcing an outright ban on polygyny and the gradual obsolescence of the practice – the Committee recommended that husbands in customary marriages be permitted to take more than one wife (SA Law Reform Commission 1998: para 6.1.13). The Act followed this recommendation, but with a significant qualification in deference to the

Parliamentary gender lobby. A husband wishing to take a second or subsequent wife must apply for a court order to approve a written contract regulating the future matrimonial property system. In this way, it was hoped that an equitable distribution of property could be guaranteed. Anecdotal evidence, however, indicates that, in the ten-year period since the Act came into force, the courts have endorsed very few (if any) such contracts. Non-observance of this provision – and, even more important, those requiring divorce actions to be processed by the family courts – will defeat one of the principal aims of the Act: to give vulnerable parties in family relationships state protection.

The courts have come to the rescue. In *Ngwenyama v Mayelane and Another* (2012), the validity of a second customary marriage had been called into question, because the husband had failed to obtain a court's approval of the necessary contract. In the court of first instance, the marriage had been declared void in accordance with the Recognition of Customary Marriages Act, but this finding was overturned by the Supreme Court of Appeal. Ndita J held that statutes had to be interpreted in the light of their scope, purpose and their overall background. She established the underlying purpose of the Act with reference to the constitutional right to equality, as well as the provisions contained in international human rights treaties and the history of inequalities suffered by the wives of polygamous marriages. In light of this inquiry, the Judge found that the Act sought to restore the dignity of such women and to ensure that every wife enjoyed equal rights.

Whether there will be compliance with all the provisions of the Customary Marriages Act is, of course, unlikely. Nevertheless, what is perhaps over-ambitious reform is justifiable when the aim is to protect women and children: goals should be set higher rather than lower. Indeed, the Law Commission was well aware that, because of financial, educational and other social disadvantages, few women (and even fewer children) would be able to act on proposed reforms. It nevertheless felt that options should be made available for a time when people would be better placed to realise their rights (SA Law Reform Commission 1998: para 2.1.28). It is much more difficult, however, to justify laws that cannot be implemented because of the inadequacies of the state infrastructure. The bodies responsible for making rights operational, that is, the Master's offices (which are responsible for overseeing the probate of wills and administration of estates), family advocates and family courts (tribunals with jurisdiction over such matters as divorce, maintenance and the custody and guardianship of minor children), are still concentrated in urban centres, to the obvious disadvantage of the rural population. Even more serious is the fact that these facilities are grossly understaffed and quite unprepared to assume responsibility for dealing with new legislation.

The New Vision of Customary Law

This somewhat disappointing catalogue of statutory reforms is offset by a dramatically different approach to customary law in the courts. Even before the arrival of a new Constitution, thinking about customary law in South Africa had begun to change. Both legal pluralism, a specialist outgrowth of anthropology, and, for want of a better term, deconstructionism had set out to debunk the predominant theory of legal positivism (Fitzpatrick 1985: 479, Gordon 1989: 46).

During the apartheid years, the low status of customary law was due largely to the positivist mindset of the legal profession. Because positivism deemed only state law as true law, customary normative orders were of marginal importance (Arthurs 1985: 3). Anthropologists, of course, could be relied upon to contest such thinking, and they produced abundant evidence showing that the positivist belief that state laws determined people's lives was not realised in reality. Few people accepted formal legal systems as their primary sources of regulation. Instead, they observed customary and other, unofficial, normative orders. Legal pluralism therefore rejected the idea that law was and ought to be the law of the State, 'uniform for all persons, exclusive of all other law, and administered by a single set of state institutions'. The positivist notion of law was denounced as ideology, 'a myth, an ideal, an illusion.' (Griffiths 1986: 12)

Deconstructionists made free use of pluralist research, and their broad aims generally coincided with those of the pluralists. Nevertheless, this school of thought was more concerned with ideology than with the day-to-day life of the legal subject. It appeared that much customary law in South Africa was an 'invented' tradition. All systems of custom are based on social practices which the communities in question accept as binding. Hence, the key test for the validity and legitimacy of customary law is how widely and deeply it is rooted in community behaviour. If the rules being applied by the State are not fully accepted by the people, they are not only invalid, but any claim to legitimacy through democratic origins in a community tradition is a sham. The law most commonly used by the legal profession – the 'official code' – bore the brunt of this attack. Opposed to this version were ethnographic texts, which more accurately describe the cultures of selected African peoples, and, in so doing, come closer to revealing a true customary law. Finally, there was the 'living' law, the system actually accepted and lived by the people (Sanders 1987: 405).

For the first time in Africa, state law-making agencies began to acknowledge the differences between official and living laws. The courts declared that only the latter deserved constitutional protection, and the Law Reform Commission used it as the basic reference for statutory reform. The living law had the merit of representing a more democratic base, while official law was condemned by '[t]raditionalists seeking to redeem the past, and modernizers attempting to discredit it'. For both, 'customary law as it stands is corrupted, inauthentic and lacking authority. It is a foreign imposition, a stranger in Africa' (Costa 1998: 534).

Another significant development in South Africa has been the emergence of an indigenous jurisprudence. Since the colonial conquest, customary laws have been considered inferior, and, as a consequence, the traffic of concepts and ideas was always from the received Roman-Dutch law to customary law. With the reception of *ubuntu* – a complex concept denoting compassion, humanity and right-minded behaviour – into the common law, this process was reversed. *Ubuntu* entered the law in a short but telling 'Postamble' to the interim Constitution. The deeply divided society that emerged from apartheid bore a 'legacy of hatred, fear, guilt and revenge'. These divisions were now to 'be addressed on the basis that there is a need for understanding but not for vengeance, a need for reparation but not for retaliation, a need for *ubuntu* but not for victimisation'. Although lacking a solid legal foundation, apart from this aspirational clause, *ubuntu* was co-opted into mainstream legal discourse by a series of judgments in the Constitutional and High Courts.

By this means, *ubuntu* has been given the function of a metanorm, one that can be used in particular factual situations where strict application of the usual rules could work a substantial injustice. Its other function has been to introduce a distinctively African source of values to the legal system. Although the values in the Bill of Rights are supposed to be universal, they are not obviously 'African'. *Ubuntu*, however, is forming 'a cohesive, plural, South African legal culture' (Keep and Midgley 2007: 30), one characterised by the ideals of reconciliation, sharing, responsibility, trust and harmony.

Conclusion

Over the last twenty years, the South African legal system has had to contend with a problem that is common to most post-colonial states: a significant gap between social classes that is marked by culture and ethnicity. Law may all too easily become a marker of cultural resistance to the interference of the central State, and, without education, income and opportunity, the disadvantaged class is less likely to accept and act on reforms promulgated by the State.

It is perhaps permissible to legislate reforms that are designed to provide goals that will be realised at a later date – so-called programmatic reform – but if significant progress is not made toward achieving those goals, the laws soon become worthless. Hence, the State must be prepared to invest considerable resources in consultation and education if reform is to take root. It must, furthermore, be prepared to develop the bureaucratic agencies responsible for enforcing the new rules, because most modern law reform requires greater state intervention in the private sphere. In this regard, the performance of the South African government is sadly wanting.

References

Books, book chapters and articles

Albertyn, C. 1994. 'Women and the transition to democracy in South Africa', *Acta Juridica*, 39: 39–63.

Arthurs, H.W. 1985. *Without the Law – Administrative Justice and Legal Pluralism in Nineteenth-century England.* Toronto: University of Toronto Press.

Beinart, W. and C.J. Bundy, 1987. *Hidden Struggles in Rural South Africa: Politics & Popular Movements in the Transkei & Eastern Cape 1890–1930.* Johannesburg: Ravan Press.

Bennett, T.W. 1985. *The Application of Customary Law in Southern Africa, the Conflict of Personal Laws.* Cape Town: Juta & Co.

—— 2004. *Customary Law in South Africa.* Cape Town: Juta & Co.

Costa, A. 1998. 'The myth of customary law', *South African Journal on Human Rights*, 14(4): 525–38.

Fitzpatrick, P. 1985. 'Is it simple to be a Marxist in legal anthropology?', *Modern Law Review*, 48(4): 472–85.

Gordon, R. 1989. 'The white man's burden: ersatz customary law and internal pacification in South Africa', *Journal of Historical Sociology*, 2(1): 41–65.

Griffiths, J. 1986. 'What is legal pluralism?', *Journal of Legal Pluralism and Unofficial Law*, 24: 1–55.

Himonga, C. and C. Bosch, 2000. 'The application of African customary law under the Constitution of South Africa: problem solved or just beginning?', *South African Law Journal*, 117(2): 306–41.

Keep, H. and R. Midgley, 2007. 'The emerging role of ubuntu-botho in developing a consensual South African legal culture', *Recht der Werkelijkheid*, 3: 29–58.

Mnisi Weeks, S. 2011. 'The Traditional Courts Bill : controversy around process, substance and implications', *South African Crime Quarterly*, 35: 3–10.

Peart, N.S. 1982. 'Section 11(1) of the Black Administration Act No 38 of 1927: the application of the repugnancy clause', *Acta Juridica*, 1982: 99–116.

Sachs, A. 1990. 'Towards a Bill of Rights in a democratic South Africa', *South African Journal on Human Rights*, 6(1): 1–24.

Sanders, A.J.G.M. 1987. 'How customary is African customary law?', *Comparative and International Law of Southern Africa*, 20(3): 405–10.

Van Kessel, I. and B. Oomen, 1997. '"One chief, one vote": the revival of traditional authorities in post-apartheid South Africa', *African Affairs*, 96: 561–85.

Reports

South African Law Reform Commission. 1998. *Report on Customary Marriages.* Project 90. Pretoria: Government Printer.

—— 1999. *Discussion Paper on Traditional Courts and the Judicial Function of Traditional Leaders.* Project 90. Pretoria: Government Printer.

South African Law Reform Commission. 2004. *Report on Traditional Courts and the Judicial Function of Traditional Leaders.* Project 90. Pretoria: Government Printer.

Cases

Bangindawo and others v Head of the Nyanda Regional Authority and another 1998 (3) SA 262 (Tk).
Bhe and others v Magistrate Khayelitsha and others 2005 (1) SA 580 (CC).
Du Plessis & others v De Klerk & another 1996 (3) SA 850 (CC).
Mhlekwa and Feni v Head of the Western Tembuland Regional Authority and another 2001 (1) SA 574 (Tk).
Ngwenyama v Mayelane and another 2012 ZASCA 94.
S v Makwanyane and another 1995 (3) SA 391 (CC).
Tongoane and others v Minister of Agriculture and Land Affairs 2010 (6) SA 214 (CC).

Legislation

Child Justice Act 71 of 2008.
Children's Act 38 of 2005.
Communal Land Rights Act 11 of 2004.
Constitution of the Republic of South Africa, Act 200 of 1993.
Constitution of the Republic of South Africa, 1996.
Native Administration Act 38 of 1927.
Recognition of Customary Marriages Act 120 of 1998.
Reform of Customary Law of Succession and Regulation of Related Matters Act 11 of 2009.
Traditional Leadership and Governance Framework Act 41 of 2003.

Chapter 15
Land Reform and Constitutional Rights

Nic Olivier, Nico Olivier and Clara Williams

Introduction

This chapter provides a brief overview of the historical background to the constitutional framework relating to land reform, as well as of the contents of, and the extent to which, the framework has been realised. The chapter starts with a summary of the pre-1994 era which was characterised by dispossession and marginalisation, including the limited land-related reforms which were implemented between 1990 and April 1994. This is followed by a discussion of the interim constitutional framework. The final Constitution provides for both the protection of the right to property (and also for expropriation and the concomitant payment of compensation), and the imposition of an obligation on the State to bring about the restoration of dispossessed land, provide access to land on an equitable basis, and ensure the security of tenure of people whose land tenure was insecure on account of racially based legislation and/or administrative practices.

The next section of this chapter deals with the national legislation, programmes and institutions established to give effect to this 1996 constitutional framework. In 2009, an enhanced paradigm, which located land reform within the broader strategic objectives (and related outcomes) of Government, was introduced by means of policy documentation, the refocusing of programmes and institutional adaptation. In 2011, the Green Paper on Land Reform was published by the Department of Rural Development and Land Reform (DRDLR), which provided for a four-tier tenure system and envisaged the establishment of a range of institutional instruments to facilitate and expedite the process of land reform. Subsequently, the current status of land reform is briefly discussed, and, in conclusion, a number of key challenges and possible options to ensure that the constitutional imperative of bringing about sustainable land reform will be realised, are identified.

Pre-1994: Dispossession and Marginalisation

Dispossession before 1913

Conflict over access to, and control over, land started soon after the Dutch East India Company established a refreshment post in the Cape in 1652 (Carey Miller and Pope 2000: 7–8). The European expansion into the hinterland led to clashes not only with the Khoi (Rugege 2004: 283–4), but also with other African communities. After several localised wars in the Eastern Cape (Du Plessis and Pienaar 2010: 77), the Transkeian Territories were annexed in 1877. Zulu-speaking communities in Natal were confined to reserves in what was known as Zululand, and in the late 1870s Griqualand East was annexed and subsequently administered as part of the Cape. In both the Cape and Natal colonies, separate legislation applied to land tenure and use until 1910 for Africans, Indians and Coloureds. In the Transvaal and the Orange Free State republics, which existed from the 1850s to 1902, land occupation and use by Africans were in principle limited to specific areas (Carey Miller and Pope 2000: 14, 17).

The period 1910–94

In terms of the Constitution of the Union of South Africa, the indirect (and very limited) representation that Africans had in the Cape Parliament continued; however, no provision was made for any form of direct or indirect representation for Africans outside the Cape Province in Parliament (Currie and De Waal 2005: 3).

The hallmark of the period 1910–48 could aptly be described as growing race-based segregation. A Department of Native Affairs was established to deal with all matters pertaining to Africans (Pienaar 2011b: 122), and the Natives Land Act of 1913 was enacted with the object of declaring illegal the ownership, occupation or use of land in South Africa by Africans outside the separate areas (Scheduled Areas) specifically identified for them (Mahomed et al. 2011: 18–19). The Scheduled Areas covered approximately 6 per cent of the surface area of the country. The Native Trust and Land Act of 1936 (ibid.: 121) provided for the acquisition of additional land (Released Areas) for Africans through the Native Trust (eventually renamed the South African Development Trust (SADT)) (Pienaar and Kamkuemah 2011: 725). The SADT was tasked with the acquisition of primarily white-owned farms which increased the amount of land available to Africans to 13 per cent of the surface area of the country (Mahomed et al. 2011: 9). Additional legislation for the management of all affairs affecting Africans in their daily lives was enacted by means of the Native Administration Act of 1927 (Rautenbach and Malherbe 2009: 17), which was the main instrument to effect forced removals of Africans. Subordinate legislation provided for specific weak tenure forms for Africans in the Scheduled and Released Areas, as well as for a separate land administration and management structure and system (see Du Plessis 2011: 56).

In 1948, this race-based segregationist framework was embedded in the ideological platform of 'separate development' or 'apartheid'. After 1948, and especially from 1959, the ideological framework focused on the consolidation of Scheduled and Released Areas into ten Bantustans or homelands. Self-government was regulated in terms of the Bantu Homelands Constitution Act of 1971 (eventually renamed the Self-Governing Territories Constitution Act). Independence was granted to four homelands: Transkei (1976), Bophuthatswana (1977), Venda (1979) and Ciskei (1981) ('the TBVCs'). Areas that could not be consolidated within the jurisdictional territories of the TBVCs and the six remaining self-governing territories, were referred to as 'SADT areas', also with a distinct statutory and administrative framework.

The national legal framework that underpinned the ideology of the temporariness of Africans in South Africa outside the homelands consisted mainly of the Natives (Urban Areas) Act of 1923 and the Natives (Urban Areas) Consolidation Act of 1945 (Pienaar 2011b: 121); the latter was replaced by the Black Communities Development Act 4 of 1984, which was premised on a changing paradigm which accepted the permanence of urban Africans.

The Group Areas Act 41 of 1950 segregated the White, Coloured and Indian groups as regards occupation, land ownership, economic activities and use of social amenities in respect of those areas not set aside for exclusive African occupation (Badenhorst, Pienaar and Mostert 2006: 587). The rights that could be obtained by Coloured and Indian people were more limited than those available to Whites (Mahomed et al. 2011: 9–10). The Group Areas Act was re-enacted in 1966 as the Community Development Act, and was based on race classification as determined in the Population Registration Act of 1950. As regards the former Coloured Mission Reserves, consolidating legislation vesting significant powers in the Department of Coloured Affairs was enacted by means of the Rural Coloured Areas Act of 1963.

Both during the 1913–48 period of segregation, and the subsequent period of apartheid, massive forced removals were implemented to ensure that Africans occupied only those areas set aside for them (Carey Miller and Pope 2000: 35). It is said that more than 6 million South Africans were dispossessed of their land from the commencement date (19 June 1913) of the Natives Land Act of 1913 till the implementation of the moratorium on forced removals in 1984. Communities and groups were also moved around within the homelands in order to implement 'betterment', irrigation, and other schemes (ibid.: 28).

1991–26 April 1994 Reforms

Following the unbanning of the liberation movements, a range of reform legislation was enacted, also in respect of land, including the Abolition of Racially Based Land Measures Act, the Upgrading of Land Tenure Rights Act, and the Less Formal Township Establishment Act (all of 1991), and the Land Titles Adjustment Act, Distribution and Transfer of Certain State Land Act, and Provision of Land and Assistance Act (all of 1993).

The most important land-related laws that were repealed were the Black Land Act of 1913, various sections of the Black Administration Act of 1927, the Development Trust and Land Act of 1936, the Group Areas Act of 1966, specific legislation applicable to Indians, the Rural Coloured Areas Act of 1963 and the Black Communities Development Act of 1984 (Carey Miller and Pope 2000: 249–52). The Advisory Committee on Non-racial Area Measures and Advisory Commission on Land Allocation were also established.

1994 Constitutional Framework

The inclusion (and content) of the property clause as s 28 of the 1993 Constitution was based on a compromise between the positions of the ANC and the National Party. For the ANC, it was of utmost importance to make sure that the property clause would not impede future land restoration or reform programmes, while the National Party endeavoured to ensure that existing property rights (especially those in the hands of white owners) would be sufficiently protected in a new dispensation (Rudman 2012: 421).

Restitution of land rights was addressed in ss 121 to 123 of the interim Constitution, which provided for a person or community to claim restitution of a land right if, amongst others, such person or community was dispossessed after a date that had to be fixed in proposed legislation (which date could not be earlier than 19 June 1913) (s 121(2)(a) and (3)).

The 1913 cut-off date is often justified with reference to the many complexities and overlapping claims that could potentially have been lodged in its absence. The Government acknowledged the fact that certain dispossessions took place prior to the Natives Land Act, but reasoned that such dispossessions could not reasonably be dealt with in terms of the judicial process provided for in the Restitution of Land Rights Act of 1994 (RLRA) and by the Land Claims Court (LCC). To cater for those excluded by the 1913 cut-off date, Government undertook to grant them priority access to land through alternative mechanisms (White Paper on South African Land Policy 1997: 4.14.2–3).

The RLRA commenced on 2 December 1994 and provides for the restitution of land rights to persons and communities dispossessed of such rights as a result of past racially discriminatory laws or practices. The RLRA is only applicable to dispossessions that took place after 19 June 1913. Section 2 sets out who is entitled to restitution of a right in land, and states that the cut-off date for claims was 31 December 1998. In the event that just and equitable compensation or another just and equitable consideration (calculated at the time of dispossession) was received, a person is not entitled to restitution.

The Commission on Restitution of Land Rights (CRLR) was established to receive all claims, investigate the merits of claims, mediate and settle disputes arising from claims, and report to the LCC on the terms of settlement in respect of successfully mediated claims (s 6).

In the course of investigating a claim, the CRLR may direct parties to attempt to settle disputes through mediation and negotiation and may refer certain matters to the LCC (ss 13–14). Section 14(3) provides that the CRLR and the parties may enter into a written agreement as to how the claim should be finalised. If the Regional Land Claims Commission then certifies that it is satisfied with the agreement and that the agreement ought not to be referred to the LCC, the agreement is effective from the date of such certification or such later date as may be provided for in the agreement.

The LCC, established by s 22, has the power to determine a right to restitution of any right in land, determine or approve compensation payable, determine the person entitled to title to land, make a declaratory order, and determine whether compensation or any other consideration received by any person at the time of dispossession of a right in land was just and equitable. Section 33 sets out the factors that must be taken into account by the LCC, including the desirability of providing restitution; remedying past human rights violations and avoiding major social injustice, the feasibility of restoration, the requirements of equity and justice, the amount of compensation or any other consideration received in respect of the dispossession, and the history of the dispossession and the current use of the land. The LCC may order the restoration of land, a portion thereof or right therein, the granting of a right in alternative state-owned land, the payment of compensation, including the claimant as a beneficiary of State programmes, or alternative relief. The LCC may also make recommendations to the Minister with regard to alternative relief for those claimants who do not qualify for the restitution of rights in land in terms of the RLRA (s 38E). The DRDLR Minister may provide financial aid to certain claimants (s 42C).

In the event that land is acquired or expropriated in order to restore or award the land to a claimant, such land vests in the State, which must then transfer the land to the claimant (s 42A(1)). Section 42D empowers the DRDLR Minister to enter into agreements with claimants for the award of land, and/or the payment of compensation.

In the event that another claim is lodged in respect of land to which (a) a court order in terms of s 35 or (b) an agreement in terms of ss 14(3) or 42D relates, an interested party may apply for the rescission or variation of the order or the setting-aside or variation of the agreement (s11(5)). Section 42E states that the DRDLR Minister may purchase, acquire in another manner, or expropriate land or a right therein for land-reform purposes. It also provides that the Expropriation Act of 1975 applies to all expropriations, and that s 25(3) of the Constitution must be adhered to in determining the compensation. (For an in-depth discussion of the RLRA, see Pienaar and Brickhill 2008: 48-52–48-64).

At an administrative level, three Land Reform Programmes were initiated:

- Restitution (the restoration of land to communities, groups, or individuals who (or whose ancestors) had been dispossessed of land on account of race-based legislation or administrative practices),
- Redistribution (the provision of support to enable access to land on an equitable basis), and
- Tenure reform (strengthening of security of tenure for those communities, groups, or individuals whose tenure was insecure on account of past race-based legislation or administrative practices).

The Development Facilitation Act of 1995 provides a framework for the identification of land to be released for redistribution purposes. Subsidisation of the purchase price and funding for support were provided in terms of the Settlement/Land and Acquisition Grant (SLAG), but no comprehensive pre- and post-settlement support programme was available to restitution and redistribution beneficiaries (for further detail, see Rugege 2004: 295–304).

1996 Constitutional Framework

In terms of the 1996 Constitution, the State is obliged to 'respect, protect, promote and fulfil' the rights contained in the Bill of Rights. Section 25 (the property clause) forms part of the Bill of Rights:

> (1) No one may be deprived of property except in terms of law of general application, and no law may permit arbitrary deprivation of property.
>
> (2) Property may be expropriated only in terms of law of general application-
> (a) for a public purpose or in the public interest; and
> (b) subject to compensation, the amount of which and the time and manner of payment of which have either been agreed to by those affected or decided or approved by a court.
>
> (3) The amount of the compensation and the time and manner of payment must be just and equitable, reflecting an equitable balance between the public interest and the interests of those affected, having regard to all relevant circumstances, including-
> (a) the current use of the property;
> (b) the history of the acquisition and use of the property;
> (c) the market value of the property;
> (d) the extent of direct state investment and subsidy in the acquisition and beneficial capital improvement of the property; and
> (e) the purpose of the expropriation.
>
> (4) For the purposes of this section-
> (a) the public interest includes the nation's commitment to land reform, and to reforms to bring about equitable access to all South Africa's natural resources; and
> (b) property is not limited to land.
>
> (5) The state must take reasonable legislative and other measures, within its available resources, to foster conditions which enable citizens to gain access to land on an equitable basis.
>
> (6) A person or community whose tenure of land is legally insecure as a result of past racially discriminatory laws or practices is entitled, to the extent

provided by an Act of Parliament, either to tenure which is legally secure or to comparable redress.

(7) A person or community dispossessed of property after 19 June 1913 as a result of past racially discriminatory laws or practices is entitled, to the extent provided by an Act of Parliament, either to restitution of that property or to equitable redress.

(8) No provision of this section may impede the state from taking legislative and other measures to achieve land, water and related reform, in order to redress the results of past racial discrimination, provided that any departure from the provisions of this section is in accordance with the provisions of section 36(1).

(9) Parliament must enact the legislation referred to in subsection (6).

So s 25 provides simultaneously for both a guarantee of protective measures for property holdings, as well as a guarantee of certain land-reform measures (Van der Walt 2004: 47, 82–3). Subsection (8) empowers the State to take legislative and other measures to achieve land reform, as long as such measures comply with the provisions of the general limitations clause, s 36, which provides for the limitation of all rights in certain circumstances. The State may, therefore, enact other legislation (in addition to s 25(7) and the RLRA) to achieve land reform (for an in-depth discussion, see Van der Walt 2011).

Section 12(1) of the Expropriation Act of 1975 refers to the so-called 'willing buyer, willing seller' principle, as well as the market value of the land concerned (Dlamini, Verschoor and Fraser 2013: 24–5). These two factors are, however, only some of the factors that need to be taken into account when calculating compensation, and are, therefore, neither determinant nor the predominant factors. The 1996 Constitution specifically states that compensation must be 'just and equitable' (s 25(3)) (Badenhorst, Pienaar and Mostert 2006: 568–78). Until recently, there has been an erroneous perception that the 'willing buyer, willing seller' principle is the sole determinant, or most important co-determinant, when calculating compensation for land that is expropriated for land-reform purposes. The principle of bringing about a just and equitable balance between the public interest (including expropriation for land-reform purposes) and the interest of the affected land owner, is paramount (Currie and De Waal 2005: 554–7). In addition, s 42E(3) of the RLRA specifically provides that the LCC must apply s 25(3) of the 1996 Constitution when determining the amount of compensation to be paid when expropriation takes place.

The White Paper on South African Land Policy (published in 1997) identified the following five key challenges to be dealt with within the context of reconstruction and development (para 2.1):

- The injustices of a racially based land dispossession of the past,
- The need for a more equitable distribution of land ownership,
- The need for land reform to reduce poverty and contribute to economic growth,
- Security of tenure for all,
- A system of land management which will support sustainable land use patterns and rapid land release for development.

As regards restitution, 79,696 claims had been lodged in accordance with the RLRA by the cut-off date of 31 December 1998. In respect of redistribution, the Provision of Certain Land for Settlement Act of 1993 was amended and renamed the Provision of Land and Assistance Act in order to provide for the proactive acquisition of land for settlement and redistribution purposes, and support to redistribution beneficiaries (see, in this regard, Pienaar and Brickhill 2008: 48-20–48-22). (See below for current status of redistribution.) In addition to SLAG, a number of other redistribution grant programmes were implemented. However, no comprehensive pre- and post-settlement support programme was implemented.

The policy and statutory framework for tenure reform was expanded during the 1996–2009 period, but is still incomplete (see also Du Plessis and Pienaar 2010: 82). The following statutory instruments were enacted:

- Extension of Security of Tenure Act of 1997,
- Prevention of Illegal Eviction from and Unlawful Occupation of Land Act of 1998,
- Transformation of Certain Rural Areas Act of 1998,
- KwaZulu-Natal Ingonyama Trust Amendment Act of 1997, and
- Communal Land Rights Act 2004 (CLRA).

However, the CLRA was declared unconstitutional by the Constitutional Court in 2010 in *Tongoane and Others v Minister of Agriculture and Land Affairs and Others* on account of the wrong parliamentary process having been followed (the CLRA should have been dealt with as a Bill that affected provinces). No new draft legislation has since been submitted to Parliament.

After 2009: An Enhanced Paradigm

In 2009, it was realised that the post-1994 rural development projects had not succeeded, and that 90 per cent of the land reform projects had either failed or were severely compromised on account of the absence of appropriate settlement support (Pienaar 2011a: 32). This resulted in a paradigm enhancement by relocating land reform within the context of comprehensive rural development, and linking it with agrarian transformation and food security. In this regard, the vision of the Comprehensive Rural Development Programme is to create vibrant, equitable and sustainable rural communities. Taking into account this new approach, DLA was reconstituted as DRDLR and the National Department of Agriculture as the Department of Agriculture, Forestry and Fisheries, each with its own minister.

The major part of redistribution funding was utilised to provide support for the recapitalisation of the above-mentioned failed and distressed land reform (restitution and redistribution) farms, by means of the Recapitalisation and Development Programme (RADP), which focused on the involvement of experienced strategic partners and the resuscitation of the on-farm infrastructure.

From 2011: Policy Shifts

The Green Paper on Land Reform (Green Paper) was published on 31 August 2011 (for a critical analysis, see Rudman 2012). It provided for an amended vision for land reform, consisting of a reconfigured single, coherent four-tier system of land tenure, clearly defined property rights, secure forms of long-term land tenure for resident non-citizens engaged in appropriate investments, and effective land-use planning and regulatory systems (Green Paper: 4).

The Government acknowledged that, 18 years after the commencement of democracy, much still needed to be done with regard to comprehensive land reform. The following challenges and weaknesses were identified as providing the rationale for the new approach to land reform (Green Paper: 5):

a. The land acquisition strategy/'willing buyer, willing seller' model (a distorted land market),
b. A fragmented beneficiary support system,
c. Beneficiary selection for land redistribution,
d. Land administration/governance, especially in communal areas,
e. Meeting the 30 per cent redistribution target by 2014,
f. Declining agricultural contribution to the GDP,
g. Unrelenting increase in rural unemployment, and
h. A problematic restitution model and its support system (communal property institutions and management).

Various task teams were appointed, and in some instances policy documents and legislation have been, or are in the process of being, drafted in respect of the new land reform policy, legislative, institutional and implementation landscape (trajectory), which consists of the following components (Green Paper: 5):

a. A recapitalisation and development programme,
b. A single land-tenure system with four tiers,
c. A Land Management Commission,
d. A Land Valuer-General,
e. A Land Rights Management Board, with local management committees,
f. Properly aligned common property institutions (CPIs), and

g. The Land Tenure Security Bill, 2010, which is an integral part of the Land Reform Programme (LRP), but is treated separately from it (see, in this regard, Pienaar and Kamkuemah 2011).

The single four-tier system represents an integrated approach to the current multiple forms of land ownership (communal, State, public and private land) and consists of:

a. State and public land: Lease hold,
b. Privately owned land: Freehold, but with limited extent,
c. Land owned by Foreigners: Freehold, but Precarious Tenure, with obligations and conditions to comply with and
d. Communally owned land: Communal Tenure, with institutionalised use rights. (Green Paper: 6)

On account of its complexity, communal tenure reform (tier (d) above) is being dealt with by means of a separate policy process.

Three new institutions will be responsible for the administration of the new land reform programme. The Land Management Commission will be responsible for the overall management of land matters, and its functions will be of an advisory, coordinating, regulatory and auditing nature. The Office of the Valuer-General will ensure that fair and consistent land values are determined whenever land is to be acquired by any entity in the national, provincial, or local spheres of government, and that the constitutional provisions as contained in s 25 are applied when land is acquired for land reform purposes. The Land Rights Management Board and the Land Rights Management Committees will be responsible for the communication of legal reforms to farm owners, farm-dwellers and potential land beneficiaries, as well as the building of institutional capacity and the development of accessible and efficient systems in respect of the recordal and registration of rights to land (Green Paper: paras 6.5–6.7).

The Policy for the RADP was released in mid-2013, and identified the following three objectives (Policy for the Recapitalisation and Development Programme 2013: 11):

- Re-establishing black commercial farmers similar to those destroyed by the 1913 Natives Land Act and the 1936 Native Trust and Land Act,
- Combating poverty, unemployment and income equality, and
- Reducing the tide of rural-urban migration.

The RADP Policy aims to recapitalise failed and distressed land reform projects transferred to land reform beneficiaries in terms of the Restitution and Redistribution Programmes. The pillars of the RADP are (a) mentorship, (b) co-management, (c) share-equity arrangements, and (d) contract farming and concessions (Policy for the Recapitalisation and Development Programme: 12–15).

Following the publication of the Green Paper, South Africa's President announced that the RLRA would be amended to re-open, for a period of five years, the lodgement of claims for the restoration of land in respect of which communities, groups, and/or individuals were dispossessed in terms of racially discriminatory legislation and/or administrative practices. Subsequently, the draft Restitution of Land Rights Amendment Bill, 2013 (2013 Bill) was published for public comment in late May 2013.

The 1997 White Paper on South African Land Policy indicated that dispossessions that took place in the former homelands were excluded from restitution claims, and that such dispossessions would be dealt with by means of other land reform programmes (especially redistribution) (Mahomed et al. 2011: 18–23). It is now acknowledged that this category of exclusions was both unconstitutional and contrary to the wording of the RLRA.

The reasoning behind the 2013 Bill is set out in paragraphs 2.1 to 2.2 of the Explanatory Memorandum:

> The following three categories were identified as being excluded by the restitution laws and programme, i.e. those who could not lodge claims by the cut-off date of 31 December 1998, those dispossessed before 1913, and those dispossessed through betterment planning schemes and not allowed to lodge their claims by the Commission on Restitution of Land Rights (CRLR). The evaluation further indicated that the research methodology that informed the restitution process was poor; that verification systems of the CRLR were inadequate, that the window period that was provided to lodge claims was too short and that the communication campaign to inform citizens about the requirement to lodge claims did not reach every corner of the country.

Based on the above, Government has decided to re-open the lodgement of claims for a period of five years (1 January 2014 to 31 December 2018), and a pro-active communication strategy will accompany this step.

Any community that had been moved on account of a betterment or any other government programme within any of the former homelands or SADT areas may submit a claim for restoration of the land from which they had been dispossessed. In addition, farm owners whose land had been acquired by means of purchase or expropriation for purposes of giving effect to the provisions of the Native Land and Trust Act of 1936 and the subsequent homeland consolidation, may, in principle, also lodge claims for the restoration of the land concerned (and if not possible, alternate land and/or monetary compensation). Government also announced in 2012 that special arrangements would be implemented to ensure that the descendants of the Khoi-San who were dispossessed of their land during the period 1652–1913 would be able to lodge claims for restoration, as well as for historical landmarks and heritage sites.

Another land reform model was proposed in the 2013 National Development Plan (NDP), Government's long-term strategic plan. Details of this model are unnecessary here, but it suffices to note that a degree of co-operative action between commercial farmers and black framers and the acquisition of land at 50 per cent of market value, are envisaged. The proposed model will in principle not impact negatively on investor confidence (National Development Plan 2013: 226–7).

Current Status of Land Reform

The exact extent of land that has been transferred to beneficiaries in terms of the Government's land reform programme is unclear. According to DRDLR, a total of 6,971,293 ha have been acquired from 1994 to 2012 (DRDLR 2013a: 34), while Parliament's Research Unit indicates that by 2012 some 7.95 million ha have been redistributed (Parliament 2013: 5). From 2009 to April 2013, agricultural land to the extent of 1,038,062 ha has been acquired for redistribution purposes (DRDLR 2013a: vi).

With regard to redistribution, the DRDLR has recently shifted its focus from a quantitative to a qualitative approach. The original target was to redistribute 30 per cent of South Africa's productive white-owned land by 2014 (amounting to 24.6 million ha), but this was replaced in 2013 by a focus on ensuring full productivity on land that has already been redistributed (Greve 2013). According to recent research, the settlement of all outstanding restitution claims, combined with historic claims, will only amount to the re-allocation of 2 per cent of white-owned commercial land, while the redistribution programme had resulted in the transfer of 7.5 per cent of white-owned farm land to claimants by the end of 2012 (Parliament 2013: 5).

A total of 79,696 land restitution claims were lodged between 1994 and 1998 in terms of the RLRA (DRDLR 2011: 40). Some 77,334 claims had been settled by May 2013, of which 71,292 were settled through financial compensation to the value of about R6.56 billion in respect of approximately 1,992 million ha of land. Only 6,042 claimants (only 7.8 per cent) therefore opted for restoration in the form of land (Commission on Restitution of Land Rights 2013: 6).

It needs to be noted that not all of the 77,334 claims settled by May 2013 have been finalised. Although no up-to-date information is available, a previous report revealed that of the 76,980 claims that were settled up to October 2012, only 59,513 had been finalised. Land claims are being settled in a phased approach, and a claim is only considered finalised once the full extent of the settled claim has been executed, that is, when all properties have been transferred or all beneficiaries have been paid (DRDLR 2013b: 11–12).

As noted, the Department's focus has shifted to ensuring the transfer of '100% developed, productive land', rather than on the quantity of land transferred (Sherry 2013). In this regard, some 696 farms have received assistance under the RADP. Of these, 389 were purchased through the Proactive Land Acquisition Strategy and the remaining 307 under land reform grants (DRDLR 2013a: 34). Some 25 per cent of the Department's budget is currently being spent on recapitalisation and development (Van der Walt 2013).

Conclusion

Notwithstanding the high hopes expressed between the 1994 RDP and the 1997 White Paper on South African Land Policy, that the far-reaching racial discriminatory injustices and dispossessions would be ameliorated, it is clear that Government's Land Reform Programme has not fully delivered 20 years after the advent of democracy. As regards restitution, notwithstanding the cut-off date for the lodgement of claims being 31 December 1998 (16 years ago), a large number of claims have not yet been legally settled. In addition, thousands of legally settled claims have not been finalised. Also, only 7.8 per cent of successful claimants have opted to have land restored, whilst the remainder have preferred financial compensation.

An evaluation of the restitution programme during the period 1994–2012 has indicated serious shortcomings which have significantly affected its efficiency, implementation and completion. Particular problems were the exclusion of claims in respect of land in the former homelands (especially betterment claims), potential claimants who could not lodge their claims as the period for lodgement was too limited, that the research methodology implemented by the CRLR was poor and the verification systems applied by the CRLR were inadequate, and that the communication campaign for the lodgement of claims was insufficient.

As regards redistribution, the process of proactively acquiring land, followed by making it available to beneficiaries, has been severely curtailed by the decision to focus budgetary allocations on the recapitalisation and development of compromised restitution and redistribution farms. In addition, in the past, business plans were not appropriately evaluated prior to the decision to make the redistribution land concerned available. There was also no uniform approach to the selection of beneficiaries as regards their suitability or expertise to manage existing commercial farms in a productive manner. The decision not to transfer redistribution land in ownership to the beneficiaries concerned, but only by means of a renewable lease, has resulted in the inability to access credit from the commercial financial sector.

After 2009, Government acknowledged publicly that 90 per cent of all then-existing land reform projects had failed, or, were at least severely compromised. The RADP seeks to revitalise the existing land reform projects by means of mentorship, co-management, share-equity arrangements and contract farming and concessions, with the view 'that all land-reform farms are 100 per cent productive'. The urgent need for a comprehensive pre- and post-settlement support programme has not yet been addressed by Government.

As regards tenure reform, significant – and near-complete – progress has been made in respect of urban areas. However, this process has not been completed in respect of the towns in the former homelands. Security of tenure for certain categories of farm workers is in the process of being strengthened. The upgrading of rights in the former coloured rural areas has not yet been finalised.

Another serious concern is the lack of a policy framework and concomitant legislation and administrative systems for the conversion of the weak, insecure and de facto informal rights to, and interests in, land in the communal areas. The invalidation of the Communal Land Rights Act by the Constitutional Court in 2010 has, amongst others, resulted in the pre-April 1994 diverse and race-based system of communal tenure still being the only framework. Rural-urban migration has been on the increase, and the timeous establishment of new, well-planned and serviced townships, formal housing and security of tenure are some of the key goals that need to be addressed by the land reform programme.

As regards the future of land reform in South Africa, a new paradigm is represented by the recent announcement by Government that the 1994–2013 quantitative approach has been replaced with the qualitative aim of bringing about land reform projects that are productive. The new framework focuses in an integrated manner on both (a) the provision of access to commercial agricultural land to those previously dispossessed and/or excluded, and (b) the productive (sustainable and beneficial) use thereof. The main components of this evolving framework are: the acceptance of the central role of agricultural transformation, food security and sustainable agricultural productivity in the NDP; the establishment of the new land administration, management and valuation structures envisaged in the 2011 Green Paper; the implementation of the RADP; the re-opening of the restitution process for a period of five years; and the planned set of special arrangements for Khoi-San communities whose ancestors had been dispossessed during the period 1652–1913. It is to be hoped that a new set of tenure and concomitant administration arrangements in respect of communal tenure reform will soon complement this evolving land reform framework.

References

Books, book chapters and articles

Badenhorst, P.J., J. Pienaar and H. Mostert, 2006. *Silberberg and Schoeman's The Law of Property*, 5th edn. Durban: LexisNexis Butterworths.

Carey Miller, D.L. and A. Pope, 2000. *Land Title in South Africa*, 4th impression. Cape Town: Juta and Co.

Currie, I. and J. De Waal, 2005. *The Bill of Rights Handbook*, 5th edn. Cape Town: Juta and Co.

Dlamini, T.S., A. Verschoor and G.C.G. Fraser, 2013. 'Exploring options in reforming South African land ownership: Opportunities for sharing land, labour and expertise', *Agrekon*, 52(1): 24–45.

Du Plessis, W. and J. Pienaar, 2010. 'The more things change, the more they stay the same: The story of communal land tenure in South Africa', *Fundamina*, 16(1): 73–89.

Du Plessis, W.J. 2011. 'African indigenous land rights in a private ownership paradigm', *Potchefstroom Electronic Law Journal*, 14(7): 45–69.

Mahomed, A., P. Benjamin, B. Barry, S. Magardie, P. Naidu and N. Yazbek, 2011. *Understanding Land Tenure Law: Commentary & Legislation.* Cape Town: Juta and Co.

Pienaar, J. and J. Brickhill, 2008. 'Land', in eds S. Woolman and M. Bishop, *Constitutional Law of South Africa*. Cape Town: Juta and Co. Ltd, vol 3, ch 48.

Pienaar, J.M. 2011a. 'Restitutionary road: reflecting on good governance and the role of the Land Claims Court', *Potchefstroom Electronic Law Journal*, 14(3): 30–48.

—— 2011b. 'Access to housing in South Africa: An overview of dimensions and mechanisms', *Journal for Juridical Science*, 36(2): 119–40.

—— and A. Kamkuemah, 2011. 'Farm land and tenure security: New policy and legislative developments', *Stellenbosch Law Review*, 22(3): 724–41.

Rautenbach, I.M. and E.F.J. Malherbe, 2009. *Constitutional Law*, 5th edn. Durban: LexisNexis.

Rudman, A. 2012. 'Re-defining national sovereignty: The key to avoid constitutional reform? Reflections on the 2011 Green Paper on Land Reform', *Stellenbosch Law Review*, 23(3): 417–37.

Rugege, S. 2004. 'Land reform in South Africa: An overview', *International Journal of Legal Information*, 32(2): 283–312.

Van der Walt, A.J. 2004. 'An overview of developments in constitutional property law since the introduction of the property clause in 1993', *South African Public Law*, 19(1): 46–89.

—— 2011. *Constitutional Property Law*, 3rd edn. Cape Town: Juta and Co.

Reports

Commission on Restitution of Land Rights, 2013. *Annual Report 2012/2013* <http://www.ruraldevelopment.gov.za/publications/annual-report/file/1996> [accessed: 11 August 2013].

DRDLR (Department of Rural Development and Land Reform), 2011. *Strategic Plan 2011–2014* <http://www.ruraldevelopment.gov.za/publications/strategic-plans/file/1824> [accessed 2 August 2013].

—— 2013a. *Annual Performance Plan 2013/2014* <http://www.ruraldevelopment.gov.za/publications/annual-performance-plans/file/1825> [accessed 3 August 2013].

Website and online material

DRDLR (Department of Rural Development and Land Reform), 2013b. *Presentation to the Portfolio Committee on Rural Development and Land Reform*, 15 May <http://d2zmx6mlqh7g3a.cloudfront.net/cdn/farfuture/

XBlxlr_bflRMEbCNEtZ_a3KxrZutBVp7leTitwjmBqs/mtime:1369041984/files/130515drdlr.ppt> [accessed: 3 August 2013].

Green Paper on Land Reform, 2011 < http://www.dla.gov.za/legislation-and-policies/file/319> [accessed: 30 July 2013].

Greve, N. 2013. 'Government not chasing 30% land redistribution target – Minister', *Engineering News* <http://www.engineeringnews.co.za/article/govt-not-chasing-30-land-redistribution-target-minister-2013-08-12?utm_source=Creamer+Media+FDE+service&utm_medium=email&utm_campaign=EngineeringNews%3A+Construction+industry+must+deal+with+%27great+anger%27+over+collusion%2C+says+Upton&utm_term=http%3A%2F%2Fwww.engineeringnews.co.za%2Farticle%2Fgovt-not-chasing-30-land-redistribution-target-minister-2013-08-12> [accessed: 13 August 2013].

National Development Plan, 2013 <http://www.npconline.co.za/MediaLib/Downloads/Downloads/NDP%202030%20-%20Our%20future%20-%20make%20it%20work.pdf> [accessed 2 August 2013].

Parliament of the Republic of South Africa, 2013. *Questions regarding the progress on land redistribution and restitution* <http://d2zmx6mlqh7g3a.cloudfront.net/cdn/farfuture/u60EKY6WxXDEckvtBkw5qdfBGZd0glSIzxhVLun8MZU/mtime:1369395741/files/130522questions.pdf> [accessed: 10 August 2013].

Policy for the Recapitalisation and Development Programme, 2013 <http://ww2.ruraldevelopment.gov.za/phocadownload/Policies/rdp_23july2013.pdf> [accessed: 13 August 2013].

Sherry, S. 2013. 'Redistribution to focus on gaining "quality land"', *Business Day*, 13 August <http://www.bdlive.co.za/business/agriculture/2013/08/13/redistribution-to-focus-on-gaining-quality-land> [accessed: 13 August 2013].

Van der Walt, S. 2013. 'Plaasproduktiwiteit tel vir Minister meer as rasteiken', *Beeld* <http://www.beeld.com/nuus/2013-08-13-plaasproduktiwiteit-tel-vir-minister-meer-as-rasteiken> [accessed: 14 August 2013].

White Paper on South African Land Policy, 1997 <http://www.google.co.za/url?sa=t&rct=j&q=white%20paper%20on%20land%20policy&source=web&cd=1&ved=0CCsQFjAA&url=http%3A%2F%2Fd2zmx6mlqh7g3a.cloudfront.net%2Fcdn%2Ffarfuture%2F63D1qO182ISnhicr9lE5VYkX7fyzKUzfxO3xg8AQJfQ%2Fmtime%3A1245423879%2Ffiles%2Fdocs%2F090617whitepaper.doc&ei=un4HUojoOO2h7AbWq4DADg&usg=AFQjCNEYP7xOfg0ZXNLcVn6gzbQkiNb-OQ&bvm=bv.50500085,d.ZGU)> [accessed 27 July 2013].

Cases

Tongoane and Others v National Minister of Agriculture and Land Affairs and Others (2010) 6 SA 214 (CC).

Legislation

Abolition of Racially Based Land Measures Act 108 of 1991.
Development Facilitation Act 67 of 1995.
Distribution and Transfer of Certain State Land Act 119 of 1993.
Extension of Security of Tenure Act 62 of 1997.
Land Titles Adjustment Act 111 of 1993.
Provision of Land and Assistance Act 126 of 1993.
Restitution of Land Rights Act 22 of 1994.
Transformation of Certain Rural Areas Act 94 of 1998.
Upgrading of Land Tenure Rights Act 112 of 1991.

Chapter 16
Green Economy, Sustainable Development and the Constitution

Tumai Murombo

Introduction

> Environment
> Everyone has the right-
> (a) to an environment that is not harmful to their health or well-being; and
> (b) to have the environment protected, for the benefit of present and future generations, through reasonable legislative and other measures that-
> (i) prevent pollution and ecological degradation;
> (ii) promote conservation; and
> (iii) secure ecologically sustainable development and use of natural resources while promoting justifiable economic and social development.
> (Section 24, Constitution of South Africa 1996)

The South African Constitution of 1996 is often lauded as unique and trend setting in modern constitutionalism. However, the hype that came with the end of apartheid and the ushering-in of a new democratic dispensation is gradually giving in to disillusionment.

Among the social, economic and cultural rights provided for by the Constitution, we find a unique innovation in the form of the right to an environment not harmful to health and well-being (Feris 2009: 132). The South African Constitution is one of a few that provide for environmental rights (Glazewski 2005: 67), especially among developing countries. Sadly, while the courts in South Africa and writers write about the Constitution as a living document, it remains ink on paper. The transformation that the Constitution not only embodies, but also is expected to deliver has not fully materialised (Sibanda 2011: 495, 498). One begins to doubt whether the transformation envisaged lies only in the Constitution itself or in the transformation of institutions, cultures, world-views, and socio-political and economic relations of power.

Can a constitution deliver transformation? This is the crux of the matter in any review of the South African Constitution. Transformative constitutionalism is a contested concept and the process of transformation is complex and contingent on a number of variables (Langa 2006: 351, Pieterse 2005: 155, Klare 1998). It may well take decades before there are visible signs of transformation in South Africa, especially with the fulfilment of socio-economic and environmental rights. The words in the Constitution and in the legislation to implement its aspirations are in many respects still far removed from the lived experiences of the people of South Africa (Langa 2011: 448). Hence, Pound's words – that law as written is often removed from reality – still holds a century later. He argued that:

> The lawyer commonly flatters himself that the vagaries of legislators are responsible for most of the divergence between law in the books and law in action; that statutes impossible of enforcement, enacted off-hand without knowledge of the situation to be dealt with, are chiefly to be blamed. No doubt, crude legislation has been a factor of no mean importance. (Pound 1910: 20–21)

While certainly this typology holds true, it is undeniable that most constitutions proclaim aspirational ideals, some of which do indeed shape legal and policy action in practice.

This chapter discusses the constitutional protection of environmental rights in South Africa and whether or not this has translated into a jurisprudence that has practical impact. Environmental rights in the Constitution are embedded in the principle of sustainable development (*Fuel Retailers Association of Southern Africa*, paras 51–3). Recently and in line with global rhetoric, discourse in South Africa is shifting towards sustainable development as being fulfilled within the framework of greening the economy to alleviate poverty. This discourse is couched mostly in calls to shift the economy from conventional sources of energy to renewable energy and clean technologies. (Sebitosi and Pillay 2008, Winkler 2005, Strydom and King 2009, Pegels 2010, Prasad and Visagie 2005, Banks and Schäffler 2006, Green Economy Accord 2011, National Climate Change Response White Paper 2012).

The so-called 'green economy', while not a new idea (Pearce, Markyanda and Barbier 1989, Milani 2000), has assumed a fundamentally and ideologically suspect posture. The failure to define sustainable development globally (Magraw and Hawke 2007: 621) and the tottering struggle to devise concepts, indicators and milestones with which to measure sustainability is succumbing to a new approach that sees capitalism and economic growth as proxies to deliver sustainable development (Brand 2012: 28). The paradox is that capitalism and unlimited economic growth are at the root of the unsustainable use of natural resources (*Fuel Retailers Association*, para 44). Sustainable development and environmental rights were developed as weapons to suppress the unsustainable spirit of consumption that has possessed the human race. The coupling of economic growth to unsustainable production and consumption has remained ever more secure and any attempts to frame sustainability in the language of the economy are bound to be futile. Economic growth must be decoupled from unsustainable use of natural resources (Fischer-Kowalski and Swilling 2011: 4).

However, the environmental lobby appears gradually to be acquiescing in the idea of sustainable development through economic growth. Indeed, the preponderance of opinion is that environmental sustainability and economic growth are compatible and can be complementary (López and Toman 2006: 3, Murombo 2008: 494, Dryzek 2007: 57). In interpreting section 24 of the Constitution, South African courts have since recognised this intertwining of environmental protection and economic development (*Fuel Retailers Association of Southern Africa*, para 44; *BP Southern Africa (Pty) Ltd*, 146). Thus the Rio+20 United Nations Commission on Sustainable Development (UNCSD) Conference, held in Rio de Janeiro in 2012, had as its theme 'a green economy in the context of sustainable development and poverty eradication and the institutional framework for sustainable development'.

Defining Green Economy

Despite being the environmental word of currency, 'green economy' does not enjoy a globally acceptable definition (Dasgupta 2011:34). The Rio+20 outcomes document, 'The Future We Want', contains a section on the green economy, but provides no guidance on what this new creature means (Clémençon 2012: 318, 'The Future We Want', 2012). Like sustainable development, the concept has such currency and attractiveness that people worry less about what it means, than what it promises to deliver. It is assumed that the green economy is the key to unlock the balance and integration that underpin the idea of sustainable development. Ocampo contends that the green economy is 'an alternative paradigm that offers the promise of growth while protecting the earth's ecosystems and, in turn, contributing to poverty alleviation' (Ocampo 2011: 4). This function of the green economy is overshadowed by its fuzziness and lack of content. This reality masks serious contestation of ideas and meaning that lies beneath the surface, and the economic inclinations of the concept. The green economy represents a new ascendance of the economic aspect of Brundtland's sustainable development over the social and environmental aspects. Ulrich Brand bluntly, and perhaps rightly, argues that 'The concept of a green economy is, like sustainable development, rather an oxymoron which intends to bundle different, partly contradictory, interests and strategies, and gives them a certain legitimacy and coherence' (Brand 2012: 29). This is all in pursuit of a solution to the global economic, financial, climate change and energy crises.

The green economy may therefore be the new way to develop in the absence of clear strategies to implement sustainable development models. However, it may also signal the death of environmental sustainability and the final stages of the commodification of natural resources in the service of capital. The green economy, as presently configured, is not synonymous with a sustainable economy. The question remains whether the green economy is up to the challenges of rectifying the repercussions of the multiple crises and of steering us off the unsustainability path (Barbier 2011: 237–8, Ocampo 2011: 4).

Who defines the green economy is likely to come to the fore when attempts are made to set indicators of what this new sustainability jargon entails (Cook and Smith 2012: 6). Certainly, it is likely that the North–South debate will resurface in the discourse about who defines which economy is green and which is brown. Despite the absence of an agreed concept of the green economy, certain strands can be extrapolated from the scant literature on the subject.

The green economy is conceived of as an approach to economic growth and development that premises such growth on the use of green technology, renewable energy and green jobs (Barbier 2011: 233). Some posit that the green economy has attained new currency since the 'triple crises of finance, energy and the environment' (Jessop 2012: 21). As a knee-jerk reaction to the 'triple crises', green-economy thinking is seen as an elixir whose long-term utility is at best dubious (ibid.). The economic logic that is lending currency to the green economy is the very logic that gave birth to the crises. A crisis of capitalism cannot be cured by greening capitalism and its embedded social and economic relations of productions (Cook and Smith 2012, Jessop 1997: 565–6). Similarly, such greening may not dislodge the very laws that legitimise these relations of production and power. Brand sums it up aptly in noting that 'In sum, the concept of a green economy seems to promise an attractive orientation out of the crisis of neoliberalism that became manifest in 2008 and has hit vulnerable countries and social groups' (Brand 2012: 28).

Others, however, see the emergence of the green economy as a promising way out of the implosion of capitalism and neoliberal policies, provided it is premised on a systematic policy integration strategy to promote sustainable development (Hamdouch and Depret 2010: 474, 476). They further argue that:

> Indeed, we see growing support for the idea that active and global environmental protection opens up real possibilities for the development of new sectors with considerable economic (growth), financial (investment) and human (jobs) potential in the short to medium-term, and probably more significant potential over the long term. In fact, the theme of 'green growth' is increasingly evident in the expression of public policies and in actors' strategies. (Ibid.: 474)

South Africa provides an illustration of how environmental law and sustainable development law have entered the service of capital, despite being projected as weapons to confront poverty and carbon-intensive unsustainable growth. The Constitution, the New Growth Path and the National Development Plan are all premised on notions of implementing sustainable development through economic growth (Government of South Africa 2010, 2012). Yet, this is as far as it goes; in reality, one is confronted by an energy-intensive economy driven by conventional fossil-fuel energy sources, environmental degradation, and painstakingly slow closure of the socio-economic inequality gap. The energy engine of the South African economy fires as much into economic growth as it concomitantly exudes air and water pollution and environmental degradation, in the shadow of which any semblance of economic growth pales into insignificance. Private-wealth creation, clothed as economic growth and progress, is exposed for what it is when one encounters the yawning gap between rich and poor, the persistence of poverty and unemployment, and stagnation in terms of the livelihoods of the most vulnerable in society. Why then does South Africa continue to deliver good Kuznets growth statistics when there are persistent socio-economic challenges? The conventional indicators of capitalist growth are proving inadequate as measures of holistic development and growth (Henderson and Sethi 2006: 1–2). This grim reality provides a good backdrop to an analysis of how the Constitution, and the laws that it has spawned, promote the green economy and new sustainable (economic) development.

The 1996 Constitution and the Green Economy Proposition

The right to an environment not harmful to health and well-being played a decisive role in reorienting environmental regulation in South Africa. Not only has it projected sustainable development as the world-view within which to think about the environment and the economy, but also how South Africa presents itself to the global community. The protection of environmental rights in s 24 is the result of South Africa embracing the notion of sustainable development (*Director: Mineral Development, Gauteng Region and SASOL Mining (Pty) Ltd v Save the Vaal Environment and Others*, para 20). In theory, sustainable development has come to define environmental regulation in South Africa and globally (*BP Southern Africa (Pty) Ltd*, para 142; *MEC for Agriculture, Conservation, Environment and Land Affairs v Sasol Oil (Pty) Ltd and Another*, para 15). The Constitution has provided the impetus for the development of an elaborate framework of environmental and natural resources regulation. Despite this, the interpretation of sustainable development and its implementation remain problematic. While the cases referred to above show the judiciary grappling with the conundrum, in nearly all the cases that have come before South African courts, there has not been clear guidance on how to implement sustainable development in practice. In some of the cases, there have been dissenting judgments illustrating the still-unsettled content of the concept, particularly as it underpins environmental rights (Feris 2009: 134). It is easy for the law and courts to provide that sustainable development requires integration and the balancing of social, economic and environmental considerations, but doing so practically is a different and often imprecise exercise.

New and revised environmental and natural resources laws have been formulated and remodelled, to align them with the spirit of sustainability. Principal among this legislation are the National Environmental Management Act of 1998 (NEMA) (the framework environmental legislation), the Minerals and Petroleum Resources Development Act of 2002 (the sustainable use of mineral and petroleum resources), and an array of Specific Environmental Management Acts (SEMAs) that deal with air quality (Air Quality Act of 2004), protected areas (Protected Areas Act of 2003), biodiversity (Biodiversity Act of 2004), waste (Waste Act of 2008), and coastal management (Integrated Coastal Management Act of 2008). Theoretically, this environmental law arsenal is impressive, but in practice its implementation and enforcement have been half-hearted. The level of legislative activity in the natural resources and environmental spheres contrasts sharply with the absence of the same vigour in the social and economic spheres of sustainable development.

Economic regulation and the social relations of production have seen little reorientation and reform towards sustainability. The economy remains largely directed towards the pursuit of profit and shareholder gratification. The workers have remained impoverished and despite some pretence at corporate social responsibility, sustainability reporting and green technology, it is proving a challenge for capitalism to transform itself into a sustainable mode of production. This is not to discount some genuine efforts by corporations to make business sustainable, but it is rather a reminder that this has often been peripheral to their core preoccupation with 'economic' sustainability. 'Welfarist' efforts to cushion the vulnerable from the effects of capital accumulation and profit maximisation have only served to antagonise the government on the one hand, and the owners of the means of production and the heavily taxed middle class on the other. It remains questionable if the law can assist here, as it is essentially a political-economic problem.

Once solved though, the economy could deliver equitable social relations and hopefully the sustainable use of natural resources, and reforming the legal superstructure and rewriting laws can assist this reordering. Skewed social relations in South Africa can be addressed through legislation and be ameliorated by welfare safety nets, but environmental laws alone cannot change these. Similarly, the nascent jurisprudence on sustainable development since 1996 has not resulted in radical changes in how industry and government think about the environment and natural resource use. When necessary, such as when the country is hosting international events of note such as the 17th Conference of the Parties to the United Nations Framework Convention on Climate Change (UNFCCC 2011) (COP 17) and World Summit on Sustainable Development (WSSD 2002), the political rhetoric turns pro-environment, but with the ever-present undertone of economic development as the priority.

Despite this criticism, South Africa has fared relatively well among developing countries in legislative reforms geared towards promoting sustainable development and environmental rights. Equally, the courts are among the first to give content to environmental rights and sustainable development on the African continent. Unequivocally, the Constitution has provided space for these developments. The quandary that confronts South Africa is how to stay true to globally appealing notions of transformative constitutionalism, the green economy and sustainable development while concurrently improving the lives of its huge population of poor citizens. Mediating economy, society and the environment in a context of poverty, unemployment and outrageous economic inequality is indeed a complex, but not insurmountable, challenge. For instance, the country has been battling to balance the need to keep the lights on and the economic engine running, while abandoning fossil fuels and promoting renewable energy. The race to meet the targets for Millennium Developments Goals (MDGs) perennially hangs like a cloud over the country. Can sustainable development still create a framework within which equilibrium and harmony can be secured?

Sustainable Development – The Quest for Equilibrium

The social, economic and cultural context of environmental regulation in South Africa has brought to the fore the inextricable complexity of the concept of sustainable development. The elusive balance between the three legs of sustainable development has become ever more intangible (Dryzek 2007: 56). The global attempt to achieve this balance through the green economy seems attractive and South Africa has warmed to the idea, as it largely comports with the country's unchanging economic regulation and models. The green economy means that South Africa can possibly justify the continued reliance on fossil fuels and energy intensive industries to create more jobs, albeit less green.

The environmental movement has gained some traction and has managed to influence legal discourse on sustainable development. However, this contrasts with the other realities, that environmental degradation continues and that the sustainable use of natural resources remains a challenge. What accounts for these dichotomies? How can sustainable development and progressive environmental laws be brought to bear on these realities? Does this imply that the social aspect of sustainable development has been forgotten (Cook and Smith 2012: 6)? South Africa has set its eyes on moving toward sustainable development through legislated environmentalism and a strong environmental civil movement, in sharp contrast with the socio-economic reality.

Implementing Sustainable Development through Environmentalism

Projecting a developmental state agenda in the face of increasing environmental consciousness was always going to be difficult. Admittedly, the levels of poverty and unemployment are high, and the 'only' supposed solution to this is job creation, through enabling economic activity that is growth oriented (Government of Republic of South Africa 2011b, 2010). This seems achievable if South Africa uses its abundantly available and cheap coal and existing brown technologies, but this is oblivious to the discounted costs of the business-as-usual approach to development and regulation. The health-care and social-welfare burdens on the State also increase in proportion to the degree to which the State allows the business-as-usual trajectory to continue.

This situation is worsened by the regular reminders of apartheid's effects and the need to address them. The development agenda has in fact become a pronounced enemy of environmentalism, which appears to be slowly giving in to the drive to redress the imbalances of the past through expedited economic development. The strong emphasis on a growing economy creates new problems for environmental governance and regulation. This is vividly illustrated by the urgency with which minerals resources are being extracted at the expense of the environment, food security (agriculture), and community livelihoods. The single-minded pursuit of job creation does not sit well with the new green agenda, as some of its tenets have long incubation periods. The transitional phase requires effective and transformative legal, policy and institutional intervention theories. The Constitution remains a key transformative tool to frame this transition.

Delivering a keynote address at the Green Economy: Pro-employment Summit, President Zuma rightly noted that:

> Underpinning such a path [to a green economy] is the requirement for government to recognise the regulatory and institutional support that will be needed to support a green economy. A green economy will require integrated strategies and plans that effectively balance economic, environmental and social development objectives. (Zuma 2010)

By including section 24 in the Constitution and by hosting the WSSD in 2002 and COP17 in 2011, South Africa is consistently signifying its intent to pursue sustainable development, which is confirmed by reforms in the field of environmental regulation. However, this must be matched by equal efforts in the economic sphere of regulation. The White Paper on Renewable Energy Policy (2004) and the Integrated Resource Plan 2 (2010) for energy resources project contradictory visions of the future energy mix, while the reality on the ground is more disheartening. Tenaciously grounding sustainability in environmentalism is perhaps a serious oversight and has led to sustainable development losing its cross-cutting integrative and balancing function. In spite of this, the judiciary in South Africa has taken decisive steps in giving content to section 24 and the function of sustainable development (*Fuel Retailers Association*, paras 57–9).

The Judiciary – Mediating the Paradox

While judicial interpretations of s 24 of the Constitution brought some theoretical lucidity, unfortunately there is little practical guidance to policy makers and decision makers on how to implement sustainability. The principal issues that have occupied the courts are how environmental impact assessment (EIA) should be used to implement sustainable development, environmental governance and the role of the three spheres of government. Broadly, the following judicial approaches can be gleaned from the environmental jurisprudence thus far:

- Section 24 of the Constitution is there not only to protect the environment but equally to promote socio-economic development, thus environmental rights are on par with other rights in the Constitution (*BP Southern Africa; MEC, Department of Agriculture, Conservation and Environment and another v HTF Developers (Pty) Ltd*, paras 25–8);
- Environmental protection and socio-economic development are not mutually exclusive but complementary and interdependent objectives. Thus in an EIA, the authority is bound to consider social, economic and

environmental impacts of a proposed activity (*Fuel Retailers Association* paras 78–9, 90);

- Sustainable development informs environmental regulation in South Africa, and
- While economic activities, such as mining, are necessary to promote development, they are subject to environmental and land-use planning regulation at the national, provincial and local levels of government, as the case may be (*Maccsand (Pty) Ltd*, paras 48–50, *Johannesburg Metropolitan Municipality v Gauteng Development Tribunal and Others*, para 45, *Le Sueur*, paras 39–40).

An exhaustive elaboration of the issues and facts of these cases is not possible given the limited scope of this chapter, yet the distilled principles do give a picture of how the courts have interpreted s 24, sustainable development and the coordination of environmental regulation across all spheres of government.

Climate Change and the Green Economy – The Future

Climate change and South Africa's contribution to greenhouse gas emissions are among the drivers of sustainable development reforms and recent green economy overtures. The Climate Change Response White Paper (2012) is part of the strategy to address green economy issues from a climate change perspective. However, it is questionable whether the White Paper adequately integrates the policy on climate change responses across sectors. The basis of the White Paper is a departure from a business-as-usual approach to climate change response, yet there is still an undertone of protecting the economy, development, jobs and the status quo. This should be read together with continued faith in fossil fuels for the near future.

Moving to a green economy requires international support through shifts in the world trade system and support for developing countries (Cosbey 2011: 58). Technology transfer must translate from paper promises to practical steps taken by the developed economies. However, since the Rio Earth Summit of 1992 and the treaties resulting from that summit that placed much faith in technology transfer, nothing significant has materialised. If anything, the stalled climate change negotiations are an indication that some of the implementing mechanisms are faced with certain failure. Technology transfer is a critical strategy for ensuring that developed economies can assist developing economies to meet their transition to low-carbon economies. The green economy presupposes this transition and therefore requires technology transfer as an integral aspect of change.

Conclusion

Over the past twenty years, the South African Constitution has certainly changed many things in the country, but the economic transformation it promises has been slow to materialise. In the environmental regulation sphere, the creation of an environmental right underpinned by sustainable development has seen policy and legislative progress, but little has changed in how the government and industry perceive and deal with natural resources. This is partly due to the complex nature of the task required in promoting integration in a social, economic, cultural and political atmosphere replete with intractable contradictions and ideological conflicts. South African courts have attempted to give meaning to environmental rights and sustainable development – yet practical guidance to policy makers and decision makers remains as elusive as the meaning of sustainable development itself. The global shift towards green economy thinking and green growth as pathways to sustainability is spreading to developing countries. However, the contestation of these new concepts and how they may entrench global inequities among states means that they remain peripheral, while conventional economic development policies remain firmly in place.

References

Books, book chapters and articles

Banks, D. and J. Schäffler, 2006. 'The potential contribution of renewable energy in South Africa', Draft Update Report. Johannesburg: Sustainable Energy and Climate Change Project.

Barbier, E. 2011. The policy challenges for green economy and sustainable economic development. Natural Resources Forum. Wiley Online Library, <www.onlinelibrary.wiley.com › ... › Natural Resources Forum › Vol 35 Issue 3> pp. 233–45 [accessed 30 June 2014].

Bodansky, D., J. Brunnee, and E. Hey, 2007. *The Oxford Handbook of International Environmental Law*. Oxford: Oxford University Press.

Brand, U. 2012. 'The Next Oxymoron? No Lessons Learned From Failures Of Implementing Sustainable Development', *Gaia-Ecological Perspectives For Science And Society*, 21(1) (March): 28–32.

Clémençon, R. 2012. 'Welcome to the Anthropocene Rio+ 20 and the meaning Of Sustainable Development', *Journal of Environment & Development*, 21: 311–38.

Cook, S. and K. Smith, 2012. 'Introduction: Green Economy And Sustainable Development: Bringing Back the "Social"', *Development*, 55 (1): 5–9.

Cosbey, A. 2011. *Trade, Sustainable Development and a Green Economy: Benefits, Challenges and Risks. The Transition to a Green Economy: Benefits, Challenges and Risks from a Sustainable Development Perspective*, UNCTAD, 40.

Dasgupta, C. 2011. 'Reflections On The Relationship Between The "Green Economy" And Sustainable Development', *UNCTAD: The Road To Rio*, 20: 33–5.

Dryzek, J.S. 2007. 'Paradigms And Discourses', in eds D. Bodansky, J. Brunnee, and E. Hey, *The Oxford Handbook Of International Environmental Law*, Oxford: Oxford University Press, pp. 44–62.

Feris, L. 2009. 'Environmental Rights And Locus Standi', in eds A. Paterson and L.J. Kotzé, *Environmental Compliance And Enforcement In South Africa-Legal Perspectives*. Cape Town: Juta & Co.

Fischer-Kowalski, M. and M. Swilling, 2011. *Decoupling: Natural Resource Use And Environmental Impacts From Economic Growth*. United Nations Environment Programme.

Glazewski, J. 2005. *Environmental Law In South Africa*. Durban: Lexisnexis Butterworths.

Government of the Republic Of South Africa. 2010. *Framework of the New Economic Growth Path (New Growth Path)*.

——. 2011a. *Economic Development Department. Accord 4*: Green Economy Accord. 29 November.

——. 2011b. Department Of Energy. *Electricity Regulations on the Integrated Resource Plan 2010–2030*. Government Notice R.400 of 2011. Government Gazette 34263.

——. 2011c. Department of Environmental Affairs. *White Paper On The National Climate Change Response*. General Notice 757 of 2011, Government Gazette 34695.

——. 2012. National Planning Commission. *National Development Plan 2030: Our Future – Make It Work*.

Hamdouch, A. and M.-H. Depret, 2010. 'Policy Integration Strategy And The Development Of The 'Green Economy': Foundations And Implementation Patterns', *Journal Of Environmental Planning And Management*, 53: 473–90.

Hayward, T. 2005. *Constitutional Environmental Rights*. Oxford: Oxford University Press.

Henderson, H. and S. Sethi, 2006. *Ethical Markets: Growing The Green Economy*. White River Junction, VT: Chelsea Green Publishing. Company.

Jessop, B. 1997. 'Capitalism and its Future: Remarks on Regulation, Government and Governance', *Review Of International Political Economy*, 4: 561–81.

——. 2012. 'Economic and Ecological Crises: Green New Deals and No-Growth Economies', *Development*, 55: 17–24.

Klare, K.E. 1998. 'Legal Culture and Transformative Constitutionalism', *South African Journal On Human Rights*, 14: 146.

Langa, P. 2006. 'Transformative Constitutionalism', *Stellenbosch Law Review*, 17: 351.

——. 2011. 'The Role of the Constitution in the Struggle Against Poverty', *Stellenbosch Law Review*, 3: 446.

López, R. and M.A. Toman, 2006. *Economic Development And Environmental Sustainability: New Policy Options*. Oxford: Oxford University Press.

Magraw, D.B. and L.D. Hawke, 2007. 'Sustainable development', in eds D. Bodansky, J. Brunnee, and E. Hey, *The Oxford Handbook of International Environmental Law*. Oxford: Oxford University Press, pp. 613–38.

Milani, B. 2000. *Designing The Green Economy: The Post-Industrial Alternative to Corporate Globalization*. Lanham, MD: Rowman & Littlefield.

Murombo, T. 2008. 'From Crude Environmentalism to Sustainable Development: Fuel Retailers', *South African Law Journal*, 125: 488–504.

Ocampo, J. 2011. *The Transition To A Green Economy: Benefits, Challenges And Risks From A Sustainable Development Perspective – Summary Of Background Papers*. United Nations Report By A Panel Of Experts To Second Preparatory Committee Meeting For United Nations Conference On Sustainable Development.

Pearce, D., A. Markandya and E. Barbier, 1989. *Blueprint For A Green Economy*. London: Earthscan and London Environmental Economics Centre and UK Department of the Environment.

Pegels, A. 2010. 'Renewable Energy In South Africa: Potentials, Barriers And Options For Support', *Energy Policy*, 38: 4945–54.

Pieterse, M. 2005. 'What Do We Mean When We Talk About Transformative Constitutionalism', *South African Public Law*, 20: 155–66.

Pound, R. 1910. 'Law in Books and Law in Action', *American Law Review*, 44: 12.

Prasad, G. and E. Visagie, 2005. *Renewable Energy Technologies For Poverty Alleviation Initial Assessment Report*. South Africa: Renewable Energy Technology (RET) Working Group.

Scholtz, A. et al. 2011. *Towards A Green Economy: Envisaging Success at Cop17*. South Africa: WWF.

Sebitosi, A. and P. Pillay, 2008. 'Grappling With A Half-Hearted Policy: The Case Of Renewable Energy And The Environment In South Africa', *Energy Policy*, 36: 2513–16.

Sibanda, S. 2011. 'Not Purpose-Made! Transformative Constitutionalism, 8 Post-Independence Constitutionalism and the Struggle to Eradicate Poverty', *Stellenbosch Law Review*, 22: 482–6.

Strydom, H. and N. King, 2009. *Environmental Management in South Africa*. Cape Town: Juta.

UNDESA (United Nations Department Of Economics And Social Affairs). 2009. *A Global Green New Deal For Sustainable Development. Policy Brief No. 12* <www.un.org/en/development/desa/policy/.../policy_briefs/policybrief12.pdf > [accessed 30 June 2014].

Winkler, H. 2005. 'Renewable Energy Policy In South Africa: Policy Options For Renewable Electricity', *Energy Policy*, 33: 27–38.

Zuma, J. 2010. Keynote Address by His Excellency, Mr Jacob Zuma, President Of The Republic Of South Africa, at the Green Economy Summit, Sandton Convention Centre, Johannesburg, 18 May <www.govza.gcis.gov.za/ node/457764> [accessed 30 June 2014].

Cases

BP Southern Africa (Pty) Ltd v MEC for Agriculture, Conservation, Environment and Land Affairs 2005(4) SA 125 (W).
Director: Mineral Development, Gauteng Region and SASOL Mining (Pty) Ltd v Save the Vaal Environment and others 1999(2) SA 709 (SCA).
Fuel Retailers Association of Southern Africa v Director-General: Environmental Management, Department of Agriculture, Conservation and Environment, Mpumalanga Province, and Others 2007 (6) SA 4 (CC).
Johannesburg Metropolitan Municipality v Gauteng Development Tribunal and Others 2010 (6) SA 182 (CC).
Le Sueur and Another v Ethekwini Municipality and Others (9714/11) [2013] ZAKZPHC 6 (30 January 2013).
Maccsand (Pty) Ltd v City of Cape Town and Others 2012 (4) SA 181 (CC).
MEC, Department of Agriculture, Conservation and Environment and another v HTF Developers (Pty) Ltd 2008 (2) SA 319 (CC).
MEC for Agriculture, Conservation, Environment and Land Affairs v Sasol Oil (Pty) Ltd and Another 2006 (5) SA 483 (SCA).

Legislation

Constitution of the Republic of South Africa, 1996.
Minerals and Petroleum Resources Development Act 28 of 2002.
National Environmental Management Act 107 of 1998.
National Environmental Management: Air Quality Act 39 of 2004.
National Environmental Management: Biodiversity Act 10 of 2004.
National Environmental Management: Integrated Coastal Management Act 24 of 2008.
National Environmental Management: Protected Areas Act 57 of 2003.
National Environmental Management: Waste Act 59 of 2008.

PART V
South Africa in Context

Chapter 17

BRICS: A Mirage of Reality

Lucia Scaffardi

Introduction

On 26 and 27 March 2013, the fifth Summit of the BRICS countries was held in Durban, South Africa. The European media gave the event little coverage, whilst the Brazilian, Russian, Indian, Chinese and South African media showed far greater interest. A wide range of issues was indeed at stake, ranging from economics to global politics, including the relevant legal perspectives.

Understanding the BRICS phenomenon from the legal angle is crucial. It is a subject rarely covered in Italian constitutionalist literature, unlike schools in North America.[1] Whilst in economic terms we are seeing an increase in the amount of work done (O'Neill 2011, Jones 2012, Nadkarni and Noonan 2012, Inks 2012, Goldstein 2011), the legal aspects of this new and unclear process cannot be neglected.

There is a strong link between the current economic situation and the decision that prompted Brazil, Russia, India, China and South Africa to establish closer ties. In fact, 'the traditional financial hot spots and the occidental economic model are losing their supremacy, because of a gravitational shift of transactions, assets and ideas towards emerging market economies that could become, if not already so, the leaders of a new economic order' (Di Plinio 2011: 100). Yet saying this phenomenon is down to mere 'parallel interests' is an oversimplification. Their cooperation proves the desire to make the voice of this important part of the world – the BRICS countries represent over 40 per cent of the world's population (ISSA 2013: 13) – be heard on a par with the West. From a legal perspective, the impact of this cooperation that we argue takes the form of a nascent 'legal network' has been unimaginable until now.

BRICS: From Acronym to Joint Action in the Inter-state Arena

The 'BRICS' acronym was introduced by Jim O'Neill, who far-sightedly predicted the economic potential of what were, at the time, four countries, without South

1 See the Wisconsin Law School <http://brics.global.wisc.edu/>, the Fordham School of Law in New York <http://law.fordham.edu/newsroom/26395.htm> and the BRICS Information Centre of the University of Toronto <http://www.brics.utoronto.ca/>.

Africa (O'Neill 2001). In doing so, he suggested a path for the creation of a new entity. Accordingly, for a while, BRIC only referred to economics, with much scepticism about further cooperation. This scepticism was shared by the actors themselves, as manifestly declared by E.G. Yasin, director of research at the State University Higher School of Economics of Moscow: 'Between the Bric countries, there is really little in common. Each of them has its own destiny, its own special character, and it will be much more difficult for them to agree among themselves than separately with Western countries' (Levy 2009). Contrary to predictions, and thanks to the collapse of the Euro-Atlantic paradigms, the reality of the BRICS is highly impressive in many respects:

> All four of the BRIC countries have exceeded the expectations I had of them back in 2001. Looking back, those earliest predictions, shocking to some at the time, now seem rather conservative. The aggregate GDP of the BRIC countries has close to quadrupled since 2001, from around $3 trillion to between $11 and $12 trillion. The world economy has doubled in size since 2001, and a third of that growth has come from the BRICs. Their combined GDP increase was more than twice that of the United States and it was equivalent to the creation of another new Japan plus one Germany, or five United Kingdoms, in the space of a single decade. (O'Neill 2011: 4)

Since 2006, when the foreign ministers of the BRICS countries first met alongside a session of the UN General Assembly, this new entity has grown considerably, both in terms of its role and of its perceived importance world-wide.

The first Summit of BRICS countries, held in Yekaterinburg, Russia, on 16 June 2009, officially launched the new organisation (Joint Statement of the BRIC Countries' Leaders 2009). Whilst it was only an initial step, the desire to provide a strong counterpoint, almost a challenge, to the dominant role played by the United States and the US dollar has been clear since the very beginning:

> We are committed to advance the reform of financial institutions, so as to reflect changes in global economy. The emerging and developing economies must have greater voice and representation in international financial institutions, whose heads and executives should be appointed through an open, transparent, and merit-based selection process. We also believe that there is a strong need of a stable, predictable, and more diversified international monetary system. (Joint Statement of the BRIC Countries' Leaders 2009: point 5)

Starting in 2009, the four countries meet regularly once a year. They have taken turns to play host, and in 2013, their first series of meetings drew to a close in Durban, South Africa; South Africa had joined the 'club' in 2010. The interesting decision-making processes adopted by the BRICS run in two directions. The first involves the 'coordination' between heads of state within the Summits; the second operates at the inter-ministerial level.

Thus, the official statements delivered in the Summits which indicate the policy guidelines for the BRICS countries are supported by the bulk of preparatory work carried out at ministerial level. The work of the BRICS 'sherpa' has increased considerably so that it now resembles a periodic consultation process. The wide range of subjects tackled in the meetings promotes and indeed legitimises inter-state cooperation at different levels. This has the knock-on effect of reinforcing relations among the partners, particularly with regard to trade, financial and economic issues (Ahdieh et al. 2007).

In addition to these (probably predictable) outcomes, there are new and unexpected ones which involve technical and scientific sectors, from technological innovation to agricultural development and protecting health and the environment. Accordingly, cooperation is actually strengthened in many sectors, with the effect of sharing skills to promote development. Adopting a multi-tasking and circular approach, the intrinsic difference of the countries makes for a positive and highly varied exchange of experiences.

Ministerial cooperation is very different from inter-state cooperation: if the former attempts to influence global dynamics or governance reform, the latter panders to the economic, political and cultural integration of BRICS countries. These interactions are still 'under construction', and it is not always easy to identify the processes that can foster a balanced development. Yet the output is significant:

> The BRICS countries have a remarkable opportunity to coordinate their economic policies and diplomatic strategies not only to enhance their position as a grouping in the international economic and financial system, but also to be a stabilisation factor for the world economy as a whole. The BRICS should increasingly harmonise and coordinate their policies with a view to sustaining their growth momentum and capacity to weather global turbulence. The benefits of cooperation are immense not only for the BRICS but also for the global economy. (The BRICS Report 2012: 168)

A clear example of this tighter cooperation is to be seen in the BRICS policies on health:

> Most of BRICS countries face a number of similar public health challenges, including universal access to health services, access to health technologies, including medicines, increasing costs and the growing burden of both communicable and non-communicable diseases. We direct that the BRICS Health Ministers meetings, of which the first was held in Beijing in July 2011, should henceforth be institutionalized in order to address these common challenges in the most cost-effective, equitable and sustainable manner. (Delhi Declaration, Point 42, 29 March 2012)

This goal coincides with the decision adopted by the health ministers in 2013 to tackle non-communicable diseases, given that 80 per cent of deaths caused by these diseases occur in countries with a low-to-average income (Delhi Health Ministers' Final Declaration, Point 4, 2012). While in Europe health issues are increasingly handled in terms of cost-cutting policies, the BRICS countries are investing in global health as a source of further development and research: 'From 2005 to 2010, Brazil's assistance spending grew each year by around 20.4%, India's by around 10.8%, China's by around 23.9%, and South Africa's by around 8%. Russia's assistance increased substantially early in the same period, before stabilizing at around US dollars 450 million per year' (GHSi 2012: 6). Needless to say, these strategies may be perceived as 'utilitarian' and aimed at each country's self-promotion, but the engagement undertaken can be measured by the extent of their research and investment in global health care.

Like traditional donors, the BRICS countries have their own motives for engaging in global health care. And there are, to be sure, reasonable concerns about their role and the effectiveness of their programmes. Yet these countries represent a potentially transformative source of new resources and innovation for global health and development. Over the long term, the BRICS can play an increasingly important role in helping to improve the health and well-being of the world's poorest countries (GHSi 2012: 92).

The dynamic process started by Brazil, Russia, India, China and South Africa to establish common interests and measures is far removed from those of its European or North American counterparts (Yu 2008). Some of these aspects are also significant on a juridical and constitutional level: an example is the strong role played by the state in all five nations, whilst on the other hand we are witnessing an ever-increasing 'divestiture' (Auby 2008) of the state in favour of the European Union, pushing the EU's economy firmly towards the free market and restricting national intervention or protectionism policies.

Against this background, what are we referring to when mentioning the BRICS? The group refrains from expressing the real nature of its setup, making any form of classification difficult. Instead, it only proves what it is not: it is no longer a summit, nor merely an international organisation.

From a legal perspective, the activities of 'the entity' show that the BRICS countries have relatively stable 'juridical flows' implemented through policy transfer, and, occasionally, fully fledged constitutional borrowing (Tebbe and Tsai 2010, Perju 2012), as they are consolidating shared action models and public policies, and imitating solutions or constitutional instruments.

An example of common public policies and coordinated actions is the agricultural and food safety sector's policy. Since 2009 and following the joint statement on food safety adopted at the Yekaterinburg (Russia) Summit, the BRICS countries have started to exchange experiences, at the levels of Heads of State and Ministers of Agriculture and their representatives. The development of specific agricultural policies has been defined during various meetings and, in 2011, the first action plan was approved. One of the most interesting actions undertaken in this sector has been the creation of a database on agricultural policies, concerning data on the production/commerce of products and agricultural technologies.

Then the question arises, should we analyse the BRICS as a group, or continue focusing attention on Brazil, Russia, India, China and South Africa as independent realities? Indeed, convergence on common problems (such as sustainability, the environment, exploitation of raw materials, and so on) needs to be analysed against the backdrop of the political and institutional frame of each country. This convergence does not mean full alignment, but a flexible model that fosters contact and exchange between independent political and juridical entities (Carducci 2012: 4).

S for South Africa: The Turning-point for the Legal Network

In the first two BRIC Summits, held in Russia and Brazil, 'many subjects were discussed … but few proposals were received, and even fewer decisions were actually taken', whereas in the Summits in India and South Africa there has been a different approach, 'anticipating perhaps a political shift' (Quercia 2011: 20). This is due to two main reasons: first, the enlargement of the range of themes discussed, so that on a purely economic-financial-commercial level, the summits took concrete steps in the field of international security, terrorism and the wars in Libya and Syria, health and the environment. Second, the fully-fledged entry of South Africa as a new member of the BRICS (Sekine 2011), as we will discuss, has contributed strengthening the BRICS 'political' side.

In 2010, just a few months after the Summit in Brasilia, the foreign ministers met in New York and approved the proposal to invite South Africa as a member of the BRIC group. The result was a new acronym strengthened with an upper-case S. Far from being just one of the many forms of 'economic and diplomatic' association described by analysts, this enlargement responds to a true political commitment of those involved.

Why have Brazil, Russia, India and China chosen South Africa as the fifth country of the network? Other African countries (such as Nigeria) could have provided greater potential, but definitely not the same political stability (O'Neill 2011: 100, Deegan 2011, Kwandiwe and Chinenyengozi 2011).

The role played by South Africa in global geopolitics, both in North/South and South/South international relations is increasingly important (Modi 2011). Its GDP accounts for over one-third of all sub-Saharan Africa, in spite of the fact that its surface area only covers 4 per cent of the continent. Approximately four-fifths of the African continent's businesses are from South Africa. On a regional level, South Africa's hegemony is even more pronounced: 80 per cent of Southern Africa's GDP is produced in South Africa, and it is the leading importer and exporter to and from neighbouring countries. The Johannesburg Stock Exchange is the continent's top financial marketplace, and ranks thirteenth world-wide (DBSA 2012). This aspect undoubtedly counted a great deal, given the financial developments we will be looking at shortly, but is not sufficient in itself. South Africa is also a member of the WTO, and the European Union is the country's most important trade partner, as approximately 40 per cent of imports and exports come from or are headed for Europe. While not yet perfectly balanced, in 2010 trade relations between the EU and South Africa were far less one-sided than those of any other African, Caribbean and Pacific country (Fioramonti 2010).

From the geopolitical angle, South African importance is well known. A founder member of the United Nations in 1945, suspended in 1974 from the General Assembly for its policy of apartheid, it was fully reinstated in 1994. Between 2007 and 2008, it was elected non-permanent member of the UN Security Council, and in 2011 it was re-elected. During the democratic transition, it was re-admitted to the Commonwealth, and joined the Non-Aligned Movement in 1994, of which it was coordinator from 1998 to 2003 (Worden 2007). It belongs to the Cairns Group, defending the interests of exporting agricultural goods economies. Since the fifth WTO ministerial meeting of Cancun, it has played a steering role in the G-20, representing developing African countries.

The BRIC group's enlargement to include South Africa indicates an evolution in the very nature of the group. The opening-up to Africa, a continent where China has important political and energy-related interests and which also represents relevant economic opportunities for India and Brazil, is important in both geopolitical and purely political terms: 'guaranteeing the BRICS clan a more planetary dimension, encompassing the African continent' (Orrù 2012: 101).

Highly significantly, the recent Durban Summit discussed the possibility of establishing a new development bank alternative to the International Monetary Fund (IMF). In addition to voicing discontent against the US dollar and the Bretton Woods institutions' hegemony, for the BRICS countries the possibility of creating a new international monetary system would give the network the chance to finance long-term economic projects and investments that the private sector might find difficult to back. In short, a BRICS bank might provide a constant flow of capital for long-term infrastructural projects, particularly in and for the group's countries, and perhaps even support for further initiatives to consolidate commercial and financial relations.

The BRICS: A Multi-centre 'Legal Network'?

A key aspect of the BRICS group is the great variability of its members' political structures: 'It must be pointed out that in the BRIC appellation each economy not only has a very diverse per capita income level but also quite dissimilar economic and political characteristics' (Das 2010: 8).

A first, very rough, classification might identify two countries as authoritarian regimes (China and Russia), and Brazil, India and South Africa as nations in transition towards consolidated forms of democracy. Following a different approach whose roots date back to the late 1990s (Mattei 1997), Brazil and Russia could be defined as belonging to the rule of political law macro-family, India and South Africa to the rule of professional law but with political hegemony and tradition still featuring heavily, and China being in an intermediate position between political and traditional rule (Ferrari 2010: 2).

The analysis of the difficult classification of BRICS countries into strictly legal categories leads us to reflect on the theoretical instruments that have been used until now. In fact, the scientific literature has either adopted a market-focused (Reitz 2009) or a rights-focused approach (Glenn 2010). Both approaches are unable to fully explain and explore the 'legal flows' of policy transfer, constitutional borrowing and constitutional dialogue, whose scope is not just cognitive, but establishes new forms of 'Community interest' (Carducci 2012: 27).

And yet, despite the difficulties in classifying these countries and the BRICS as a group, several elements must be taken into consideration to have a better understanding of the phenomenon. Quite often, the enforcement and respect for fundamental rights, even when recognised in the Constitutions, is blatantly inconsistent in several of these countries. In these immense geopolitical entities, basic victories are a long way off from being fully implemented. We could take education as an example, with very high illiteracy rates, or health care, where the fragile nature of health entitlement results in high child-mortality rates, or the absence of drugs for fighting pandemic diseases (such as HIV first and foremost), not to mention workers' rights.

And even first-generation rights, such as freedom of thought and expression, are not fully guaranteed. Civil liberties and political rights are still partly denied in some of these countries. The Freedom House charts for 2013 show impressive differences among BRICS countries in the exercise of political rights (PR) and civil liberties (CL). Brazil is considered a free country, with a score of 2 for PR and 2 for CL, on a scale from 7 to 1. South Africa too has been recognised a free country, with the same scores as Brazil. Similarly, India is a free country with a score of 2 for PR and 3 for CL. In Russia and China though, the situation is different: Russia is not a free country, with scores of 6 and 5 for PR and CL. If possible, the situation is even worse in Beijing: China is not classified as a free country and scores 7 for PR and 6 for CL (Freedom in the World 2013). As a matter of fact, China has been frequently singled out, in Freedom House's documents, for its IT censorship and lack of public information.

If we consider poverty, in spite of the very good economic performance of recent years in Brazil, Russia, India and China, the number of poor people remains extremely remarkable, so that their '676 million poor constitute more than half of poor people worldwide' (Goldstein 2011: 33) and South Africa's inclusion would only worsen the situation. The added value of policy making at BRICS level, however, might ensure that policy transfers trigger processes improving people's quality of life through food-safety programmes, health policies and environmental sustainability. Indeed, the transformations that are occurring within the BRICS are probably the result of the approach adopted. These countries have not set up a radical group whose goal is to revolutionise or overturn global governance; they have engaged in the creation of a legal network. Having identified a need for reform, the approach is to tackle the status quo in a gradual way and on several fronts.

The process has been sketched from a virtuous angle, although the distances to be covered to achieve progressive implementation targets are considerable.

But can these distances be bridged? Without doubt, due to economic growth, 'the BRICS can play a very important role in helping to improve the health and well-being of the world's poorest countries' (GHSi 2012: 11): this not only indicates a campaign within the BRICS, but also an external one in which members of the BRICS appear to be leaders that drive developing countries forwards.

The core question consists in the adoption of suitable government policies: having abandoned the Rostow model, based on an optimistic vision of capitalism and the free market (Rostow 1960), we need to decide if, with regard to economic growth, it is better to have a weak executive open to pluralist motions, or a strong one 'with an iron fist' capable of guiding the economic change that globalisation has brought. Accordingly, we find a new and different line of thought between the processes that have developed in the BRICS countries and those we are analysing in our own nations.

Conclusion

These five countries have given a different, albeit still unshaped, form to the new century. They are reforming not just trade and the economics, but even the law. Acknowledging this fact does not mean we are glorifying the process underway, but instead attempting to understand what evolutions might arise (and are partly already in place) in terms of state law, in countries that differ greatly in geographical and legislative terms. The BRICS countries are beginning to share objectives, but do not necessarily want to use the same instruments to pursue them. As already mentioned, there are convergences that affect each country's legal system and even their Constitutions. But, if the EU requires new member states strongly to review their constitutional and legal systems, the BRICS group has been using what may be described as 'soft policy transfer'.

This form of 'dialogue' between the BRICS countries today involves 'juridical flows', the results of which cannot be termed 'transplants' but are instead purposive forms of 'legal borrowing' (Scheppele 2003: 296, Frankenberg 2010: 563). They are the result of the decisions taken in the inter-governmental sessions. From the transposition of models, we see a shift towards procedures, with a direct, and we argue positive, impact on the overall legal system. In this way, the foundations for solid legal 'bridges' between different systems are laid (Tebbe and Tsai 2010: 463).

The BRICS countries have abandoned part of their independence in sharing common policies. But they have not given up their sovereignty and they have not homogenised their economic systems; neither have they abandoned some forms of 'State capitalism' in the name of an Anglo-liberalist approach. If the EU integration process is based on the transfer of binding law-making powers from national to supra-national actors, and while the creation of the so-called 'global law' has empowered new actors such as multinational companies, NGOs, public-private hybrid institutions, or global extra-national systems, with the BRICS we are facing a completely different phenomenon. More research will tell us whether we are facing a new concept of a multi-centre inter-state order. In particular, working on the legal and constitutional frame of this legal network seems fascinating and promising, and will contribute to understand if the BRICS is a mirage or reality (Armijo 2007).

References

Books, book chapters and articles

Ahdieh, R.B., Z. Lee, S. Ragavan, K. Noonan and C.W. Francis, 2007. 'The Existing Legal Infrastructure of BRICs: Where Have We Been and Where Are We Going?', *Northwestern Journal of Technical and Intellectual Property*, 5: 503 ff.

Armijo, L.E. 2007. 'The BRICs countries (Brazil, Russia, India, and China) as analytical category: mirage or insight?', *Asian Perspective*, 31(4): 7–42.

Auby, J.B. 2008. 'Is legal globalization regulated? Memling and the business of baking camels', *Utrecht Law Review*, 4(3): 210–17.

Carducci, M. 2012. 'Il BRICS come "Legal Network" e le sue implicazioni costituzionali', in *Liber amicorum, in on. di Carlo Amirante*, Arcavacata di Rende: UniCal.

Das, D.K. 2010. 'Another perspective on globalization', *Journal of International Trade Law & Policy*, 9: 46–63.

Deegan, H. 2011. *Politics South Africa*. London: Harlow.

Di Plinio, G. 2011. 'Nuove mappe nel caos. Lo Stato e la costituzione economica della crisi globale', in eds G. Cerrina Ferroni and G.F. Ferrari, *Crisi economico-finanziara e intervento dello stato. Modelli comparati e prospettive.* Torino: Giappichelli.

Ferrari, G.F. 2010. 'Sistemi giuridici: origine e diffusione', in ed. idem, *Atlante di Diritto pubblico comparato*. Torino: Utet.

Fioramonti, L. 2010. *European Union Democracy Aid : supporting civil society in post-aparthcid South Africa*. London: Routledge, 2010.

Frankenberg, G. 2010. 'Constitutional Transfer: The IKEA Theory Revisited', *International Journal of Constitutional Law*, 8(3): 563–79.

Glenn, H.P. 2010. *Legal Traditions of the World: Sustainable Diversity in Law*. Oxford: Oxford University Press.

Goldstein, A. 2011. *BRIC. Brasile, Russia, India, Cina alla guida dell'economia globale*. Bologna: Il Mulino.

Inks, R. 2012. *Emerging Economies: The Geopolitics of the BRICS Nations*. Austin, TX: Stratfor.

ISSA (International Social Security Association) 2013. *BRICS. Social Security Coverage Extension in the BRICS – A Comparative Study on the Extension of Coverage in Brazil, the Russian Federation, India, China and South Africa.*

Geneva: ISSA <http://apsredes.org/site2013/wp-content/uploads/2014/03/2-BRICS-report-final.pdf> [accessed 10 July 2014].

Jones, S. 2012. *BRICs and Beyond: Lessons on Emerging Markets*. Chichester: John Wiley and Sons.

Kwandiwe, K. and E. Chiencyengozi, 2011. *Governance in the 21st Century*, Pretoria: HSRC Press.

Levy, C.J. 2009. 'Emerging Powers Prepare to Meet in Russia', *New York Times*, 15 June.

Mattei, U. 1997. 'Three Patterns of Law: Taxonomy and Change in the World's Legal Systems', *American Journal of Comparative Law*, 45(1): 5ff.

Modi, R. 2011, *South–South Cooperation*. Basingstoke: Palgrave.

Nadkarni, V. and N.C. Noonan, 2012. *Emerging Powers in a Comparative Perspective: The Political and Economic Rise of the BRIC Countries*. London and New York: Continuum.

O'Neill, J. 2001. *Building Better Global Economic BRICs*, Goldman Sachs Global Economic Paper No. 66.

——. 2011. *The Growth Map. Economic Opportunity in the BRICs and Beyond.* London: Penguin Books.

Orrù, R. 2012. 'L'ordine costituzionale sudafricano post-apartheid: luci ed ombre nell'orizzonte dei BRICS', in ed. L. Scaffardi, *BRICS: Paesi emergenti nel prisma del diritto comparato*. Torino: Giappichelli.

Perju, V. 2012. *Constitutional Transplants, Borrowing, and Migrations*, Boston College Law School Legal Studies Research Paper No. 254.

Quercia, P. 2011. 'Il contesto geopolitico dell'emersione di Brasile, Russia, India e Cina', in eds P. Quercia and P. Magri, *I BRICs e noi. L'ascesa di Brasile, Russia, India e Cina e le conseguenze per l'Occidente*. Milano: ISPI.

Rostow, W.W. 1960. *The Stages of Economic Growth: A Non-Communist Manifesto*. Cambridge: Cambridge University Press.

Scheppele, K.L. 2003. 'Aspirational and Adversative Constitutionalism: The Case for Studying Cross-constitutional Influence through Negative Models', *International Journal of Constitutional Law*, 1(2): 296–324.

Sekine, E. 2011. 'The Impact of the Third BRICS Summit', *Nomura Journal of Capital Markets*, 3(1): 1–6.

Tebbe, N. and R.L. Tsai, 2010. 'Constitutional Borrowing', *Michigan Law Review*, 108: 459–522.

Yu, P.K. 2008. 'Access to Medicines, BRICS Alliances, and Collective Action', *American Journal of Law, Medicine & Ethics*, 34: 345–94.

Worden, N. 2007, *The Making of Modern South Africa*. Oxford: Blackwell.

Reports

BRICS 2012. *The BRICS Report. A study of Brazil, Russia, India, China and South Africa with Special Focus on Synergies and Complementarities*. Oxford: Oxford University Press.

DBSA 2012. *The State of South Africa Economic Infrastructure.*
Freedom House 2013. *Freedom in the World* <http://www.freedomhouse.org/reports> [accessed 30 June 2014].
GHSi 2012. *Shifting Paradigm. How the BRICS are reshaping Global Health and Developments* <http://ghsinitiatives.org>.

Website and online material

Delhi Declaration <http://www.brics5.co.za/about-brics/summit-declaration/fourth-summit/>.
Delhi Health Ministers' Final Declaration <http://pib.nic.in/newsite/erelease.aspx?relid=91533>.
Joint Statement of the BRIC Countries' Leaders, Yekaterinburg, 16 June 2009 <http://archive.kremlin.ru/eng/text/docs/2009/06/217963.shtml> [accessed 30 June 2014].

Chapter 18

From Import to Export? Some Signs of the External Circulation of South African Constitutional Jurisprudence

Andrea Lollini

Introduction

Section 39 of the 1996 South African Constitution allows judges to make use of foreign law in interpreting the Bill of Rights. Due to this provision, the South African Constitutional Court (CC) has developed an innovative hermeneutical technique based on extra-systemic inferences. A hallmark of one of the most controversial contemporary constitutional transformations, the use of extra-systemic interpretative inferences has become one of the main features of South African constitutional interpretation (Webb 1998, Hogg 1998).

Although the South African CC was not the first constitutional jurisdiction to operate in a *dialogue* with foreign courts, the Constitution of post-apartheid South Africa is the only text with an express provision enabling the judges to use extra-systemic parameters for interpreting it.

The phenomenon of the global interaction between national supreme courts is now commonly used and is growing rapidly. Some examples might be useful for sketching out this controversial development in current constitutionalism. The most active constitutional courts in their use of foreign law include the Supreme Courts of Canada and Israel, and one should note the frequent references that constitutional judges in Latin American countries such as Argentina, Brazil and Colombia make to the Supreme Court of the United States (L'Heureux-Dube 1998, Rivlin 2009). The Indian Supreme Court as well as the constitutional courts of Central and Eastern European countries are also examples of courts systematically using foreign argumentative inferences. Unexpected comparative references may also be tracked down in the jurisprudence of France's *Cour de Cassation* (Canivet 2005).

As the spaces in which judges from different countries can meet, exchange views and share judicial problems multiply, the phenomenon of circulation of legal materials among national supreme courts grows in size and intensity. Some example are the first two World Conferences of constitutional and supreme courts held in Cape Town in 2009 and in Rio de Janeiro in 2011 under the umbrella of the Venice Commission, as well as a number of networks of judges in several regional contexts. Other significant examples include the European forum of Constitutional Courts as well as the African forum of Francophone countries (Orrù n.d.).

During the last decade, this major transformation in contemporary world constitutionalism has captured the interest of an increasing number of scholars. Despite the unwillingness of some United States Supreme Court judges to refer to foreign legal materials, North American scholars were the first to craft definitions of this phenomenon. Anne Marie Slaughter was probably the first to use the metaphor of 'dialogue', speaking of an ongoing 'dialogue between courts'. In this perspective, public law doctrine has developed a broad and detailed classification of the phenomenon, speaking of: a) *cross-judicial influence* (Thiruvengadam 2001); b) *cross-constitutional influence* or *cross-constitutional fertilisation*; c) *judicial transplant* (Choudhry 1998); d) *trans-judicial communication* or *judicial dialogue* (ibid.); e) *trans-judicial borrowing* or *precedent borrowing* (Scheppele 2003). This last definition explicitly connects the entire phenomenon with Anglo-American law, which follows the binding precedent principle (in its various forms). Thus modern precedent-borrowing between constitutional judges would be an expansion of a typical common law format that evolved from a historically common practice among the judges of Commonwealth countries. Beginning in the nineteenth century, these judges largely used foreign court precedents, generally British ones and in particular those of the Privy Council. Currently, the phenomenon of 'borrowing' precedents and interpretative solutions or argumentation models goes well beyond the legal rationale and the geo-cultural borders that defined the relationship between the British Empire's centre and its peripheries.

The analysis of constitutional court rulings in legal systems that have adopted new constitutional texts (such as Canada in 1982, or South Africa in 1996) or in legal systems such as Israel's shows that judges increasingly resort to practices of comparing constitutional law, expressly referring to and citing rulings and interpretive solutions of constitutional courts, including those of the Romano-Germanic tradition. Interpretive solutions are now being actively sought and borrowed by courts from different legal traditions, a practice that no longer arises out of subordination.

It is no longer a question of verifying the existence of this phenomenon as a fact: the evidence is simply irrefutable. The issue is, rather, to analyse how these extra-systemic parameters are integrated in the interpretive phase and how the comparative method is actually used. Legal scholars are polarised between a celebratory view of this phenomenon and radical scepticism. However, even if the comparative constitutional hermeneutic includes the risk that its use could give judges an uncontrollable and arbitrary freedom when interpreting and applying the law, it is progressively becoming a resource for constitutional judges (Osiatynski 2003, Childress 2003, Klug 2003).

South African Constitutional Jurisprudence: From Import to Export?

As we have already mentioned, s 39 of the Constitution (headed by 'Interpretation of the Bill of Rights') states that the CC 'may' take foreign law into consideration. Endowed with this power, the Court has been able to develop a pioneering practice of interpretation, and, as a result, South Africa has quickly become a 'model' examined by scholars world-wide.

South African constitutionalist doctrine cites three main reasons for this provision: first, the need for international legitimacy after decades of isolation under the apartheid regime, which had ignored international standards on fundamental rights; second, the search for international *repères* capable of aiding the interpretative work of an entirely new constitutional text (the Constitution drafters became increasingly aware of the lack of reference points in the previous regime based on a segregationist rationale, and third, introducing judicial review in South Africa would have required a period of legal and cultural 'learning'. For these reasons, post-apartheid South Africa had to make a virtue of necessity. Acting as a listener, referring to interpretative models of other constitutional judges, calling upon widespread legal institutional culture and breathing life into a courageous constitutional compromise, it tried to make up for its decades-long cultural and legal alienation.

Since its very first decisions in 1995, the CC has incorporated a large volume of foreign law such as precedents, judicial solutions, interpretive tests, argumentative schemes, or foreign examples of legislative solutions.

Even if the unexpected post-segregation political transition, the modernity of the new democratic Constitution, and the challenging task of implementing the post-apartheid constitutional system were solid reasons for keeping the international spotlight on Johannesburg, this innovative hermeneutic approach has contributed to increasing the international consideration of the new South African democratic constitutionalism (Lollini 2007: 2009). The country has rapidly become an interesting experimental laboratory of modern constitutionalism for both the sensitive nature of the constitutional issues (such as redressing inequalities, developing social rights and enforcing fundamental ones) and the specificity of constitutional interpretation. In this context, the constitutional system is the target of a growing body of comparative analysis, studies and surveys.

Until now, however, strictly in terms of constitutional jurisprudence, the new system has been mostly perceived as an importing system. Most of the scientific efforts made by international scholars in comparative law concentrate on a specific perspective: the incoming foreign laws incorporated by the South African judges.

However, there are signs of what might become a new trend in the future. In some cases, the CC has moved from the simple act of 'learning' from important foreign constitutional experiences to 'teaching' other countries within the liberal-democratic constitutional tradition. In other words, South Africa has slightly shifted from being an importer to being an exporter of new constitutional experiences and experiments.

This role reversal can be evaluated by looking at the constitutional jurisprudence of some of the most significant legal systems from which South Africa has often imported legal elements. More recently, one can also observe some South African legal references incorporated by constitutional judges of important western countries.

As confirmation of this claim, we will cite examples of Canadian and Israeli constitutional jurisprudence. The amount of evidence, however, is limited, and our hypothesis will require testing in the future with further data. This is due to the fact that it is difficult to proceed with a comprehensive analysis of the entire jurisprudence of several constitutional jurisdictions. The only research strategy available is to proceed with a case-by-case methodology. In conclusion, even if the data are not completely sufficient to generate truly scientific evidence, the appearance of South African legal references in the jurisprudence of both the Canadian and Israeli Supreme Courts demonstrates, at least, that South African constitutional law is no longer a merely importing culture but it is also an exporting legal system.

Examples from the Supreme Court of Canada

One of the first cases we examine is *Arsenault-Cameron v. Prince Edward Island*, which constitutes a basic pattern of use of South African constitutional jurisprudence. In this case, what is simply interesting to note is the fact that the Canadian Supreme Court considers South Africa side by side with far more commonly considered legal traditions. The judges sitting in Ottawa discovered similarities in legal reasoning between the following national high courts: 'The same reasoning was adopted by the Constitutional Court of South Africa ... It reviewed the similarity of the tests in the United Kingdom, the United States, Australia and Canada' (para 4).

In the later Canadian case of *United States v. Burns*, South African legal parameters were incorporated in a more delicate controversy and a more focused way. Hence, the Canadian Supreme Court referred to a very important South African constitutional landmark: the 1995 decision in which the Johannesburg judges declared the death penalty unconstitutional.

In particular, the Supreme Court of Canada had to decide whether extradition without assurances infringed fugitives' constitutional rights to remain in or enter Canada and violated s 6(1) of the Canadian Charter of Rights and Freedoms. In this case, the respondents were wanted on three counts of aggravated first-degree murder in the state of Washington. If found guilty, they would face either the death penalty or life in prison without parole. The case appears to be even more complicated because the respondents were both Canadian citizens and were 18 years old. Even if the Minister of Justice for Canada, after evaluating the respondents' particular circumstances, including their age and their Canadian nationality, had ordered their extradition pursuant to s 25 of the Extradition Act without seeking assurances from the United States under article 6 of the extradition treaty between the two countries that the death penalty would not be imposed or, if imposed, would not be carried out, the British Columbia Court of Appeal in a majority decision ruled that the unconditional extradition order would violate the mobility rights of the respondents under s 6(1). The Court of Appeal thus set aside the Minister's decision and directed him to seek assurances as a condition of surrender.

The Supreme Court had to weigh several clashing arguments in favour of or against the extradition without assurance, grounding its reasoning in the balancing test employed in two previous similar cases: *Kindler v. Canada* and *Reference Re Ng Extradition*. The Supreme Court held:

> The 'shocks the conscience' language signals the possibility that even though the rights of the fugitive are to be considered in the context of other applicable principles of fundamental justice, which are normally of sufficient importance to uphold the extradition, a particular treatment or punishment may sufficiently violate our sense of fundamental justice as to tilt the balance against extradition. The rule is not that departures from fundamental justice are to be tolerated unless in a particular case it shocks the conscience. An extradition that violates the principles of fundamental justice will always shock the conscience. (para 286)

As one of the major countries opposed to the death penalty in the international arena, Canada has not only abolished this form of punishment, but it also supports international initiatives opposing extradition without assurances, combined with its international advocacy of the abolition of the death penalty itself. For this reason, the Court had to account for the fact that the Canadian sense of fundamental justice views capital punishment as unjust and something to be stopped. On the contrary, however, the Court also had to consider the risk that Canada could be transformed in a sort of 'safe haven' for dangerous fugitives. In balancing arguments against and in favour of the extradition, the Court considered also that the 'death row phenomenon' in itself is another factor that weighs against extradition without assurances.

In conclusion, the Court affirmed that:

> A review of the factors for and against unconditional extradition therefore leads to the conclusion that assurances are constitutionally required in all but exceptional cases. This case does not present the exceptional circumstances that must be shown. A balance which tilted in favour of extradition without assurances in *Kindler* and *Ng* now tilts against the constitutionality of such an outcome. (para 290)

It is clear that the judges sitting in Ottawa were dealing with a very controversial case. The gravity of the crime and the fatal consequences the two young Canadians faced if extradited to the US shocked public opinion. In this perspective, the Canadian judges looked for support to the South African CC in *Makwanyane* (1995). During this case, the Court decided on unconstitutionality against a substantial degree of public opinion in favour of maintaining capital punishment.

For this reason, the Canadian judges incorporated the South African judicial experience through the following statement:

> While we affirm that the 'balancing process' set out in *Kindler* and *Ng* is the correct approach, the phrase 'shocks the conscience' and equivalent expressions are not to be taken out of context or equated to opinion polls. The words were intended to underline the very exceptional nature of circumstances that would constitutionally limit the Minister's decision in extradition cases. The words were not intended to signal an abdication by judges of their constitutional responsibilities in matters involving fundamental principles of justice. In this respect, Canadian courts share the duty described by President Arthur Chaskalson of the Constitutional Court of South Africa in declaring unconstitutional the death penalty in that country. (para 67)

The Canadian court then expressly quoted the words of Chaskalson P in *Makwanyane* (1995):

> Public opinion may have some relevance to the enquiry, but, in itself, it is no substitute for the duty vested in the Courts to interpret the Constitution and to uphold its provisions without fear or favour. If public opinion were to be decisive, there would be no need for constitutional adjudication. The protection of rights could then be left to Parliament, which has a mandate from the public, and is answerable to the public for the way its mandate is exercised. The very reason for establishing the new legal order, and for vesting the power of judicial review of all legislation in the courts, was to protect the rights of minorities and others who cannot protect their rights adequately through the democratic process. Those who are entitled to claim this protection include the social outcasts and marginalised people of our society. It is only if there is a willingness to protect the worst and the weakest amongst us that all of us can be secure that our own rights will be protected. (para 88)

It seems that Canada and South Africa have created a sort of hermeneutic circuit on this specific issue. Even if it cannot be established whether that circuit may be defined as 'dialogue between Courts', it must be said that the issue of the death penalty, death row and extradition with assurance shows a reciprocal reference between the two Courts. This circular movement started in 1995 when the South African CC widely quoted two Canadian precedents, *Kindler* and *Ng*, in the *Makwanyane* case. In this context, it was for the South African Court to pay 'deference' *vis-à-vis* the more established Canadian constitutional experience.

However, the above mentioned data derived from the *United States v. Burns* case reveals a sort of feedback. In a more recent Canadian case on a similar legal issue, the judges in Ottawa discussed the balancing test established in *Kindler* and *Ng*, considering also the words, ideas and reasoning contained in the *Makwanyane* case. Both courts gradually looked to foreign colleagues as a source of useful arguments for the legal reasoning of their decisions. This practice, at least regarding this specific issue, created a chain of mutual interactions crafting a hermeneutic circuit.

I refer to *R v Hall*, where the Canadian Supreme Court dealt with an extremely violent case of murder that caused significant public concern. Once arrested, the person accused of the murder applied for bail. The judge, however, denied bail under s 515(10)(c) of the Criminal Code in order 'to maintain confidence in the administration of justice', considering the highly charged aftermath of the murder and the strong evidence implicating the accused. A superior court judge dismissed the accused's habeas corpus application challenging the constitutionality of s 515(10)(c). The Court of Appeal confirmed the decision as did the Supreme Court in a five to four decision.

As in the previous case, social pressures outside the Court affected a strictly judicial decision. In this case, it was the collective fear about the murder's harsh and violent profile that deeply unsettled public opinion. Here again, the South African experience seems to have been extremely helpful to the Canadian constitutional judges. The CC had successfully resolved a very similar case characterised by the same public perplexities and fears. It is interesting to note how the Canadian judges incorporated South African judicial elements in the following part of the decision:

> Aside from this lack of an empirical foundation for the section, our attention was not drawn to any provision similar to s 515(10) in comparable legal systems. The only enactment in the same vein as s 515(10) is the South African provision allowing for bail to be denied, 'where in exceptional circumstances there is the likelihood that the release of the accused will disturb the public order or undermine the public peace or security'. This provision was challenged in *S v. Dlamini*, 1999 (4) SA 623 (CC), as being contrary to the constitutional right to be released from detention if the interests of justice permit, subject to reasonable conditions. The Constitutional Court of South Africa upheld the provision under the analogue to s 1 (at p 659-60). (para 115)

The Canadian Court then quoted from the South African decision, as follows:

> It would be irresponsible to ignore the harsh reality of the society in which the Constitution is to operate. Crime is a serious national concern, and a worrying feature for some time has been public eruptions of violence related to court proceedings. In the present context we are not so much concerned with violent public reaction to unpopular verdicts or sentences, but with such reactions to unpopular grants of bail. There is widespread misunderstanding regarding the purpose and effect of bail. The ugly fact remains, however, that public peace and security are at times endangered by the release of persons charged with offences that incite public outrage. Experience has shown that organised community violence, be it instigated by quasi-political motives or by territorial battles for control of communities for commercial purposes, does subside while ringleaders are in custody. Their arrest and detention on serious charges does

> instil confidence in the criminal justice system and does tend to settle disquiet, whether the arrestees are warlords or druglords. (para 115)

The Canadian Court then continued:

> It is obvious that in Canada no comparable social conditions exist, either currently or in the foreseeable future, which would justify s 515(10) under s 1. Moreover, the provision in question in *Dlamini* is more narrowly drawn than the provision under appeal here, and indeed seems more akin to the 'public safety' ground under s. 515(10)(b). As a result, in my opinion, the respondent has failed to identify a sufficiently pressing and substantial objective that is furthered by s. 515(10)(c). (para 115)

In *Grant v Torstar Corp. et al.*, the Canadian Supreme Court incorporates several foreign extra-systemic inferences into the legal reasoning. In particular, a number of common law countries are analysed in a comparative perspective. South African legal and judicial elements, as well as the fundamental principle of free expression entrenched by the post-apartheid Constitution are directly quoted by the judges sitting in Ottawa as possible solutions for the Canadian case.

Developments in South Africa have generally paralleled those in the other jurisdictions just discussed, the UK most particularly. In *Du Plessis*, the Constitutional Court of South Africa considered and rejected an argument that the common law of defamation should be liberalised and constitutionalised along the lines of *Sullivan.* The court held that s 15 of the Constitution – the free expression guarantee – did 'not mandate any particular rule of common law' (p. 885) because the guarantee does not apply directly to disputes between private litigants. However, echoing the Canadian 'Charter values' approach, it held that the common law ought to be developed by courts in a manner consistent with constitutional values (para 82).

A number of countries with common law traditions comparable to those of Canada have moved in recent years to modify the law of defamation to provide greater protection for communications on matters of public interest. These developments confront us with a range of possibilities. The traditional common law defence of qualified privilege, which offered no protection in respect of publications to the world at large, situates itself at one end of the spectrum of possible alternatives. At the other end is the American approach of protecting all statements about public figures, unless the plaintiff can show malice. Between these two extremes lies the option of a defence that would allow publishers to escape liability if they can establish that they acted responsibly in attempting to verify the information on a matter of public interest. This middle road is the path chosen by courts in Australia, New Zealand, South Africa and the United Kingdom (para 85).

As a general comment on this selection of Canadian judgments, what is interesting to note is that the South African democratic constitutional system is frequently considered side by side with the most prominent common law countries. This fact appears to confirm the hypothesis that the new South African constitutional system is now perceived as a stable member of the international family providing solid legal suggestions for solving national judicial disputes.

Examples from the Supreme Court of the State of Israel

The hypothesis that South Africa has become an exporting jurisdiction is confirmed by Israeli court decisions. An analysis of Israeli jurisprudence shows that a significant number of South African references has been incorporated by the judges sitting in the Jerusalem Supreme Court.

In *Adalah Legal Centre for Arab Minority in Israel and others v Minister of Interior and others*, the Supreme Court of Israel, as a High Court of Justice, had to verify the constitutionality of the Citizenship and Entry into Israel Law no. 5763/2003. This law, approved by the Knesset as a reaction to harsh terrorist attacks, almost neutralised the family reunification rights of Palestinians living outside Israel with family members living within Israel's boundaries. In this case, the Supreme Court had to decide whether or not the right to live in family union is a fundamental right connected to the right to human dignity and, for this reason, protected by the Basic Laws of the State of Israel.

To decide this sensitive issue, Justice Barak, after a general reference to the 'most enlightened nations', of which Israel is held to be part, looked for similar cases decided by foreign constitutional courts. For this particular case, the jurisprudence of the CC appeared to be a solid point of reference for the President of the Israeli Court. The use of South African judicial parameters is contained in Justice Barak's legal reasoning as follows:

> Israel *has joined the most enlightened nations* that recognize – subject to qualifications of national security, public safety and public welfare – the right of family members 'to live together in the place of their choice'. Indeed, the constitutional right of the Israeli spouse – a right that derives from the nucleus of human dignity as a constitutional right – is 'to live together in the place of their choice'. (p. 20)

The question of the relationship between human dignity as a constitutional right and the right to family life in general, and the right to realise this right by means of living together in a family unit in particular, arose in the case of *Dawood v Minister of Home Affairs*. The judgment was given by the Constitutional Court of South Africa (p. 25): 'In summary, we *have seen* that the right to family life is not merely a basic right in common law, but a constitutional right enshrined in the right to human dignity' (p. 27).

In *Gila Louzon v. Government of Israel*, the Supreme Court, acting as the High Court of Justice, dealt with a case regarding the constitutionality of the National Health Insurance Law. As President Beinisch pointed out:

> … the petitioners suffer from various forms of cancer. The petitioners' doctors referred them for medicinal treatment, and when these petitions were filed, the petitioners' required medications were not included in the basket of health services that receives public funding under the provisions of the National Health Insurance Law. The petitioners had difficulty in purchasing the medications independently, and this was the basis for their petition to this Court requesting that we instruct the respondents to include their medications in the publicly-funded health services basket. The petitioners argue that the decision to omit these medications from the health services basket approved for 2005 violated their constitutional rights, it was unreasonable, and it discriminated against them adversely vis-à-vis other patients whose required medications were included in the basket. (p. 6)

It is interesting to note how comparative inferences are used in order to evaluate the constitutional status of the right to health in Israel. Judges in Jerusalem deemed the South African constitutional interpretation of social rights to be an important point of reference. In fact, over the last decade, the CC had developed a particular interpretation and enforcement of the social rights enshrined in the 1996 Constitution. The way in which the Supreme Court of Israel incorporates South African judicial parameters appears to be consistent. In the following statement, South African law appears to operate as a guideline for interpreting Israeli provisions regarding the right to health:

> On the internal constitutional level, the constitutions of many states, including Canada and the U.S.A, do not confer explicit constitutional status upon the right to health. The constitutional law of these states protects only limited aspects of this right. On the other hand, s 27 of the South African Constitution confers explicit constitutional status upon the right of access to medical treatment. However, the South African Constitution adds that the state must take *reasonable* legislative and other measures, *within its available resources*, to achieve *the progressive realization* of each of these rights. It should be noted that the constitutions of India and Holland expressly entrench the right to promote public health, but this right is not enforceable by the judiciary and it is only a type of fundamental principle that is intended to guide the actions of the executive and the legislative authorities. (p. 19)

Private (res.) Raphael Yissacharov v. Chief Military Prosecutor et al, decided by the Israeli Supreme Court, constitutes another example of the international role played by South African precedent. The appellant, imprisoned for being absent from the army without leave, was found with a dangerous drug in his possession. During interrogation, the interrogator failed to inform the appellant of his right to consult a lawyer. This omission, which was not mentioned by the prosecution, was considered by the trial court to have been illegal and intentional. In the end, the appellant argued that he made this confession because the interrogator had failed to inform him of his right to consult a lawyer, and, as a consequence, that it should not be admissible as evidence. As stated by the Supreme Court, under Israeli law, there was no statutory or case-law precedent for the exclusion of evidence obtained illegally. The defence argued that the court should adopt such a doctrine based on the *Basic Law on Human Dignity and Liberty* adopted in 1992.

The legal void claimed by the applicant prompted the Supreme Court to operate a wide interpretation of the existing legal system manifesting, as a consequence of that, judicial activism. In order to solve this legal issue, the Court proceeded with a comparative analysis looking at strategies adopted by foreign colleagues in similar circumstances. In this regard, the opinion of the majority of the judges is the following:

> In view of the normative change in the Israeli legal system introduced by the Basic Law on *Human Dignity and Liberty*, and in the absence of legislation on this issue, the time has come to adopt a case law doctrine of inadmissibility for illegally obtained evidence … The criterion for excluding illegally obtained evidence is that the evidence should be excluded if admitting it would substantially violate the right of the accused to a fair trial, considering the circumstances of each case on its merits. (para d)

It is interesting to note how the Israeli judges focused the national judicial issue by comparison with some reputed democracies with a criminal system comparable to Israel's, and South Africa is expressly mentioned among them. Alongside other important common law countries, South Africa is viewed as a system capable of exporting useful experience to Israel. This appears to be confirmed in the following part of the judgment: 'Indeed, in Canada, South Africa and the United States the duty to give notice of the right to consult a lawyer applies not only with regard to persons under arrest but also with regard to suspects who are detained for the purposes of interrogation' (p. 30).

A comparative look at other legal systems that are similar to our legal system shows that the aforesaid three questions led to the development of two main models of doctrines for the exclusion of illegally obtained evidence. One model is expressed in the exclusionary rules practised in the United States. The second model is the one practised in the other common law countries, including Canada, England, South Africa and Australia. Let us therefore turn to examine closely the inadmissibility doctrines practised in these countries, in order to obtain inspiration from the arrangements adopted by them on the matter under discussion. Obviously, the comparative perspective does not bind us in formulating a doctrine that is appropriate for our legal system, and reference to legal systems that are fundamentally similar to our legal system is merely intended to broaden our horizons and benefit from the experience of those countries, in so far as this experience is relevant for the purposes of the legal position in Israel (p. 87).

Conclusion

The case sample presented here is certainly not sufficient to demonstrate scientifically the creation of a sort of hermeneutic circuit for a stable trend of exportation. At the moment, the data come only from Canadian and Israeli jurisprudence. Creating a more accurate picture will require comparative analysis with other constitutional systems. Limited as they are, the examples none the less are significant. The Canadian Supreme Court borrowed South African judicial elements for highly sensitive cases. Moreover, in all the examples analysed, the post-apartheid legal system is considered side by side with the most consolidated democratic constitutional traditions and as a source of comparative inspiration.

Due to the asymmetries that still characterise South African society, the CC is constantly confronted with challenging legal issues that could transform the 1996 constitutional promise into a constitutional reality. Indeed, the Court's decisions are gradually becoming a source of inspiration for other constitutional cultures specifically for the complexity of the issues it deals with in terms of enforcing fundamental and social rights, fighting against inequality and harmonising a multicultural society. In this regard, the CC's insistence on developing the path toward a constitutional democracy while learning from more experienced countries appears to have yielded its first results of exporting national judicial solutions.

References

Books, book chapters and articles

Canivet, G. 2005. 'The Practice of Comparative Law by the Supreme Courts: Brief Reflections on the Dialogue between the Judges in French and European Experience', *Tulane Law Review*, 80: 1377–400.

Childress, D.E. 2003. 'Using Comparative Constitutional Law to Resolve Federal Questions', *Duke Law Journal*, 53: 193–222.

Choudhry, S. 1998. 'Globalization in Search of Justification: Toward a Theory of Comparative Constitutional Interpretation', *Indiana Law Journal*, 74: 819ff.

Hogg, P.W. 1998. 'Canadian Law in the Constitutional Court of South Africa', *South African Public Law*, 1.

L'Heureux-Dube, C. 1998. 'The Importance of Dialogue: Globalization and the International Impact of the Rehnquist Court', *Tulsa Law Journal*, 34: 15ff.

Klug, H. 2003. 'The Dignity Clause of the Montana Constitution: May Foreign Jurisprudence Lead the Way to an Expanded Interpretation?', *Montana Law Review*, 64: 133ff.

Lollini, A. 2007. 'Legal Argumentation Based on Foreign Law. An Example From Case Law of the South African Constitutional Court', *Utrecht Law Review*, III(I).

—— 2009. 'Confronting Comparative Methods: Approaches to Using Extra-Systemic Parameters by the Canadian Supreme Court and the South African Constitutional Court', in eds A.S. Muller et al., *Highest Courts and Internationalisation of Law.* The Hague: Hague Academic Press, pp. 165–82.

Orrù, R. n.d. 'Informal judicial cross fertilization and the system of Conferences between Constitutional Courts and equivalent bodies' <http://www.juridicas.unam.mx/wccl/ponencias/12/206.pdf> [accessed 22 June 2014].

Osiatynski, W. 2003. 'Paradoxes of Constitutional Borrowing', *International Journal of Constitutional Law*, 1(2): 244–68.

Rivlin, E. 2009. 'Thoughts on Referral to Foreign Law, Global Chain-Novel, and Novelty', *Florida Journal of International Law*, 21: 1–27.

Scheppele, K.L. 2003. 'Aspirational and Aversive Constitutionalism: The Case for Studying Cross-Constitutional Influence through Negative Models', *International Journal of Constitutional Law*, 1(2): 296–324.

Thiruvengadam, A.K. 2001. 'Legal Transplants through Judiciaries: Cross-judicial Influences on Constitutional Adjudication in the Post World War II Era. A Study in Comparative Constitutional Law Focusing on Theoretical and Empirical Issues', Paper on the Issue of Transjudicial Borrowings. New York: New York University.

Webb, H. 1998. 'The Constitutional Court of South Africa: Rights Interpretation and Comparative Constitutional Law'. *University of Pennsylvania Journal of Constitutional Law*, 1: 205–83.

Cases

Adalah Legal Centre for Arab Minority in Israel and others v. Minister of Interior and others HCJ, 7052/2003.

Arsenault-Cameron v. Prince Edward Island [1999] 3 S.C.R. 851.

Gila Louzon v. Government of Israel, HCJ, 3071/2005.

Grant v. Torstar Corp [2009]; SCC, 61.

Kindler v. Canada (Minister of Justice), [1991] 2 S.C.R. 779.

Private (res.) Raphael Yissacharov v. Chief Military Prosecutor et alii, Supreme Court of Israel sitting as Court of Criminal Appeals, CrimA 5121/98.

R v. Hall [2002] 3 SCR 309, 2002 SCC 64.

Reference Re Ng Extradition (Can), [1991] 2 S.C.R. 858.

S v Dlamini 1999 (4) SA 623 (CC).

S. v. Makwanyane 1995 (3) SA 391.

US v. Burns [2001] 1 S.C.R. 283; 2001 SCC 7.

Index

For Product Safety Concerns and Information please contact our EU representative GPSR@taylorandfrancis.com
Taylor & Francis Verlag GmbH, Kaufingerstraße 24, 80331 München, Germany

www.ingramcontent.com/pod-product-compliance
Ingram Content Group UK Ltd.
Pitfield, Milton Keynes, MK11 3LW, UK
UKHW022015180926
475701UK00003B/370
9780367600013